ALG

8^{50}

A Bibliography of
General Histories of Economics
1692-1975

A Bibliography of
General Histories of Economics
1692-1975

Richard S. Howey

THE REGENTS PRESS OF KANSAS

Lawrence

Library of Congress Cataloging in Publication Data

Howey, Richard S., 1902–
A bibliography of general histories of economics,
1692–1975.

Bibliography: p.
Includes index.
1. Economics—History—Bibliography. I. Title.
Z7164.E2H68   [HB75]   016.33'009   81-17696
   ISBN 0-7006-0219-4   AACR2

Contents

List of Tables

Preface

At this point, it may be helpful to comment on the expression "general histories of economics." As used in this bibliography, the unqualified word "histories" will ordinarily refer to "general histories of economics." Here, the word "general" implies that the authors *intended* their histories to cover the whole of economics, that is, to treat all ages, all countries, and all economic subjects. Whenever authors explicitly restricted their histories with regard to time, to place, or to economic content, it was clear that they had intended their histories to be "special" rather than "general." A strict interpretation of this definition of "general" was not adhered to in the early years of the period under consideration, when the boundaries of the subject were yet in doubt and, accordingly, when it was hard to distinguish between "general" and "special" histories. For this and other reasons, some items were included in these early years that, had they appeared later, would have been rejected. The fact that special histories outnumbered general histories was a sufficient reason for having excluded them from this bibliography.

Before 1890 the title of a general history might be *History of Political Economy*, whereas after 1900 it might be either *History of Economics* or *History of Economic Thought*. "Political economy" was the first name for the subject that, between 1890 and 1900—for reasons that are not obvious—came, in the English language, to be called "economics." In a way, the change was helpful, since the term "political economy" had no adjectival form. The change in terms from "political economy" to "economics" was also disadvantageous in two ways. In the first place, the change was often not adopted in foreign languages. In the second place, it left us with two names for much the same thing. The relations between the two expressions are variously interpreted. In this bibliography the relations are as follows: "political economy" and "economics" have essentially the same meaning; "economics" is preferred for the overall term, and for the most up-to-date context; "political economy" is largely restricted to the nineteenth century.

In the following bibliography, an asterisk (*) placed after an entry number designates a history in the University of Kansas Library. Collectively, the starred entries provide a catalog of the general histories of economics at the University of Kansas. These 499 starred entries constitute the largest single collection of general histories of economics to be found anywhere. The magnitude of the Kansas collection stimulated and facilitated the compilation of this bibliography.

Originally, my intention to catalog the general histories of economics at the University of Kansas was part of a plan to compile a more complete bibliography of the general histories of economics than any that was then available. Fulfillment of the plan required that I make two additions to the Kansas general histories: first, those histories that are located in other libraries; and second, those that are described in accessible bibliographies but that are not located in any libraries.

In order to assure reasonable consistency and precision, the 499 histories at the University of Kansas were bibliographically examined. Most of the 265 histories that were found in other libraries were likewise examined, chiefly by visits to the libraries themselves but also by means of interlibrary loans. Unfortunately, the 234 histories that appeared only in other bibliographies—they were most often subsequent editions or translations—in some cases brought bibliographic inconsistencies with them.

The plan to compile this bibliography was inspired by the desire to increase the existing scant knowledge of the historiography of economics. The word "historiography," as here employed, denotes a "history of histories previously written." In this somewhat restricted sense, Orestes Popescu, in *On the Historiography of Economic Thought: A Bibliographical Survey* (1964), was the first writer to use the word in connection with the histories of economics. At that time, he used the word sparingly, once in his title, and once in his text. It probably has had no further similar use since that year.

In accord with the aim of the plan just mentioned, this bibliography includes basic material for further study of the histories of economics. It can be briefly described as a definitive, international, annually arranged listing of all the general histories of economics, accompanied by historical annotations.

By itself, it can serve as a *bare bones* "history of histories previously written" for anyone who looks through the entries from 1692 to 1975 and who takes into account Appendix A (which lists a large sample of the mini-histories that have appeared in the general textbooks on economics published since 1840), Appendix B (which provides information on the development of university courses in the history of economics), and Appendix C (which examines the role of translations). Such a scanning would first disclose the fashioning of the histories of economics concurrently with the public acceptance of its original name, "political economy." From that start to the present, this bibliography will furnish an impression of the number, the distribution through time, the nationality, and the scope of the original editions. Also it will bring out both the concentrations of later editions and the spread of the histories—through translations—to forty-six countries on five continents. Some measure of the merit of each individual history is given by its subsequent editions and by the remarks of reviewers. This sort of bibliographic brush with the facts and events of the historical record should change—for the better, in many ways—any view (or more likely any fragments of a view) of the historiography of economics that is now explicitly or implicitly held.

This bibliography contains two kinds of histories: first, short (essay-length) histories, most often chapters in early general textbooks on political economy; and second, long (book-length) histories. The short histories have the lesser historiographic weight. Further, earlier (pre-1839) short histories have much more weight than do those that came later: before 1839 they were predecessors, while afterwards they increasingly became summaries of long histories. The year 1839 stands out as the date when long histories first commanded enough attention at home and abroad to justify subsequent editions. These subsequent editions deserve notice for several reasons, one being that they measure the relative merits of book-length histories. This is not the case with essay-length histories, where the measurement is of the books in which the histories are but small parts.

Roughly half (226) of the "subsequent" editions of book-length histories are later editions published in their home countries, and half (275) are translations that were published in foreign countries. The uncommon use of the word "translation" in this bibliography rests on the supposition that every nation, in some sense, has its own unique language or set of languages. Therefore, it is possible to speak of American, Argentine, Austrian, Belgian, Brazilian, British, Canadian, Cuban, Indian, Mexican, and Swiss translations. This supposition facilitated the accurate use, in the notes and in Appendix C, of the word "translations" to designate the movement of histories among nations.

Consideration of the dissimilarities between long and short histories and between their first and subsequent editions led to corresponding differences in the way the histories are presented in this bibliography. Basically, the intention was to present every independently published edition of all book-length histories but only as many essay-length histories as feasible. The main features of this presentation are shown in the chart.

Book-length Histories	Essay-length Histories
Every edition is fully described in a separately numbered entry.	Every pre-1839 first edition is fully described in a separately numbered entry.
Every numbered entry of a first edition contains the dates and "nationalities" of all its subsequent editions (later editions and translations).	Every numbered entry of a first edition contains the dates and "nationalities" of all its subsequent editions (later editions and translations).
Every numbered entry of a subsequent edition supplies the date and "nationality" of its first edition.	Appendix C lists a sample of post-1839 first editions.
Comments on the entries are largely restricted to numbered first editions.	Comments on the entries are largely restricted to numbered first editions.

Every entry in this bibliography provides the ordinary facts regarding both the work and its author; gives the location of a copy, either in a library or in some other bibliography; tells whether there are other editions (including translations), whether the author has written other histories, and often adds a comment, which may be either short, giving no more than the university at which the author was a professor, or long, especially in the case of early influential histories. As a convenience, the "nationality" of each history is taken to be that of the city mentioned on its title page. In the notes, statements—particularly those on priority—have been given without such qualifying adverbs as "probably" and "possibly," in order to encourage further scrutiny of them. The mention of reviews, which has been casual, is intended to display in some degree the tenor of contemporary reception. The notes both introduce related matters and give added bibliographic information.

All the other university disciplines also have their general histories. They appear in the subject catalogs at university libraries under headings ranging from "Astronomy-History" to "Zoology-History." These resulted from the conviction that history could be studied, not only for the enjoyment or usefulness of historical knowledge itself, but also for the light that it throws on the subject matter of other disciplines.

The idea of extracting indirect profit from history was prevalent in German universities early in the nineteenth century. It passed by steps to the universities of other countries. It enjoyed marked success in its application to political economy, which, at the time, was being slowly drawn into the curricula of the growing universities of the world. A comparison would probably show that economics has had more of these histories than any other discipline. It is regrettable that we have no overall account of these disciplinary histories and almost no accounts of the histories in individual disciplines. It is difficult to ascertain the extent to which the fortune of the historical method is changing at the present.

I acknowledge my indebtedness to all the earlier lists of histories of economics, as well as to the collections of numerous libraries, especially those of the University of Kansas Library, the New York Public Library, and Columbia University Library. I also deeply appreciate the aid of many people, particularly of Linda, Kathé, Monika, and especially Anita Williams.

Richard S. Howey

Bibliographies Containing Histories
Not Located in Libraries

BEPI: A Bibliography of English Publications in India, 1976. [Delhi]
"Biblio." [Catalogue des ouvrages parus en langue française dans le monde entier. Paris.]
Bibliografia brasileira. [Rio de Janeiro]
Bibliografia brasileira mensal. [Rio de Janeiro]
Bibliografia nazionale italiana. [Firenze]
Blagojević, [Obren], *Ekonomske doktrine,* p. 475. [Beograd]
Boletim bibliográfico brasileiro. [Rio de Janeiro]
Brinkman's Catalogus van boeken. [Amsterdam]
Catalogo cumulativo, 1886–1957, del bollettino delle pubblicazioni italiane. [Firenze]
Catálogo general de la librería española. [Madrid, Instituto Nacional del Libro Español]
Catalogo generale della libreria italiana. [Milano]
Chuprov, [Aleksandr Ivanovich], *Riechi i stat'i,* III, 577. [Moskva]
Cumulative Book Index. [New York]
Deutsches Bücherverzeichnis. [Leipzig]
Flamant, [Maurice], "Indications bibliographiques," *Revue d'économie politique* 65 (1955): 1046. [Paris]
Gómez Granillo, [Moisés], *Breve historia.* [México]
Impex. [Delhi]
Index translationum. [Paris]
Indian Books in Print. [Delhi]
Indian National Bibliography. [Calcutta]
International Bibliography of Economics. [London]
Jugoslovenska retrospektivna bibliografsha grada. [Beograd]
Kayser, [Christian Gottlob], *Vollständiges Bücher-lexicon.* [Leipzig]
La Librairie française. [Paris]
Libros en venta. [New York]
Libros españoles. [Madrid]
Livraria Portugal. [Lisboa]
Livros novos. [São Paulo]

Lyster, [T. W.], "Bibliography of . . . Ingram," *Leabharlann,* III (1909). [Dublin]

Mizuta, [Hiroshi], *History of Economic Thought Newsletter,* April 1970. [Bristol]

Morgenstern, [Oscar], and Schams, [Ewald], "Eine Bibliographie der allgemeinen Lehrgeschichten der Nationalökonomie," *Zeitschrift für Nationalökonomie* 4 (1933). [Wien]

Norsk bokfortegnelse. [Oslo]

Palau [y Dulcet, Antonio], *Manual del librero hispano-americano.* [Barcelona]

Popescu, [Oreste], *On the Historiography of Economic Thought.* [Neuchâtel]

Remer, [Charles F.], and Kawai, [Saburo], *Japanese Economics.* [Ann Arbor]

Šoškić, [Branislav], "Bibliografija," *Razvoj ekonomske misli.* [Beograd]

Svendsen, [Knud Erik], "Eine Bibliographie der allgemeinen Lehrgeschichten der Nationalökonomie: 1933–1958," *Zeitschrift für Nationalökonomie* 20 (1960). [Wien]

Svensk Bok-katalog. [Stockholm]

2

A Bibliography of
General Histories of Economics
Published from 1692 to 1975

An entry that is preceded by a number with an asterisk (*) is in the University of Kansas Library.

1   Morhof, Daniel Georg (1639–91; professor at Rostock, then at Kiel) "Politicus" [and] "Oeconomicus" [in] *Polyhistor, sive de notitia auctorum et rerum commentarii.* Lubecae: Sumptibus Petri Boeckmanni, 1688–92. 4°.
In University of Wisconsin Library.
Other editions: 1695, 1708, 1714, 1732, 1747.

First book to acknowledge the existence of a branch of learning akin to the one somewhat later called "political economy" and now known as "economics." The eleventh edition of the *Encyclopaedia Britannica* described Morhof's book as "a kind of encyclopaedia of the knowledge and learning of his time" (18:836). Morhof stressed the importance of "Politicus" and "Oeconomicus" as subjects, included mainly German writers (Seckendorff, Obrecht, Becher, etc.), but also mentioned Xenophon and *England's Treasure.* He concluded that economics had been developed largely by *illiterati,* rather than by scientific investigators.

Smith had a copy of the 1747 edition in his library.[1] In 1860 Kautz described Morhof as "der erste Literarhistoriker unserer Wissenschaft."[2] Morhof's attention to political economy was recognized by Roscher (1875), Cannan (1896), and Surányi-Unger (1922).[3]

Morhof published the first (1682) survey in German of European literature, *Unterricht von der teutschen Sprache und Poesie* (Kiel: J. Neumann).

2*   Réal de Curban, Gaspard de (1682–1752)
La Science du gouvernement, tome huitième, contenant l'examen des principaux ouvrages composés sur des matières de gouvernement. Amsterdam: Arkstée & Merkus, 1764. xvi, 767 p. 26.5 cm.

Furnished sketches of the authors' lives and summaries of their main books, arranged by countries and by years: indispensable parts of the history of ideas.

It included works by Bodin, Botero, Locke, Mariana, Montchrétien, Oresme, Seckendorff, and Sully.

3   Schreber, Daniel Gottfried (1708–77; professor at Leipzig)
     "Geschichte der Cameralwissenschaften als Universitätswissenschaften"
     [pp. 7–83 in his] *Zwo Schriften von der Geschichte und Nothwendigkeit der Cameralwissenschaften in so ferne sie als Universitätswissenschaften anzusehen sind.* Leipzig: in Verlag der Dyckischen Buchhandlung, 1764. 19.5 cm.
     In University of Chicago Library.

"Cameralism," the general subject out of which "political economy" evolved in Germany, had become a university subject prior to the establishment of two professorships for the subject in 1727. The bibliographer of Cameralism, Magdalene Humpert, listed five "Geschichte der Kameralistik" published from 1750 to 1764, of which four are unavailable in the United States.[4] Schreber's, the fifth history, was little more than a bibliography with historical intent. It contained mostly German writers (Morhof was one), but also mentioned Davenant and Petty. The direct influence of Cameralist histories on subsequent histories was negligible. In 1766, Johann Gottfried Hunger published a bibliographic addition.[5]

4   [Dupont de Nemours, Pierre Samuel] (1739–1817)
     De l'origine et des progrès d'une science nouvelle. À Londres, et se trouve à Paris: chez Desaint, Libraire, rue de Foin, 1768. 2, 84 p. 18.5 cm.
     In Columbia University Library.
     Later editions: 1846 (in Daire, *Collection des principaux économistes*), 1910 (in Dubois, *Collection des économistes*). Translations: Swiss, 1768; German, 1770 (or 1772 or 1773).

First of Dupont's articles on the Physiocrats. At this date, any examination of a group of writers was a notable contribution toward general history.

More descriptive and less historical than the title suggested. Its fragment of history was found in the pages near the beginning, where Dupont considered Montesquieu, Gournay, Quesnay, the Marquis de Mirabeau, and Mercier de la Rivière.

Written by the youngest of the Physiocrats.

5*   [————]
     "Catalogue. Des écrits composés suivant les principes de la science économique" [2:191–202 in] *Éphémérides du citoyen, ou bibliothèque raisonnée des sciences morales et politiques.* Paris: Chez Lacombe, 1768.

The second (see nos. 4 and 7) of Dupont's three articles on the Physiocrats.

Supplied to satisfy readers of *De l'origine et des progrès d'une science nouvelle* who had regretted the omission of a list of the writings of Quesnay's followers.

Listed 45 entries on Physiocracy ordered by date from 1757 to 1768.

6   Beccaria, Cesare Bonesana, Marchese di (1738–94)

[A short history contained in] *Prolusione letta dal regio professore nelle scuole palatine Marchese Cesare Beccaria Bonesana, nell' apertura della nuova cattedra di scienze camerali.* Milano: Galeazzi, 1769. 16 p. In-4°. In Bibliothèque Nationale.

Later editions: 1769 (Firenze: Allegrina); 1770 ([2:18–19 in] *Opere diverse del marchese Cesare Beccaria Bonesana*); 1804 ([19:187–88 in *Parte moderna*] Custodi, *Scrittori classici italiani di economia politica* [no. 24 in this bibliography]); 1822 ([pp. 384–85 in his] *Elementi di economia pubblica con varii opuscoli*); 1854 ([pp. 216–17 in] *Le opere di Cesare Beccaria*); 1958 ([1:375–76 in] *Opere* [also dated 1971]). Translations: British, 1769; French, 1769 ([6:133–49 in] *Éphémérides du citoyen, ou bibliothèque raisonnée des sciences morales et politiques*); Swiss, 1769.

A purported general history of political economy, incidentally contained in the introductory lecture of a Milanese professorship "di scienze camerali," it was a noteworthy achievement without precedent. The promise to include this short rudimentary history in the proposed lectures had been given the year before in the author's *Piano d'istruzioni per la cattedra di scienze camerali o sia di economia civile.*

This untitled landmark history is set down here in the following 183 words of its 1769 English translation.

> In France, Lewis the XIVth, and his minister Colbert, awakened trade almost instantaneously. . . . In the meantime the light of those sciences that are most useful to humanity began to shine forth in Europe. . . . The profound spirit of philosophy and observation extended itself to public oeconomics and commerce. Already the English had received from Bacon the first seeds of these sciences, which other illustrious men of that nation have since developed and brought to light. In France the Marischal Vauban was the first who spoke the unknown language of oeconomical reasoning, resembling in this, as well as in the profession of arms, the great Xenophon, who has left us the only ancient monument we have upon this branch of politics. But the more thorough cultivation of this science was reserved for our days when Melon, the immortal Montesquieu, Ustaritz [*sic*], Ulloa, the philosopher Hume, the abbé Genovesi (founder of it in Italy) together with many others, have carried it to that height, that nothing more seems wanting unless the last and not least difficult lineaments, to render it perfect, and of general and certain utility.

It is interesting that the first history should make so strong a claim for the perfection of the subject.

The first argument over the proper contents of a history of political economy appeared in Dupont's footnotes to the French translation. These footnotes were nine times the length of Beccaria's "succinta storia." In them, Dupont repeated his assertion, made in *De l'origine* (no. 4 in this bibliography) that the subject had started with Montesquieu's *De l'esprit des lois* in 1748 and that nothing important had appeared subsequently until the discovery of Physiocracy by

5

Gournay and Quesnay. His footnotes explicitly disclaimed, or modified, Beccaria's claims to the inclusion of Vauban, Melon, Uztariz, Ulloa, Hume, and Genovesi. He expressed astonishment that Beccaria had omitted mention of Gournay, Quesnay, Mirabeau, and de la Rivière.[6]

Beccaria's short history had ties to other early views on the subject: a tie to the "scienze camerali," which earlier had had a history by Schreber (no. 3 in this bibliography); ties to his French contemporaries Dupont and Morellet (nos. 4, 5, 7, and 8 in this bibliography); and a less direct tie to Adam Smith (no. 10 in this bibliography), whose library held a copy of Beccaria's 1770 *Opere diverse*, which contained the Italian version of the *Prolusione*, as well as a copy of the 1769 issues of the *Éphémérides du citoyen*, in which was found the French translation with Dupont's critical notes. Smith's library lacked, in its catalogue, a copy of the English translation that possibly had been sponsored by Hume.

7*   [Dupont de Nemours, Pierre Samuel] (1739–1817)
    "Notice abrégée des différents écrits modernes qui ont concouru en France à former la science de l'économie politique" [1:xi–lii; 2:v–xlviii; 3:v–xxx; 4:iii–xxiv; 5:v–xlvii (i); 6:5–52; 8:5–38; and 9:5–78 in] *Éphémérides du citoyen, ou bibliothèque raisonnée des sciences morales et politiques.* Paris: Chez Lacombe, 1769.

Dupont's last and chief article on the Physiocrats, which he identified as "cette Histoire abrégée des Écrits économiques."

An eightfold expansion of his *Catalogue* (1768) which corrected a few slips, added a section on writers before 1756, inserted names of Physiocrats omitted from his *Catalogue,* and presented new comment on the Physiocratic writings, it was not a general history, but principally a year-by-year commentary on the writings of *les philosophes économiques,* from 1756 to 1768, written by one of them.

This was one of the first publications to use the term "économie politique."[7]

Stephan Bauer called it the "first sketch of a history of economics" ("Éphémérides," in Palgrave, *Dictionary,* 1:744), and Schumpeter followed his lead (*A History of Economic Analysis* [no. 574 infra], p. 227).

8*   Morellet, André (1727–1819)
    "Catalogue d'une bibliotheque d'économie politique, formée pour le travail du nouveau Dictionnaire de commerce" [appended to his] *Prospectus d'un nouveau Dictionnaire de commerce . . . en cinq volumes in-folio, proposés par souscription.* Paris: Chez les Frères Estienne, 1769. 34 p. 28 cm.

Joseph Garnier wrote (1853) that the *Prospectus* was "remarquable à divers titres et très intéressant pour l'histoire de la science" ("Morellet [André]," in Charles Coquelin et Gilbert Urbain Guillaumin, *Dictionnaire de l'économie politique* [Paris: Guillaumin et Cie], 2:252). The part most interesting for the history of political economy was the "Catalogue."

The expression "économie politique" was barely known in 1769. The "Catalogue" furthered its recognition as a blanket term to embrace such distinct subjects as agriculture, commerce, money, prices, taxes, and usury, among others, which had long been discussed by writers, as well as to include the few attempts, expressly those of the Physiocrats, to find generalizations enveloping these distinct subjects. The delineation of the scope of the term "political economy" was a prerequisite to the development of its history. The "Catalogue," in which the term "économie politique" appeared twenty-one times, helped to make known, in detail, a satisfactory prerequisite delineation. It listed 739 entries, dated from 1535 to 1769 and divided into 38 subject divisions. The median date was 1756.

It also directly helped to establish an annual (and thus chronological in a degree) list of the main books on political economy, a second prerequisite to the development of its history. There had been earlier lists,[8] but the "Catalogue" was better. It provided the facts for a degree of chronology in that all but 35 of the items were dated. Further, most subdivisions were roughly, many were almost entirely, and several were completely annual in arrangement.

Morellet listed authors' names for only one-third of the items: anonymity in political economy was still the rule. The distribution among languages, shown below, indicates the extent to which the list was international. The absence of books in German, a major language with an extensive literature in all fields of study, is notable.

French	346
English	299
Latin	52
Italian	41
Spanish	1
	739

The "Catalogue" has connections with subsequent attempts to write a history of political economy. Its first was with Smith, who originated the historical ideas of "The Mercantile System" and "The Agricultural Systems" (see no. 10 infra). These two ideas provided basic useful generalizations that had been extensively used by later historians of political economy. Morellet, according to John Rae, had become one of Smith's "fastest friends in France" during the time that Smith spent at Paris in 1766 (*Life of Adam Smith* [London: Macmillan & Co., 1895], p. 200). Morellet later corresponded with Smith, and he probably gave Smith the copy of the "Catalogue" found in Smith's library. If it came to Smith in the year of its publication, it arrived when he was in Kirkaldy working on the *Wealth of Nations*.

Morellet was also connected with Peuchet, who wrote an early sketch of a history of political economy (see no. 20 infra). Morellet, who had been asked by the publishers in 1769 to prepare a new edition of Savary's *Dictionnaire universel du commerce,* announced the new dictionary in the *Prospectus* but never completed the work, although he retained the hope of doing so until the French Revolution cut off financial assistance from the government. He turned over his collected materials to Peuchet, one of his assistants.

The *Prospectus* later received notice in two major histories: by Blanqui

7

(1837: *Histoire de l'économie politique* [no. 85 infra], p. 62) and McCulloch
(1845: *The Literature of Political Economy* [no. 98 infra], p. 62).

9* Young, Arthur (1741–1820)
   "Examination of False Propositions" [chapter 3 in his] *Political Arith-
   metic*. Containing Observations on the Present State of Great Britain;
   and the Principles of her Policy in the Encouragement of Agriculture.
   Addressed to the Oeconomical Societies established in Europe. London:
   Printed for W. Nicoll, 1774 (reprinted, New York, 1967). 21.5 cm.
   Translations: French, 1775; German, 1777.

Contained a rudimentary history of political economy that linked several earlier
writers together and criticized their errors. The desire to search out the sources
of present errors was a recurring incentive to the examination of the history of
political economy. Young was the first to present the Physiocrats to English
readers.

10* Smith, Adam (1723–90)
    "Of Systems of Political Economy" [fourth book in his] *An Inquiry into
    the Nature and Causes of the Wealth of Nations*. London: W. Strahan
    and T. Cadell, 1776. 28 cm.

    The later editions and translations of the *Wealth of Nations* were more
    numerous by far than those of any other book contributing to the his-
    toriography of economics. A bibliography of 128 later editions and
    106 translations published through 1938 is found in "A Catalogue of
    Smithiana," part of *The Vanderblue Memorial Collection of Smithiana*
    ("Publication Number 2 of the Kress Library of Business and Eco-
    nomics" [Cambridge, Mass.: Harvard University Press, 1939]). The
    Vanderblue catalogue listed the following 48 translations published be-
    fore 1878: German, 1776–78, 1776–92, 1794–96, 1796–99, 1799, 1810,
    1846–47, 1861; Dutch, 1778–79, 1796; Danish, 1779–80; French, 1779–
    80, 1781, 1786, 1788, 1790–91, 1791–92, 1794, 1800–1801, 1802, 1809,
    1822, 1843, 1859, 1860; Swiss, 1781, 1791, 1792 (2 editions), 1797, 1801;
    American, 1789, 1796, 1804, 1811, 1816, 1818, 1871, 1876, 1877; Italian,
    1790–91, 1851 (2 editions); Spanish, 1794, 1805–6; Russian, 1802–6,
    1866; Austrian, 1814. The following 4 later editions and 37 trans-
    lations appeared after 1938. Later editions: 1950, 1954, 1961, 1976.
    Translations: American, 1947, 1952, 1961, 1963, 1966; Chinese, 1964;
    Czechoslovak, 1958; East German, 1963–75; Egyptian, 1959; French,
    1950; German, 1974; Greek, 1948; Hungarian, 1959; Italian, 1945,
    1973; Japanese, 1950, 1959–66, 1963–65, 1968, 1969, 1974; Korean,
    1959 (2 editions), 1960, 1961; Mexican, 1958; Polish, 1954; Romanian,
    1962–65; Russian, 1962; Spanish, 1947, 1949–55, 1956, 1961; Turkish,
    1948, 1955; Yugoslav, 1952, 1970.

The enumeration of Adam Smith's many accomplishments should be extended
to acknowledge his contribution to the writing of the history of political economy.
The "Fourth Book" was a source from which early historians of political

economy drew authoritative major generalizations. In it Smith had recognized, before anyone else did, the simplifying possibility of gathering earlier writers into two groups, the writers on the Mercantile System and the French writers on the Agricultural Systems, later known as the Physiocrats. In adding a system of his own—the "Industrial System," as it came to be called—he presented a third main historical grouping. Early short histories often did little more than elaborate the three Smithian subdivisions. To this day, most histories show the influence of Smith's groupings.

No one before Smith had written of "systems" of political economy prominently enough to be recognized and remembered: he created both the idea and the term.[9] No one previously had written of the totality of the ideas associated with his "Mercantile System" under any name. Smith elucidated the concept, and he supplied the memorable phrase to designate it. Although the Physiocrats had described their own works, they had not effectively related them to other, especially earlier, writers. Smith's application of the idea of "systems" to political economy was an innovation that was handy, and thus attractive, to most later historians of political economy. The many editions and translations of the *Wealth of Nations* assured a swift and widespread acceptance of the historical concepts of the "Mercantile System" and the "Agricultural Systems."

Smith has not received credit for his historiographic contribution. Bibliographers of the histories of political economy have always omitted his name. The critical literature on Smith contains nothing on his place as a historian of political economy. Roll may be the only historian who has identified Smith with the histories of political economy. He wrote: "Interest in the development of economic science is little more than a hundred years old. There are a few unimportant works in the eighteenth century, and there is a book in the *Wealth of Nations* which surveys earlier systems of political economy" (*A History of Economic Thought* [no. 389 infra], p. 13). Two centenaries have failed to give him his historiographic due.

Smith's role in the development of a history of political economy may have been overlooked because it was not labeled as such and because it was overshadowed by his other lines of thought. In his "Plan of the Work" he had mentioned the "different theories of political economy" and had said that "I have endeavoured, in the Fourth Book, to explain, as fully and distinctly as I can, those different theories, and the principal effects which they had produced in the different ages and nations." However, the "different ages" aspect did not stand forth in the "Fourth Book" in the way his "Plan" had promised. The force of Smith's suggestion only becomes clear when the general histories of the next fifty years are examined serially.

11*   Dohm, Christian Conrad Wilhelm von (1751–1820; professor at Cassel)
      "Ueber das physiocratische System" [2:289–324 in] *Deutsches Museum.*
        Leipzig: in der Weygandschen Buchhandlung, 1778. 20 cm.
      Translation: Austrian, 1782.
First writer after Smith, whose *Wealth of Nations* he had read in translation, to use the idea of a "system" in looking at the Physiocrats.

12* Büsch, Johann Georg (1728–1800; professor of mathematics; founder and director of the Handlungs-Akademie at Hamburg)
   "Von dem physiokratischen System überhaupt" [Zweiter Theil, pp. 535–45 in his] *Abhandlung von dem Geldsumlauf in anhaltender Rücksicht auf die Staatswirtschaft und Handlung.* Hamburg und Kiel: bey Carl Ernst Bohn, 1780. 21 cm.
   Later editions: 1800, 1827.

Another adoption of Smith's idea of "systems." Büsch was influenced by Dohm.

13* [Pfeiffer, Johann Friedrich von] (1718–87; professor at Mainz)
   Berichtigungen beruehmter Staats- Finanz- Policei- Cameral- Commerz- und oekonomischer Schriften dieses Jahrhunderts. Frankfurt am Main: in der Esslingerschen Buchhandlung, 1781–84. 6 v. 19 cm.

Similar in intention to Réal de Curban's *La Science du gouvernement* (1764), it contained abstracts and criticisms of the works of 30 mid-eighteenth-century writers on social thought. Most were German Cameralists, but also included were Necker, Locke, Genovesi, Smith, Verri, Mirabeau, Letrosne, and Stewart. Pfeiffer did not relate these writers with each other or to any generalization on the development of political economy. He provided a source from which it was possible to form an opinion on change in social thought.

14 Will, Georg Andreas (1727–98; professor at Altdorf)
   "Geschichte und Literatur der Physiokratie" [pp. 4–50 in his] *Versuch über die Physiokratie, deren Geschichte, Literatur, Inhalt und Werth.* Nebst dem berühmten Abrégé des principes de l'Économie Politique Sr. Durchlaucht des Herrn Marggrafen von Baden. Nürnberg: bei Gabriel Nicolaus Raspe, 1782. 22 cm.
   In Kress Library at Harvard.

Improved on Dupont's and Smith's earlier histories in that it looked at the Physiocrats from a distance. It influenced later writers.

15 Condorcet, Marie Jean Antoine Nicolas Caritat, Marquis de (1743–94), and others.
   Bibliothèque de l'homme public; ou analyse raisonnée des principaux ouvrages françois et étrangers, sur la politique in général, la législation, les finances, la police, l'agriculture, & le commerce en particulier, & sur le droit naturel & public. Paris: Chez Buisson, 1790–92. 28 v. 20 cm.
   In University of Michigan Library.

A display of ideas that a history of political economy would have to take into account. It presented analyses of the works of many writers in a manner similar to Réal de Curban, *La Science du gouvernement* (1764), and to Pfeiffer, *Berichtigungen* (1781–84). They wrote mostly on politics, but a few, such as Bodin, Sully, Hume, Locke, Mirabeau, and Smith wrote on political economy.

16 Stewart, Dugald (1753–1828; professor at Edinburgh)

"Account of the Life and Writings of Adam Smith, LL. D." [3:55–137 in] *Royal Society of Edinburgh, Transactions, 1794.* 26 cm. First read before the Royal Society of Edinburgh on 21 January and 18 March 1793. In Columbia University Library.

Later editions: 1795 (2). Translations: French, 1797, 1799; Swiss, 1799.

Influential, since the development of the history of political economy made use of biography. An even wider circulation came from its use in editions of the *Wealth of Nations,* sometimes in complete form but more often as an abridgment. This union of Smith's biography with the *Wealth of Nations* began with a German translation (1799), next appeared in Garnier's French translation (1802), found its way to England and Scotland (1805), and then to the United States (1811).

17 Schmalz, Theodor Anton Heinrich (1760–1831; professor at Königsberg) "Industrie-System" [,] "Mercantil-System" [, and] "Oekonomie-System" [pp. 388–420 in his] *Encyclopaedie der Cameralwissenschaften.* Königsberg: bey Friedrich Nicolovius, 1797. 20 cm.

In University of Chicago Library.

Later editions: 1819, 1823.

Other histories by Schmalz: 1808, 1818.

First to call the "system" of Smith the "Industrie System." It compared the three systems but did not discuss their chronology.

18 Voss, Christian Daniel (1761–1821; professor at Brunswick) "Das Merkantil-oder Handelssystem" [,] "Oekonomisches oder Physiocratisches System" [, and] "Das (Smithsche) Oekonomie-Industrie System" [Dritter Theil, 2:76–396 in his] *Handbuch der allgemeinen Staatswissenschaft nach Schlözers Grundriss.* Leipzig: in der Weidmannischen Buchhandlung, 1798. 20 cm.

In Yale University Library.

Arranged a long discussion of the three systems in chronological order.

19* Walther, Friedrich Ludwig (1759–1824; professor at Giessen) "Das Handelssystem" [,] "Das physiocratische System" [, and] "Industrie System" [pp. 374–77 in his] *Lehrbuch der Staats-Wirthschaft.* Giessen: bey Georg Friedrich Heyer, 1798. 19 cm.

An implicitly historical arrangement of the three systems.

20* Peuchet, Jacques (1758–1830) "Discours préliminaire" [1:xi–xvi, in his] *Dictionnaire universel de la géographie commerçante.* Paris: Chez Blanchon, an vii [1799]. 27 cm.

A result of the "Dictionnaire" that Morellet had projected thirty years earlier (see no. 8 supra). Peuchet had been an assistant to Morellet.

It was the second survey of political economy from early times and in different countries, thirty years after Beccaria's (no. 6 in this bibliography). The simplicity of this reduction of the literature of political economy to a few generalizations is admirable.

Peuchet defined "political economy"; commented on the "multitude des écrits," starting with Xenophon (also mentioned by Beccaria), and continuing to the end of the eighteenth century; noted the diversity of opinion expressed by these writers; generalized that the English had first discovered "les principes à suivre dans les discussions sur cette importante partie de l'ordre social," supporting this view with the assertion that, when Petty wrote his *Political Arithmetic* (Peuchet gave the date as 1676), the subject was scarcely known in France; and maintained that, from 1730, the subject had progressed rapidly in France, Sweden, and some of the states of Germany. "On vit," Peuchet wrote, "paraître une multitude d'écrits, où toutes les questions relatives aux droits de la propriété et à la liberté du commerce furent discutées avec plus ou moins de profondeur et d'exactitude." These remarks served to introduce the Physiocrats. He incorporated Dupont's defense of the Physiocrats, which named all the principal members of the sect and explained their doctrines, and pointed out, at the end, that the term "économie politique" now referred not only to the works of Quesnay and his disciples but also to the later works by Smith and others.

21   Sempere y Guarinos, Juan (1754–1830)
      Biblioteca española económico-política. Madrid: en la imprenta de Sancha, 1801–21. 4 v. 14.5 cm.
      In Kress Library at Harvard.

First publication in Spain on the history of political economy. It contained extracts, and comments thereon, from the publications of 18 Spanish political economists from the fifteenth to the eighteenth century, arranged somewhat chronologically with biographical sketches.

It was a national, rather than general, history of political economy.

22*   Garnier, Germain, Comte (1754–1821)
      "Un exposé sommaire de la doctrine de Smith, comparée avec celle des économistes français" [and] "Sur le système des économistes" [1:i–xviii and 5:258–83 in] Adam Smith, *Recherches sur la nature et les causes de la richesse des nations.* Traduction nouvelle . . . par Germain Garnier. Paris: Chez H. Agasse, 1802. 21 cm.
      Later editions: 1809, 1822, 1843, 1859, 1860, 1880–81.

Garnier used the three systems in organizing a history. He began with the observation that the study of political economy had escaped the attention of the ancient philosophers; skipped the Mercantile System, although later described Smith's "Book IV" as a polemical treatise "où l'auteur s'est proposé de combattre les divers systèmes d'économie politique soutenus jusqu'à lui, et surtout celui qu'il nomme *système mercantile*" (1:xxvii); and found that the first political economists had been French and English writers who had discussed the relative advantages of agriculture and commerce at the end of the seventeenth century. He held that "un système complet sur la formation et la distribution des richesses" (1:ii) had to wait until the mid eighteenth century. This "système complet" was that of the Physiocrats, to which many pages were given, mentioning only Quesnay by name, but stating and criticizing the doctrines of the school in detail. The rest of the history described Smith's system as the successor to that of the Physiocrats.

The reader could obtain a capsule view of the history of political economy from these few remarks on the main turns taken by economic literature in the past.

23   Buhle, Johann Gottlieb Gerhard (1763–1821; professor at Göttingen and Moscow)
      "Geschichte der Theorie der Staatswirthschaft in England" [5:481–768 and 6:3–50 in his] *Geschichte der Künste und Wissenschaften seit der Wiederherstellung derselben bis an das Ende des achtzehnten Jahrhunderts.* Göttingen: bey Johann Friedrich Röwer, 1803–4. 8°.
      In University of Cincinnati Library.

Entirely a description of the works of Hume, Smith, and Stewart. It was called a "Geschichte" on the ground that later political economy depended on these three authors.

24*   [Custodi, Pietro] (1771–1842), ed.
      Scrittori classici italiani di economia politica. Milano: Nella Stamperia e Fonderia di G. G. Destefanis, 1803–16 (reprinted, Rome, 1966–77). 50 v. 21.5 cm.

Each of the 31 authors who were included was given a biographical sketch, usually prepared by the editor. These sketches, together with the accompanying republication of the authors' most important writings, formed a bulky history of Italian political economy.

25*   Malthus, Thomas Robert (1766–1834)
      "Of the Definitions of Wealth" [,] "Agricultural and Commercial Systems" [,] "Different Effects of the Agricultural and Commercial Systems" [, and] "Of the Bounty on the Exportation of Corn" [chapters 8, 9, and 10 in his] *An Essay on the Principle of Population; or, a View of its Past and Present Effects on Human Happiness; with an inquiry into our Prospects Respecting the Future Removal or Mitigation of the Evils which it Occasions.* A New Edition, very much Enlarged. London: Printed for J. Johnson in St. Paul's Church-Yard by T. Bensley, 1803. 27.5 cm.
      Later British editions: 1806, 1807, 1817, 1826, 1872, 1878, 1888, 1890. Translations: German, 1807, 1879, 1900; American, 1809, 1890; French, 1809, 1823, 1824, 1845, 1852, 1889; Belgian, 1841; Spanish, 1846, 1848, 1849, 1905; Italian, 1946.
      Later history by Malthus: 1820.

This expansion of the part of the 1798 edition that dealt with the Physiocrats and Smith used Smith's expressions "Agricultural Systems" and "Commercial System" and helped to spread a rudimentary version of the history of political economy.

26* Say, Jean Baptiste (1767–1832)

"Discours préliminaire" [1:xii–xxiii in his] *Traité d'économie politique, ou simple exposition de la manière dont se forment, se distribuent, et se consomment les richesses.* Paris: Chez Deterville, 1803. 19.5 cm.

Later editions: 1814, 1817, 1819, 1826, 1841, 1861, 1876. Translations: Spanish, 1804, 1813, 1814, 1816, 1817, 1821, 1836, 1838; German, 1807, 1818, 1826, 1831; Austrian, 1814; Italian, 1817; Danish, 1818; British, 1821; American, 1821, 1824, 1827, 1830, 1832 (2 editions), 1834, 1836, 1841, 1842, 1843, 1845, 1846, 1847, 1848, 1851, 1852, 1853, 1855, 1857, 1858, 1863, 1865, 1867, 1869, 1880; Swedish, 1823; Belgian, 1827 (2 editions); Dutch, 1857.

Other histories by Say: 1826, 1828.

The importance of Say's history was due, in part, to the *Traité*'s wide sale both in and out of France and to Say's personal influence, particularly on Blanqui.

This influential history mentioned the Romans (their first mention in a history of political economy), Sully, Vauban, Montesquieu, Voltaire, Quesnay, Mercier de la Rivière, the Marquis de Mirabeau, Raynal, Condorcet, Condillac, Turgot, Smith, Stewart, and Garnier. It avoided the use of Smith's terms "Mercantile System" and "Agricultural Systems" and did not follow the lines of Peuchet or Garnier. Say remarked that "il n'y avait pas d'Économie politique avant *Smith*" (1:xx). Say also thought that nothing substantial had been written on political economy since. He offered his own *Traité* as the first improvement. Consequently Say's history recounted the faults of earlier writers, and, to a lesser extent, Smith's inadequacies.

27 Sismondi, Jean Charles Léonard Simonde de (1773–1842)

"Introduction" [1:4–11 in his] *De la richesse commerciale, ou principes d'économie politique, appliqués à la législation du commerce.* Genève: Chez J. J. Paschoud, an XI [1803]. 20 cm.

Another history by Sismondi: 1819.

Sismondi evaluated the ideas of the Mercantilists, Physiocrats, and Smith. He showed a familiarity with Peuchet (2:393–94 n) and Garnier (1:96 n), although he did not mention their histories.

28* Weber, Friedrich Benedict (1774–1848; professor at Frankfurt an der Oder)

"Geschichte der verschiedenen Staatswirthschaftssysteme" [and] "Geschichte des physiokratischen und Merkantilsystems insbesondere" [pp. 85–94 in his] *Einleitung in das Studium der Cameralwissenschaften; nebst dem Entwurf eines Systems derselben.* Berlin: bei Heinrich Frölich, 1803. 17 cm.

Other histories by Weber: 1804, 1813, 1819.

This history gave Quesnay his due, listed the principal Physiocrats, and supplied the names of their German followers. It slighted the Mercantile System, and finished with a chapter on the "Geschichte der Cameralwissenschaften als solche."

"Erläuterung ihres Hauptgrundsätzes und ihrer Systeme" [and] "Von der Literatur der Staatswirthschaft" [1:9–37 and 43–60 in his] *Systematisches Handbuch der Staatswirthschaft mit vorzüglicher Rücksicht auf die Literatur derselben.* Berlin: bei Heinrich Frölich, 1804. 18.5 cm.
In Columbia University Library.
Other histories by Weber: 1803, 1813, 1819.

Discussed the Physiocrats, Mercantilists, and later writers, with extensive bibliography, but without reference to other histories.

30* Jakob, Ludwig Heinrich von (1759–1827; professor at Halle and Kharkov) "Geschichte und Literatur der National-Oekonomie" [pp. 8–12 in his] *Grundsätze der National-Oekonomie oder National-Wirtschaftslehre.* Halle: bey dem Verfasser und in Commission der Ruffschen Verlagshandlung, 1805. 19 cm.
Later editions: 1809, 1814, 1825.
Another history by Jakob: 1821.

An interest in foreign books (he had translated Say's *Traité* and Thornton's *Paper Credit*) and his position as a critic of the Physiocrats and a sympathizer with Smith equipped the author to prepare this history.

31* Hufeland, Gottlieb (1760–1817; professor at Landshut [earlier at Jena and Würzberg, later at Halle], active in spreading Smith's doctrines) "Vorrede" [1:ix–xxxiv in his] *Neue Grundlegung der Staatswirthschaftskunst, durch Prüfung und Berichtigung ihrer Hauptbegriffe von Gut, Werth, Preis, Geld und Volksvermögen mit ununterbrochner Rücksicht auf die bisherigen Systeme.* Erster Theil. Giessen: Tasche u. Müller, 1807. 23 cm.
Later edition: 1815.

Mentioned Smith, Garnier, Sismondi, and Say, all of whom had written historical sketches.

32 Schmalz, Theodor Anton Heinrich (1760–1831; professor at Königsberg) "Vom Merkantil-System" [,] "Vom Industrie-System" [and] "Vom Oekonomie-System" [pp. 116–51 in his] *Handbuch der Staatswirthschaft.* Berlin: F. Maurer, 1808. 20.5 cm.
In Kress Library at Harvard.
Translation: Danish, 1817.
Other histories by Schmalz: 1797, 1818.

33* Ganilh, Charles (1758–1836)
"Plan de l'ouvrage" [1:i–xxxii in his] *Des Systèmes d'économie politique, de leurs inconvéniens, de leurs avantages, et de la doctrine la plus favorable aux progrès de la richesse des nations.* Paris: Chez Xhrouet, 1809. 21 cm.
Later edition: 1821. Translations: German, 1811; American, 1812;

British, 1812; Austrian, 1814.
Another history by Ganilh: 1815.

Contained the most extensive treatment of the Mercantile System since Adam Smith, introducing the following names: Raleigh, Misselden, Mun, Roberts, Fortrey, Davenant, and King in England; Johan de Witt in Holland; Serra, Genovesi, Muratori, and Corniani in Italy; and Richelieu and Colbert in France.

Edward C. K. Gonner mentioned Ganilh's "extensive acquaintance with the economic literature of his own time, of which he wrote a history, probably his most important work" ("Ganilh, Charles," in Palgrave, *Dictionary*, 2:183).

34* Harl, Johann Paul, Ritter von (1773–1842; professor at Erlangen)
"Geschichte der Staatswirthschaft und ihrer Wissenschaft" [and] "Staats-wirthschaftliche Literatur" [1:108–38 in his] *Vollständiges Handbuch der Staatswirthschafts- und Finanz-Wissenschaft, ihrer Hülfsquellen und Geschichte, mit vorzüglicher Rücksicht, sowohl auf die älteste als auch auf die neueste Gesetzgebung und Literatur.* Erlangen: in der Expedition des Kameral-Korrespondenten, 1811. 19.5 cm.

Cited Garnier, Jakob, Lueder, Say, Schmalz, Sismondi, Voss, Walther, and Weber, who had written similar embryonic histories.

35* Weber, Friedrich Benedict (1774–1848)
"Zur Geschichte der politischen Oekonomie; theils in ihrer Ausübung und Anwendung selbst, theils besonders als Wissenschaft" [1:24–45 in his] *Lehrbuch der politischen Oekonomie.* Breslau: bey Carl Friedrich Barth, 1813. 22.5 cm.
Other histories by Weber: 1803, 1804, 1819.

Weber added a bibliography on the "Literatur der politischen Oekonomie" of 116 entries, divided into subjects and subdivided by language (1:45–64). He also had bibliographies on public finance (2:431–33) and on Physiocracy (1:346–49). Finally he explained the policies of the three systems (1:349–99).

36* Ganilh, Charles (1758–1836)
"Introduction" [1:1–24 in his] *La Théorie de l'économie politique, fondée sur les faits résultans des statistiques de la France et de l'Angleterre; sur l'expérience de tous les peuples célèbres par leurs richesses; et sur les lumières de la raison.* Paris: Chez Deterville, 1815. 21.5 cm.
Another history by Ganilh: 1809.

An interpretive history.

Ganilh held that "économie politique" had not emerged until the mid-eighteenth century, when speculation and conjecture had been first applied generally to human thought; that dependence of thought on empirical fact had led the Mercantilists to associate commerce with national wealth; that the Physiocrats had ignored the facts on which earlier writers had concentrated and developed their own speculations; that Smith had given a "réfutation des deux systèmes empirique et économiste," and that Smith's work had been criticized in the nineteenth century by Spence, Malthus, and Thornton.

37* Storch, Heinrich Friedrich von (1766–1835)
"Des différens systèmes sur la nature et les sources de la richesse nationale" [1:115–61 in his] *Cours d'économie politique, ou exposition des principes qui déterminent la prospérité des nations.* St. Pétersbourg: imprimé Chez A. Pluchart et Comp., 1815. 21 cm.
Translations: German, 1819–20; French, 1823; Italian, 1853.

Storch cited Smith, Say, Sismondi, Jakob, Hufeland, Ganilh, and Schmalz, who had prepared histories. He followed a common pattern: mention of the Greeks; then sections on the Mercantile System, the Agricultural System, and the Industrial System.

38 Pryme, George (1781–1868; professor at Cambridge)
"Introductory Lecture" [and] "Of Different Systems of Political Economy" [in his] *A Syllabus of a Course of Lectures on the Principles of Political Economy.* Cambridge, England: J. Smith, 1816. 26 p.
In Seligman Collection at Columbia.
Later editions: 1819, 1852, 1859.

Pryme outlined the history of political economy as follows: "Is necessarily a Science of late origin—Rise of it in Italy—Spain—French Economists—Adam Smith—subsequent writers." Listed lectures on the "Ancient System" (Sparta, Rome, Athens), the "Commercial System" (Colbert, Child, Mun, Gee, Davenant, Steuart), the "Agricultural System" (Quesnay, Mirabeau, Turgot, Garnier), and the "Character of Dr. Smith's 'Wealth of Nations.' "

39* Hauterive, Alexandre Maurice Blanc de Lanautte (1754–1830)
"Histoire de l'économie politique" [pp. 345–48 in his] *Élémens d'économie politique.* Paris: Chez Fantin, 1817. 21 cm.
First use of expression "Histoire de l'économie politique" as a title (p. 377).

40 Lueder, August Ferdinand (1760–1819; professor at Göttingen and Jena)
Kritische Geschichte der Statistik. Göttingen: Johann Friedrich Röwer, 1817. xvi, 855 p. 20 cm.
In John Crerar Library.

Relevant because it applied history to an allied subject.[10] Statistics in 1817 resembled descriptive political economy. This book had an introduction, "Hohe Wichtigkeit der Geschichte der Statistik."

41* Schmalz, Theodor Anton Heinrich (1760–1831; professor at Königsberg)
"Mercantil-System" [,] "Industrie-System" [, and] "Oeconomie-System" [1:242–96 in his] *Staatswirtschaftslehre in Briefen an einen teutschen Erbprinzen.* Berlin: bei August Rücker, 1818. 20 cm.
Translation: French, 1826.

Other histories by Schmalz: 1797, 1808.
More expository than historical.

42* Mill, James (1773–1836)
"Economists" [3:708–23 in] *Encyclopaedia Britannica, Supplement* to the fourth, fifth, and sixth editions. Edinburgh: Archibald Constable, 1819. 27 cm.

Discussed the Physiocrats. It contained the first use of the English expression "History of Political Economy."

43* Silva Lisboa, José da, Visconde de Cayrú (1756–1835)
"Origem da sciencia da economia politica" [1:10–108 in his] *Estudos do bem-commum e economia politica, ou sciencia das leis naturaes e civis de animar e dirigir a geral industria, e promover a riqueza nacional, e prosperidade do estado.* Rio de Janeiro: Na Impressão Regia, 1819–20. 23 cm.

First history published outside Europe, first history clearly divided nationally, and first history to include Portuguese writers. Other nationalities included were English, Italian, French, Swiss, and German.

44* Sismondi, Jean Charles Léonard Simonde de (1773–1842)
"Objet de l'économie politique et origine de cette science" [1:13–59 in his] *Nouveaux principes d'économie politique, ou de la richesse dans ses rapports avec la population.* Paris: Chez Delaunay, 1819. 21 cm.
Later editions: 1827, 1951. Translations: Italian, 1819, 1854; Spanish, 1834; Russian, 1897, 1936; German, 1901–2; Polish, 1955.
Another history by Sismondi: 1803.

Offered a detailed history of political economy. It began with the Greeks and the Romans; then looked successively at the views of the ministers of Charles V, the Mercantile System, and the Agricultural System; and finished with a discussion of Smith and a mention of his successors, including Ricardo.

It was the development of an article inserted in the *Edinburgh Encyclopaedia,* which had begun publication in 1810. Because of publication lag, the volume containing Sismondi's article did not appear until 1830 (16:39–43).

45* Weber, Friedrich Benedict (1774–1848)
"Geschichte der einzelnen Staatswirthschaftssysteme insbesondere" [pp. 123–33 in his] *Entwurf einer Encyklopädie und Methodologie der Cameralwissenschaften.* Berlin: bei Duncker und Humblot, 1819. 20 cm.
Other histories by Weber: 1803, 1804, 1813.
Treated the Physiocratic, Mercantile, and Smithian systems.

46* Malthus, Thomas Robert (1766–1834)
"Introduction" [pp. 2–3 in his] *Principles of Political Economy Con-*

sidered with a View to their Practical Application. London: John Murray, 1820. 21.5 cm.

Later British editions: 1836, 1951. Translations: French, 1820, 1846; American, 1821; Italian, 1873, 1973.

Earlier history by Malthus: 1803.

Very slight history of political economy which appeared in a successful book.

47* Maslov, Stepan Alekseevich (1793–1879)
Dissertatio inauguralis De natura atque fundamento nec non origine et successu variorum systematum oeconomiae politicae, quam e decreto amplissimi ordinis juridico-politici Universitatis Caesareae Mosquensis pro gradu doctoris elaboravit publiceque defendet Stephanus Maslow, disciplinarum juridico-politicarum Magister. Mosquae: Augustus Semen, 1820. xii, 67 p. 21.5 cm.

First university dissertation on the history of political economy, and first separately published monograph on the general history of political economy. It was divided into discussions of the Commercial, Agricultural, and Industrial systems. Maslov was familiar with Garnier, Say, Ganilh, and Sismondi, writers who had published short histories.

Cossa wrote that this dissertation belonged "to the domain of the history of economic literature" (*An Introduction to the Study of Political Economy* [no. 169 infra], p. 452).

48 Müller, Johann Anton
Chronologische Darstellung der italienischen Klassiker über National-Oekonomie, nebst einigen ausführlichen Abhandlungen über die Freyheit des Getreidehandels, und die Ausfuhr der rohen Produkte. Pesth: Hartleben, 1820. xii, 316 p. 8°.

In University of Michigan Library.

Contained a bibliographical-biographical account of the authors in Custodi's *Scrittori classici italiani,* followed by longer studies of Bandini, Paoletti, Arco, Genovesi, Algarotti, Verri, and Scottoni.

49* Jakob, Ludwig Heinrich von (1759–1827)
"Kurze Geschichte und Bücherkunde der Finanzwissenschaft" [1:5–21 in his] *Die Staatsfinanzwissenschaft, theoretisch und praktisch dargestellt, und erläutert durch Beyspiele aus der neueren Finanzgeschichte europäischer Staaten.* Halle: bey Hemmerde und Schwetschke, 1821. 20.5 cm.

Translations: Spanish, 1850, 1855–56.

Another history by Jakob: 1805.

An annotated subject bibliography that traced the history of public finance from the Greeks to Smith.

50* Lotz, Johann Friedrich Eusebius (1770 or 1771–1838; declined a professorship at Bonn)

"Geschichte und Literatur der Staatswirtschaftslehre" [1:5–21 in his] *Handbuch der Staatswirtschaftslehre*. Erlangen: bei Joh. Jak. Palm und Ernst Enke, 1821. 21 cm.
Second edition: 1837.

This history discussed Greek, Roman, and medieval political economy. It then considered the Mercantile, Physiocratic, and Industrial systems, citing such writers of histories as Smith, Garnier, Say, Sismondi, and Jakob.

51   McCulloch, John Ramsay (1789–1864)
"Sketch of the Progress of Commercial Science in England in the Seventeenth Century, Part I" [pp. 22–23 in no. 261 (19 January 1822) of] *The Scotsman*. Edinburgh.
No more parts were published.
In Newberry Library.
Other histories by McCulloch: 1823, 1824, 1825 (2 entries), 1826, 1828, 1845.

This is the first of eight publications by which McCulloch augmented and improved the history of political economy. For the first time, a writer based his history on a careful, methodical survey of the literature of political economy. This procedure gave his work freshness. Earlier histories had resulted from hearsay, tradition, second-hand sources, and unverified recollection. McCulloch also brought to his task a vigor which resulted in widespread publication that rivaled Smith's or Say's.

On 17 April 1822 McCulloch wrote to Ricardo that the "history of the different theories and opinions entertained respecting commerce has long been a favourite subject with me" (David Ricardo, *The Works and Correspondence of David Ricardo* [Cambridge, England: At the University Press for the Royal Economic Society, 1952], 9:186). Perhaps his early relish for books had predisposed him toward this history. McCulloch wrote that his bookishness had developed during the youthful hours spent in his grandfather's library (*A Catalogue of Books, the Property of a Political Economist, with Critical and Bibliographical Notes* [London, 1862], p. v). As a consequence he collected, over half a century, the largest library on political economy of its time (ibid.). He early read authors who themselves had written histories: in his first publication (1816), a nonhistorical pamphlet, he had quoted Dupont, Young, Smith, Peuchet, Malthus, Say, Ganilh, and Sismondi—names found in this bibliography.[11]

McCulloch showed his awareness of the compass and content of the literature of political economy by the number of authors he mentioned, by the various editions he quoted, and by the little known tracts he examined. His bibliographical skill may have been polished by the appearance of Robert Watt's *Biblioteca Britannica*.[12] Also useful to McCulloch were the Advocates Library and the Library of the Signet.

"I have sent along," McCulloch explained to Ricardo, ". . . a copy of a small Tract which I wrote with the intention of publishing in the Scotsman—I found, however, that it was too long; and that the million who read Newspapers would much rather have the space occupied by it filled with the accounts of murders, assassinations, and so forth—I only printed a dozen of copies of this Tract and it serves merely for the purpose of keeping as it were the main points in my view" (*Works and Correspondence,* 9:186). No copy of this "small tract" has been located. Perhaps there also were earlier traces of a history of political economy in the lectures on political economy that he gave in Edinburgh in 1820/21.

52* Oberndorfer, Johann Adam (1792–1871; professor at Landshut)
"Schicksal der Nationalökonomie" [pp. 14–57 in his] *System der National-ökonomie aus der Natur des Nationallebens entwickelt.* Landshut: bei Philipp Krüll, 1822. 20.5 cm.

Dealt with the Ancient World, the Middle Ages, the Mercantile System, the Physiocratic Systems, the Smithian System, and developments since Smith.

53* Say, Louis Auguste (1774–1840)
Considérations sur l'industrie et la législation, sous le rapport de leur influence sur la richesse des états, et examen critique des principaux ouvrages qui ont paru sur l'économie politique. Paris: J. P. Aillaud, 1822. 414 p. 20 cm.

Say examined the principal works on political economy by Dupont, Smith, Canard, Lauderdale, Ganilh, Ricardo, Malthus, J. B. Say, Destutt de Tracy, and Saint-Chamans in separate analytical chapters that, taken together, comprised a historical survey.

54* McCulloch, John Ramsay (1789–1864)
"Political Economy—Definition and History" [7:216–33 in] *Encyclopaedia Britannica, Supplement* to the fourth, fifth, and sixth editions. Edinburgh: A. Constable, 1823. 27 cm.
Other histories by McCulloch: 1822, 1824, 1825 (2 entries), 1826, 1828, 1845.

Remained in the *Britannica* until the ninth edition (1885).

"I have been obliged to interrupt the writing of my Lectures," McCulloch informed Ricardo 22 June 1822, "in order to write a general article on Political Economy for the Supplement to the Encyclopaedia Britannica—I was very averse to engage in this undertaking, but I could not get it avoided—I have not time to execute it as I could wish" (Ricardo, *Works and Correspondence,* 9:206). It has been said that this article may have contained the full text of the small tract of which he had printed a dozen copies earlier but of which no copy survives (ibid., 9:187 n.1). It did contain the part that he had inserted the year before in the *Scotsman.* On March 25 Ricardo acknowledged receipt of a "separate copy," spoke of the "valuable historical sketch" that it contained (ibid., 9:275), and urged him to publish it independently in order to increase the number of his readers (ibid.).

55* Rau, Karl Heinrich (1792–1870; professor at Heidelberg)
"Verschiedene Grundansichten über die Entstehung des Volksvermögens"

[p. 78 in his] *Grundriss der Kameralwissenschaft, oder Wirthschaftslehre für encyklopädische Vorlesungen.* Heidelberg: Neue Akademische Buchhandlung von Karl Groos, 1823. 21.5 cm.

Another history by Rau, 1826.

Short outline of the Commercial, Physiocratic, and Smithian systems.

56* McCulloch, John Ramsay (1789–1864)
"Rise, Progress" [pp. 19–72 in his] *A Discourse on the Rise, Progress, Peculiar Objects, and Importance, of Political Economy: Containing an Outline of a Course of Lectures on the Principles and Doctrines of that Science.* Edinburgh: Archibald Constable and Co., 1824. 22 cm.
Later edition: 1825 (enlarged but containing no major changes). Translations: French, 1825; Polish, 1828.
Other histories by McCulloch: 1822, 1823, 1825 (2 entries), 1826, 1828, 1845.

Rewritten version of his 1823 history.

57 Saint-Chamans, Auguste Louis Philippe, Vicomte de (1777–1860)
"Les Trois systèmes principaux d'économie publique" [pp. 278–319 in his] *Nouvel essai sur la richesse des nations.* Paris: Le Normant Père, 1824. 21 cm.
In University of Chicago Library.

Colbert, Mun, Petty, Ustariz, and Melon typified the Mercantile System; Quesnay represented the Physiocratic System; Smith comprised the third system; and Say was also mentioned.

Included in 1852 as part of his *Traité d'économie politique.*

58 Blanqui, Jérôme Adolphe (1798–1854)
"Esquisse historique de l'origine et des progrès de l'économie politique" [1:37–48 in] *Le Producteur, journal de l'industrie, des sciences et des beaux-arts.* Paris: Chez Sautelet et Cie, 1825.
In Princeton University Library.
For other histories by Blanqui, see entry for 1837–[1838] edition.

First historical publication by a writer who became a leading historian of political economy.

Blanqui was a protégé of Say's who shared his interest in the history of political economy.

59* Bosellini, Carlo (1764–1827)
"Progressi delle scienze economiche sino al terminare del secolo passato" [25:280–305; 26:5–52, and] "Progressi delle scienze economiche dal principio del secolo fino al presente" [27:267–92, 28:50–62, 182–97; and 29:54–73, 175–97 in] *Giornale Arcadico di scienze lettere, ed arti.* Roma: Antonio Boulzaler, 1825–26. Also published, without alteration, in two volumes dated 1825 and 1826. Reprinted and carefully annotated "a cura di Miriam Rotondò Michelini" [pp. 495–624 in vol. 2

of] Bosellini, *Opere complete* (Torino: Fondazione Luigi Einaudi, 1976). I have not been able to locate any copy of a second edition (1827), said to contain additions (see *Biographie universelle, ancienne et moderne, Supplément,* vol. 59 [Paris: Chez L. G. Michaud, 1835], p. 35).

A long history which dealt with the Greeks and the Romans; at more length with the writers of the seventeenth and eighteenth centuries, divided into national groups; and finally took the account from Smith to 1825.

Bosellini failed to impress his contemporaries.[13]

60*   McCulloch, John Ramsay (1789–1864)
      "Rise and Progress of the Science" [pp. 7–60 in his] *The Principles of Political Economy: with a Sketch of the Rise and Progress of the Science.* Edinburgh: William and Charles Tait, 1825. 21.5 cm.
      Later editions: 1829 (abridged), 1830, 1839 (abridged), 1843, 1849; the historical sketch was dropped from the 1864 imprint but reinserted in the 1870 imprint (also dated 1872, 1878, 1886). Translations: Portuguese, 1830 (abridged); German, 1831; French, 1851, 1863; Belgian, 1851, 1863; Italian, 1853 (historical sketch omitted); Spanish, 1855, 1889.
      Other histories by McCulloch: 1822, 1823, 1824, 1825 (entry next below), 1826, 1828, 1845.

Carried McCulloch's history to a large, widespread audience. It followed the text of the second edition of the *Discourse* (1825), except that it omitted writers after Smith, since their views were discussed in the later nonhistorical chapters.

61*   ⸻
      "Rise of the Science in Modern Europe" [pp. 18–48 in his] *Outlines of Political Economy: Being a Republication of the Article upon that Subject Contained in the Edinburgh Supplement to the Encyclopaedia Britannica.* Together with Notes Explanatory and Critical, and a Summary of the Science. By Rev. John M'Vicar, A.M., Professor of Moral Philosophy and Political Economy in Columbia College, New York. New York: Wilder & Campbell, 1825 (reprinted, New York, 1966, with introduction by Joseph Dorfman). 24 cm.
      Other histories by McCulloch: 1822, 1823, 1824, 1825 (entry next above), 1826, 1828, 1845.

Prepared as a textbook for American colleges.[14] M'Vicar's footnote "Economical Science in America" (pp. 44–48) was, as Dorfman noted, "the first venture on what might be called the history of political economy in the United States" ("Introductory Essay" of 1966 reprint, p. 8).

62*   Blanqui, Jérôme Adolphe (1798–1854; "Professeur d'Histoire et d'Économie industrielle à l'École spéciale de commerce de Paris")
      "Introduction historique" [,] "Biographie des économistes les plus célèbres" [, and] "Bibliographie ou catalogue des meilleurs écrits sur l'économie

politique" [pp. 1–28 and 215–44 in his] *Précis élémentaire d'économie politique*. Paris: Aux Bureaux de l'Encyclopédie Portative, 1826. 12 cm.
Later editions: 1840, 1842, 1857. Translations: German, 1828 (seventeen German authors added to the "Bibliographie"), 1855 (dropped the "Bibliographie"); Spanish, 1843; Danish, 1858 (lacked the "Introduction historique" and the "Bibliographie").
For other histories by Blanqui, see entry for 1837–[1838] edition.

A revision and extension of Blanqui's "Esquisse historique" of 1825, which repeated Blanqui's mention of "le beau tableau qu'il [Say] a tracé des progrès de la science économique" and spoke also of the *Discourse* which McCulloch had just published "sur les progrès de l'économie politique" (pp. 7–8). His "Bibliographie" was to play a part in his history of 1837.

63*   Cooper, Thomas (1759–1839; president and professor of chemistry and political economy at South Carolina College)
"On the Rise and Progress of the Science of Political Economy" [pp. 1–14 in his] *Lectures on the Elements of Political Economy*. Columbia, S.C.: printed by Doyle E. Sweeny, at the Telescope Press, 1826. 21.5 cm.
Second (unchanged) edition: 1829.

Third American textbook to include a history of political economy. First was Say (1821) and second, McCulloch (1825). It was modeled on McCulloch's *Discourse*.

64*   [McCulloch, John Ramsay] (1789–1864)
Historical Sketch of the Rise and Progress of the Science of Political Economy. Edinburgh: printed by A. Balfour & Co., 1826. 96 p. 22 cm.
Other histories by McCulloch: 1822, 1823, 1824, 1825 (2 entries), 1828, 1845.

Although prepared and printed as the "Introductory Discourse" in McCulloch's edition of Smith's *Wealth of Nations* (1828), it was first used as a noncommercial limited edition of 24 copies which were distributed as gifts.[15] At least 15 percent longer than the historical part of McCulloch's *Discourse* (1824), it contained everything in his earlier historical versions, plus new material and selections from the nonhistorical sections of earlier books,[16] and was by far the best history to date. If a history of the histories were to ignore the maxim "ce le premier pas qui coute," it could well begin with this *Historical Sketch*.

It started with the lofty view that the study of political economy would not only increase material well-being but also, and more importantly, that the study would improve higher thought and speculation, since they, in turn, rested on a material base.

Next it considered why neither the ancient philosophers nor the members of the medieval universities had studied political economy. It found that the ancients were misled by their antipathy toward the mechanical and commercial arts, a survival from a time when the warrior was the most useful citizen, and that the control of the early universities by the Church removed the incentive for them to examine political economy. The entry of political economy into

24

universities had to wait until the Church began to lose its hold on speculative thought.

Its immediate beginning was connected with the high regard in which the precious metals were held, an esteem that had led early governments to prevent their exportation on the ground that national welfare depended on a large supply. The seventeenth-century idea that, through trade, a nation could influence the size of its own stock of gold and silver started the discussion of political economy.

The discussion of the Mercantile System began with Mun, as had Smith's. This was followed by a consideration of Child, an anonymous pamphlet *Interest of Money Mistaken* (1668), Locke, and Harris. McCulloch's subsequent discussion of the progress of commercial science in Great Britain showed how the errors of these Mercantilists were exposed. The principal error of the early writers was found to rest on their belief that durable imports were better for the country than nondurable ones, gold and silver being properly held to be the most durable goods.

The steps in the breakdown of the predilection for durable goods were explained. The initial step was in the pamphlet *England's Great Happiness: or, a Dialogue between Content and Complaint* (1677), later attributed to Houghton. Although McCulloch did not identify the author as John Houghton, he did call it a "remarkable tract" whose "influence was far too feeble to arrest the current of popular prejudice" (pp. 28–29). After a digression on the merits of Petty's publications, another step was found in North's pamphlet *Discourses upon Trade*, which was said to contain "a far more able statement of the true principles of commerce than any that had then appeared" (p. 32). Unluckily, its suppression, soon after publication in 1691, prevented any considerable circulation and thus diminished its influence. A few years later, Barbon, in *A Discourse Concerning Coining the New Money Lighter* (1696), argued strongly against limiting durable exports (especially gold and silver). The pamphlet *The Considerations [up]on the East India Trade* (1701), later attributed to Martyn, was highly regarded for its refutation of "the various arguments advanced in justification of the prohibition against importing East India goods" (p. 41).

The care with which McCulloch examined the pamphlets of the seventeenth century on political economy was unprecedented. Smith, the first writer to investigate the Mercantile System, had mentioned none of the four pamphlets that McCulloch uncovered. Nor are they in the catalogue of Smith's library. Two were in Morellet's "Catalogue."

After introducing these four critical pamphlets, this history appraised the subsequent leading English writers up to Adam Smith. Davenant was judged not to have had "any material effect in accelerating the progress of sound commercial science" (p. 45). Stewart's favorable judgment of Vanderlint's *Money answers all Things* (1734) and Smith's approval of Decker's *An Essay on the Causes of the Decline of the Foreign Trade* (1744) were both accepted (pp. 45–46). Hume's *Political Discourses* (1752) failed to satisfy completely, because it lacked both a "systematic view of the effects of commerce" and "any analysis of the sources of wealth" (p. 48). Harris's *An Essay upon Money and Coins*

(1757) was rated as "perhaps, on the whole, the best economical treatise that had appeared prior to the publication of the *Wealth of Nations*" (ibid.). Steuart's *An Inquiry into the Principles of Political Oeconomy* (1767) was looked down on (pp. 49–50).

McCulloch defended, at this point, the completeness of his histories.[17] He next elaborated the reasons that had led him "to treat of the progress of economical science in England at such considerable length." This was the first attempt of a historian to justify the writing (or reading) of the history of political economy. McCulloch listed several inducements: (1) "the interest and importance of the subject," (2) "because it has hitherto been very imperfectly investigated," and (3) "in order to form a just estimate of the merits of Dr. Smith" (p. 50). A further inducement of another kind was that its study defended the English against the contention by "Say and some other continental writers" that the "Italians and French were the first who discovered and established the correct principles of commercial intercourse" (pp. 50–51).[18] In McCulloch's opinion neither the English nor the French subverted the Mercantile System before Smith.[19]

McCulloch credited Quesnay with having "the unquestionable merit of being the first who attempted to investigate and analyze the sources of wealth, *with the intention of ascertaining the fundamental principles of Political Economy;* and who, in consequence, gave it a systematic form, and raised it to the rank of a science" (p. 58). McCulloch admitted Quesnay's "merit of originality," but he added that he had been "anticipated in several of his peculiar doctrines by some English writers."[20]

McCulloch had an interest in forerunners, especially obscure ones.[21] He listed the Physiocrats, noted their principal works, selected Mercier de la Rivière as the "ablest expositor of this system," and concluded that the Physiocrats had "powerfully contributed to accelerate the progress of economical science" (pp. 56–66).

McCulloch had two major criticisms of the *Wealth of Nations*. His first was that the Physiocrats had mislead Smith into favoring agriculture over manufacturing and the home trade over foreign trade. But Smith's greater error lay in his faulty or non-Ricardian theory of value and rent.

The judgments in McCulloch's *Historical Sketch* still provide a fair guide to the development of political economy from the beginning through Ricardo.

65   Rau, Karl Heinrich (1792–1870; professor at Heidelberg)
     "Geschichte der politischen Oekonomie" [pp. 19–42 in his] *Grundsaetze der Volkswirtschaftslehre* [vol. 1 of his] *Lehrbuch der politischen Oekonomie*. Heidelberg: C. F. Winter, 1826. gr. 8°.
     In Kress Library at Harvard
     Later editions: 1833, 1837, 1841, 1847, 1855, 1863, 1868. Translations: Belgian, 1839; Italian, 1855.
     Another history by Rau: 1823.

Rau began with the Greeks, then discussed the Physiocratic System, the Commercial System, and the Smithian System. An extensive bibliography listed

26

major publications on the history of political economy.

66 Say, Jean Baptiste (1767–1832)
"Esquisse historique des progrès de l'économie politique" [pp. 257–74 in]
Encyclopédie progressive. Paris: au Bureau de l'Encyclopédie Progressive, 1826. 21 cm.
In Newberry Library.

A restudied version of the history in the author's *Traité* (1803). Part of this material is found in his *Cours* (1828).

67 Strelin, Georg Gottfried (1750–1830)
"Die Nationalökonomie oder Nationalwirthschaft" [pp. 137–80 in his]
Versuch einer Geschichte und Literatur der Staatswissenschaft. Erlangen: bei Johann Jakob Palm und Ernst Enke, 1827. 20.5 cm.
In University of Michigan Library.

Consisted of bibliographical notes organized around the ideas of the Mercantile, Physiocratic, and Industrial systems.

Strelin said: "Jede Wissenschaft hat ihre Geschichte und bedarf auch ihrer. Die Staatswissenschaft hat sie noch nicht, vermuthlich weil sie, als Wissenschaft, noch zu neu ist" (p. v). He thought that the previous works of Jakob and Lotz were not comprehensive enough.

68 Blanqui, Jérôme Adolphe (1798–1854)
"Essai sur les progrès de la civilisation industrielle des principales nations européenes" [38:598–612 in] *Revue encyclopédique*. Paris, 1828.
In Princeton University Library.
For other histories by Blanqui, see entry for 1837–[1838] edition.

Another step in the development of Blanqui's history.

Said by Joseph Marie Quérard (*La Littérature française contemporaine* [Paris: Daguin Frères, 1842], 1:597, 612) to have been the substance of the course given by Blanqui at the Athénée in 1828, a course that served as the basis for his *Histoire* published in 1837.

69 Flórez Estrada, Alvaro (1766–1854)
"Del orijen de esta ciencia" [,] "Del Sistema Mercantil" [,] "Del Sistema Agricola" [,] "Del Sistema Industrial" [, and] "De los nosteriores progresos de la Economía Política" [1:17–51 in his] *Curso de economía política*. Londres: Publicado e impreso por D. M. Calero, 17, Frederick Place, Goswell Road, 1828. 21 cm.
In Kress Library at Harvard.
Translations: French, 1831, 1833; Spanish, 1835, 1848, 1850, 1852; Venezuelan, 1840.

Influenced by McCulloch, whose article in the *Encyclopaedia Britannica* Flórez called "una obra maestra."

70* McCulloch, John Ramsay (1789–1864)

"Introductory Discourse" [1:i–xcvi in] Adam Smith, *An Inquiry into the Nature and Causes of the Wealth of Nations.* J. R. McCulloch, ed. Edinburgh: printed for Adam Black and William Tait, 1828. 23 cm. Other histories by McCulloch: 1822, 1823, 1824, 1825 (2 entries), 1826, 1845.

A modification of the author's *Historical Sketch* (1826), which had an extensive circulation, remaining in print into the twentieth century.

71*   Pecchio, Giuseppe (1785–1835)
    Storia della economia pubblica in Italia, ossia Epilogo critico degli economisti italiani, preceduto da un'introduzione. Lugano: G. Ruggia e Comp., 1829. 310 p. 23 cm.
    Later editions: 1832, 1849, 1852, 1903. Translations: French, 1830; German, 1841.

Discussed the authors that Custodi had reprinted in his 50-volume *Scrittori classici,* the state of the science after 1789, the relation between the Italian and the English authors, and the influence that the economists exercised on reforms in eighteenth-century Italy.

It was not a *general* history of political economy but one that did influence subsequent general histories. Rabbeno said that "the success of the work was, however, perhaps beyond its merits" and that "to expound superficially in a series of biographical and bibliographical sketches the lives and principal theories of a certain number of authors does not by any means constitute a history of the science" (Palgrave, *Dictionary,* vol. 3 [1901], p. 86).

72*   Rabenius, Lars Georg (1771–1846)
    "National ekonomiens lärdoms-historia" [pp. 13–27 in his] *Lärobok i national-ekonomien.* Upsala: Palmblad & C., 1829. 23 cm.

Surveyed the history from the Greeks to the Industrial System. It gave the usual Mercantile-Physiocratic-Industrial System presentation and was the first history of political economy in Swedish other than translations; accordingly it included Swedish authors. It contained no mention of McCulloch.

73*   Say, Jean Baptiste (1767–1832)
    "Histoire abrégée des progrès de l'économie politique" [6:351–422 in his] *Cours complet d'économie politique pratique; ouvrage destiné à mettre sous les yeux des hommes d'état, des propriétaires fonciers et des capitalistes, des savans, des agriculteurs, des manufacturiers, des négocians, et en générale de tous les citoyens, l'économie des sociétés.* Paris: Rapilly, 1829. 20.5 cm.
    Later editions: 1833, 1840, 1852. Translations: German, 1830 (Stuttgart), 1830 (Heidelberg), 1833, 1845; Belgian, 1832, 1836, 1837, 1840, 1843, 1844, 1845; Italian, 1834, 1835.

A longer sketch than the one found in Say's *Traité* (1803), it was the result of his lectures at the Conservatoire des arts et métiers. See also his "Esquisse historique" (1826). Say quoted McCulloch often.

74* Steinlein, Karl (1796–1851; "Privat-Docenten der Staats-Wissenschaften" at München)

"Geschichte und Literatur der Volks-Wirthschafts-Lehre" [pp. 1–218 in his] *Handbuch der Volks-Wirthschafts-Lehre, mit drei synoptischen Tafeln.* Erster Band [no more published], enthaltend die Einleitung mit der Literatur, die Grundlehren, und einen Theil der Lehre von der Production. München: in Commission der literarisch-artistischen Anstalt, 1831 (reprinted, Frankfurt, 1969). 22 cm.

A bibliography of political economy which contained enough introductions and annotations to entitle it also to be classed as a history.

75* Coux, Charles de

[Pp. 39–50 in his] *Essais d'économie politique.* Paris: Aux Bureau de l'Agence Générale pour la Défense de la Liberté Religieuse, 1832. 22 cm.

"Discours prononcé à l'ouverture d'un cours d'économie politique."

76* Lawrence, William Beach (1800–1881)

"History of Political Economy" [pp. 1–38 in his] *Two Lectures on Political Economy,* Delivered at Clinton Hall, before the Mercantile Library Association of the City of New York, on the 23d and 30th of December, 1831. New York: G. & C. & H. Carvill, 1832. 23 cm.

Included a discussion of the teaching of political economy in England and the United States.

77* Baumstark, Eduard (1807–89; professor at Greifeswald)

"Volkswirthschaftslehre" [pp. 535–45 in his] *Kameralistische Encyclopädie: Handbuch der Kameralwissenschaften und ihrer Literatur für Rechts- und Verwaltungs-Beamte, Landstände, Gemeinde-Räthe und Kameral-Candidaten.* Heidelberg: Karl Groos, 1835. 22 cm.

Divided according to the three systems; followed by a considerable bibliography.

78* Fix, Théodore (1800–1846)

"Coup d'oeil sur la science de l'économie politique" [and] "De l'économie politique en Allemagne" [17:258–91 and 21:148–70 in] *La France littéraire.* Paris: Bureau de la France Littéraire, 1835.

Emphasized German publications. Kautz referred to these surveys as "die hübsche Abhandlungen von Th. Fix" (*Theorie und Geschichte der National-Oekonomik* [no. 115 infra], 1:40).

79* Rotteck, Carl Wenzeslaus Rodecker von (1775–1840; professor at Freiburg im Breisgau)

"Von den drei Hauptsystemen der Nationalökonomie" [4:81–119 in his] *Lehrbuch der ökonomischen Politik.* Stuttgart: Hallberger'sche Verlagshandlung, 1835. 20 cm.

Covered the Mercantile, Physiocratic, and Smithian systems.

80*   Schön, Johann (1802–39; professor at Breslau)
      "Ursprung der Volkswirtschaftslehre" [pp. 9–26 in his] *Neue Unter-
      suchung der Nationalökonomie und der natürlichen Volkswirtschafts-
      ordnung*. Stuttgart und Tübingen: in der J. G. Cotta'schen Buch-
      handlung, 1835. 21.5 cm.

Mentioned the histories of Smith, Garnier, Say, Lotz, Ganilh, McCulloch,
Steinlein, Jacob, and Sismondi. It treated the Greeks, St. Thomas Aquinas (first
appearance in a history of political economy), the Mercantile System, the Physiocratic System, and the Industrial System down to McCulloch.

81   Augustinis, Matteo de (1779–1845)
      "Discorso storicocritico sulla economia sociale" [13:39–61 in] *Il progresso
      delle scienze, delle lettere e delle arti*. Napoli, 1836.
      In University of Minnesota Library.

Critical Italian summary, embracing mainly the three systems, "mercantile,"
"agricola," and "industriale."

82   Villeneuve-Bargemont, Jean Paul Alban de (1784–1850)
      "Cours sur l'histoire de l'économie politique" [1:83–90, 223–29, 269–74,
      421–35, 509–22; 2:15–23, 85–95, 168–75, 241–49, 321–34; 3:14–26, 165–
      77, 332–47, 401–16; 4:90–104, 161–76, 254–74, 321–39; 5:11–36, 85–98,
      172–92, 245–61, 325–47; 6:7–17 in] *L'Université catholique, recueil
      religieux, philosophique, scientifique et littéraire*. Paris: Imp. de E. J.
      Bailly, 1836–38.
      In University of Illinois Library.
      Later edition: 1841 (reprinted, 1970). Translation: Belgian, 1839.

Before this serial publication was completed, the first volume of Blanqui's
Histoire de l'économie politique en Europe (1837) had appeared. It was the
case of an appearance, in the same year and city, of two influential histories of
new description, prepared by two authors in complete independence of each other.

Before 1837 the general histories usually had been parts of other works;
thereafter they increasingly became separate volumes.

Three-twelfths of the book was devoted to an examination of the literature
of political economy since 1600, four-twelfths to political and social history of the
same period, and five-twelfths to history before 1600.

83*   Blanqui, Jérôme Adolphe (1798–1854; professor at the École speciale du
      commerce, at the Athénée royale de Paris, and at the Conservatoire des
      arts et métiers)
      *Histoire de l'économie politique en Europe, depuis les anciens jusqu'à
      nos jours, suivie d'une bibliographie raisonnée des principaux ouvrages
      d'économie politique*. Paris: Guillaumin, Libraire-éditeur, 1837–[1838].
      2 v. (xxviii, 432; 480 p.) 20.5 cm.
      Later editions: 1842, 1845, 1860, 1882. Translations: Belgian, 1839;
      Spanish, 1839; German, 1840; Dutch, 1851–52; American and British,

1880 (reprinted, 1968); Russian, 1895; Japanese, 1952.
Other histories by Blanqui: 1825, 1826, 1828.

Differed from earlier histories in that it incorporated a great deal of political, economic, and social history.[22] The historical background (especially in the earlier parts) was often implied from the institutions, monuments, and jurisprudence of the different countries. Early political economy was treated at relatively greater length: 516 pages were given to the period before Quesnay, leaving less than 300 to finish the history. It was the first history to include socialists (St. Simon, Fourier, and Owen). These socialists also were discussed at the end of Villeneuve-Bargemont's *Histoire* in a section published after the appearance of Blanqui's second volume.[23] For some time afterwards, histories of political economy followed Blanqui's example by ending their histories with the socialists.

The "Bibliographie raisonnée" (in this edition, haphazardly arranged, but with an author index) was a list of the notable volumes on political economy said to be "le plus étendu qui ait paru jusqu'à ce jour" (1:xxiii).

Blanqui's reputation as a disciple of J. B. Say helped his *Histoire* to receive recognition. Quérard called it "un livre qui seul suffit pour fonder une réputation durable" (*Littérature française contemporaine,* 1:593). Ewald Schams, in his review of past histories, said that it "hat die Qualität des ersten, geschlossenen, alle Nationen und Lehrmeinungen umfassenden Geschichtswerkes" ("Die Anfänge lehrgeschichtlicher Betrachtungsweise in der Nationalökonomie," *Zeitschrift für Nationalökonomie* 3 [1931]: 57). In short, it was the first substantial general history of political economy. In turn, the *Histoire* added to Blanqui's own reputation. He became a member of the Académie des sciences morales et politiques.

84*   Lavergne-Peguilhen, Moritz von (1801–70)
"Von den bestehenden Staatswirtschaftslehren" [pp. 328–45 in his] *Die Bewegungs- und Productionsgesetze.* Königsberg: E. J. Dalkowski, 1838. 21 cm.

Divided into the three systems, with most attention to the third, which included ten German writers.

85*   Blanqui, Jérôme Adolphe (1798–1854)
Histoire de l'économie politique en Europe, depuis les anciens jusqu'à nos jours. Bruxelles: Ad. Vahlen, 1839. 215 p. 24.5 cm.
This pirated translation lacks the "Bibliographie raisonnée."
See entry for first (1837–[1838]) edition.

Listed in Marx's *Gesamtausgabe* as part of a *Sammelwerk* also containing Rossi's *Cours d'économie politique* (pp. 215–429) and Buret's *De la misère des classes laborieuses en Angleterre et en France* (pp. 429–694).[24] The date of the *Sammelwerk* was given as 1843. The date of the part containing Blanqui's *Histoire* was later given as 1839 and 1842 in Kautsky's edition of Marx's *Theorien* (1905) and as 1839 (but not 1842) in the new edition of the *Theorien* redone from the original manuscript in 1954.[25] Marx resided in Brussels from 1845 to 1848.

86 ──────

Historia de la economía política en Europa desde los tiempos antiguos hasta nuestros dias. Traducción de José Carasa. Madrid: Nicolás Arias, 1839. xvi, 508 p. 4°.
Listed in Palau.
See entry for first (1837–[1838]) French edition.

87 Schmitthenner, Friedrich Jacob (1796–1850)
"Geschichte der Staatswissenschaft" [pp. 36, 42–43, 46–48, 63–64, 84–90, 95–107, 137–47, in his] *Zwölf Bücher vom Staate, oder systematische Encyklopädie der Staatswissenschaften. Band 1: Grundlinien der Geschichte der Staatswissenschaften, der Ethnologie, des Naturrechtes und der Nationalökonomie.* Zweite Auflage. Giessen: Georg Friedrich Heyer, 1839. 8°.
In University of Michigan Library.
Had no first edition with same title; perhaps the author's *Grundriss* (1830) was assumed to be the first edition.

88* Villeneuve-Bargemont, Jean Paul Alban de (1784–1850)
Histoire de l'économie politique. Bruxelles: La Société Nationale, 1839. 682 p. 21 cm.
French editions: 1836–38, 1841.
A pirated edition.
Courtois wrote that this book was "even more than Blanqui's work with a nearly similar title—rather a history of facts than of ideas" and noted that it showed "wide reading compared to that of Blanqui" (Palgrave, *Dictionary,* vol. 3 [1901], p. 626).

89* Blanqui, Jérôme Adolphe (1798–1854)
Geschichte der politischen Oekonomie in Europa von dem Alterthume an bis auf unsere Tage, nebst einer kritischen Bibliographie der Hauptwerke über die politische Oekonomie. Aus dem Französischen übersetzt, mit Anmerkungen versehen, mit einem Auszug aus des Grafen G. Pecchio Geschichte der politischen Oekonomie in Italien vermehrt, und mit einem theils ergänzenden, theils berichtigenden Epilog begleitet von Dr. F. J. Buss. Karlsruhe: Druck und Verlag von Ch. Th. Groos, 1840 (reprinted, Glashütten im Taunus, 1971). 2 v. (xvi, 335; 647 p.) 20.5 cm.
See entry for first (1837–[1838]) French edition.
First long history of political economy available in German. It encouraged lectures on the subject in the German universities, which were the first universities to offer separate courses of lectures on the history of political economy, a

significant occurrence, since the history of political economy was to become principally a university subject.

90* Daire, Eugène (1798–1847), ed.
   Collection des principaux économistes. Paris: Guillaumin et Cie, 1840–48. 15 v. 24.5 cm.

Assisted in the study of the history of political economy by gathering, in one set of volumes, outstanding international works on political economy. All non-French works were translated into French. The volumes contained historical introductions, usually by Daire.

91* "The History and Moral Relations of Political Economy" [8:291–311 in] *The United States Magazine and Democratic Review.* Washington, D.C., 1840.

Influenced by McCulloch, whose history was said to be "the first, and . . . most complete, history that has been given of the rise and progress of the science" (p. 298 n). It mentioned American writers, who had made "but few advances" over the English (p. 304).

92* "Political Economy—History of the Science" [8:338–42 in] *The Penny Cyclopaedia of the Society for the Diffusion of Useful Knowledge.* London: Charles Knight and Co., 1840. 30 cm.

Drew from Custodi, Pecchio, and McCulloch.

93* Villeneuve-Bargemont, Jean Paul Alban de (1784–1850)
   Histoire de l'économie politique, ou études historiques, philosophiques et religieuses sur l'économie politique des peuples anciens et modernes. Paris: Guillaumin, 1841 (reprinted, 1970). 2 v. (480, 454 p.) 21 cm. Earlier edition: 1836–38. Translation: Belgian, 1839.

Villeneuve-Bargemont said that after he first had seen Blanqui's history, he suspended indefinitely "la mise au jour" of his own promised work, on the ground that a second publication on an already exhaustively treated subject would be regarded as "intempérative ou superflue." He later consented to this Paris edition, when he had realized the extent that his history differed from Blanqui's, especially in its religious emphasis, and when he had discovered that it already had been pirated in 1839 (1:5–6).

94* Blanqui, Jérôme Adolphe (1798–1854)
   Histoire de l'économie politique en Europe, depuis les anciens jusqu'à nos jours, suivie d'une bibliographie raisonnée des principaux ouvrages d'économie politique. Deuxième édition. Paris: Guillaumin, Libraire, 1842. 2 v. (468, 494 p.) 21.5 cm.
   See entry for first (1837–[1838]) edition.

Unchanged from the first edition except that the bibliography was enlarged and arranged alphabetically.

33

95* Rossi, Pellegrino Luigi Edoardo (1787–1848)
"Introduction à l'histoire des doctrines économiques" [2:201–23 in]
Journal des économistes. Paris, 1842 (reprinted, in Rossi, *Mélanges d'économie politique d'histoire et de philosophie,* 1857).

The first of a course of lectures on "l'histoire des doctrines économiques" at the Collège de France. The remaining lectures were never published.

It consisted of general statements on the history of "doctrines économiques." In it, Rossi made first use of the expression "l'histoire des doctrines économiques," which became the expression by which this subject was known in France and which later was employed in the laws and regulations that required the subject to be taught in connection with certain degrees.

96* Bianchini, Lodovico (1803–71; a government official who wrote on political economy, served after 1845 as professor at Naples)
Della scienza del ben vivere sociale e della economia e degli stati. Parte storica e di preliminari dottrine. Palermo: Stamperia di Francesco Lao, 1845. xvi, 508 p. 27 cm.
Later edition: 1857.

Patterned after the histories of Blanqui and Villeneuve-Bargemont. Although it skipped the ancient world and began with Charlemagne, it was still almost half again as long as Villeneuve-Bargemont's *Histoire* (1836–38). The added length came mainly in the section after 1800, which treated Italy, France, Great Britain, Germany, and other nations. Each chapter first discussed the main political events of the period and then followed with a brief mention of the principal political economists and their chief publications. This work listed more than 100 German writers, with slight characterization and evaluation of their works. It was the first major history to pay attention to German economists. Say, McCulloch, Blanqui, and Villeneuve-Bargemont had mentioned few of them: this was a neglect that had to do less with the relative quality or quantity of the German output than with the fact that no major German general history or German Custodi had appeared.

97* Blanqui, Jérôme Adolphe (1798–1854)
Histoire de l'économie politique en Europe, depuis les anciens jusqu'à nos jours, suivie d'une bibliographie raisonnée des principaux ouvrages d'économie politique. Troisième édition. Paris: Guillaumin, Libraire, 1845. 2 v. (xxiv, 378; 430 p.) 18 cm.
See entry for first (1837–[1838]) edition.

No material change from second edition.

98* McCulloch, John Ramsay (1789–1864)
The Literature of Political Economy: A Classified Catalogue of Select Publications in the Different Departments of that Science, with Historical, Critical, and Biographical Notices. London: Longman, Brown, Green, and Longmans, 1845 (reprinted, London School of Economics, 1935; and New York, 1964). xiii, 407 p. 22 cm.

Other histories by McCulloch: 1822, 1823, 1824, 1825 (2 entries), 1826, 1828.

Intended, according to its author, to be "in some measure a history of Political Economy, as well as a critical catalogue of the principal economical works" (p. viii). To that end he had taken every means "to become acquainted with the history of the science."

Akin to his *A Catalogue of Books, the Property of a Political Economist, with Critical and Bibliographical Notices,* of which an edition (with somewhat different title) of 30 copies was privately printed in 1856 and an enlarged and annotated public edition was offered in 1862.

99* Sandelin, Pieter Alexander (1777–1857)
      "Histoire de l'économie politique" [3:438–55 in his] *Répertoire général d'économie politique ancienne et moderne.* La Haye (The Hague): P. H. Noordendorp, 1847. 24 cm.

Contained the standard account beginning with the Greeks, continuing through the three systems, and ending with a bibliography of more recent books on political economy. Blanqui's *Histoire* was not mentioned. Other volumes had long articles on Malthus, the Physiocrats, Ricardo, Say, Sismondi, and Turgot; as well as short ones on minor political economists.

100* Twiss, Travers (1809–97; professor at Oxford)
      View of the Progress of Political Economy in Europe since the Sixteenth Century. A Course of Lectures delivered before the University of Oxford in Michaelmas Term, 1846, and Lent Term, 1847. London: Longman, Brown, Green, and Longmans, 1847 (reprinted, New York, 1974). xv, 298 p. 22 cm.

Shorter than the histories of Blanqui, Villeneuve-Bargemont, and Bianchini, it skipped the early periods.

Twiss listed his indebtednesses: put McCulloch first and Say second, called the books of Blanqui and Villeneuve-Bargemont "valuable publications," and acknowledged the influence of Custodi and Daire. Although he disclaimed "novel views," he spent almost half his first lecture on *A Brief Conceipte of English Policy,* a pamphlet that had not previously been described in any history.[26] Twiss used this pamphlet as additional evidence to support the view that "more clear and correct views on the subject of money than any which were made public in Italy during the sixteenth or seventeenth century are to be found in an English work" (p. 17). Although Twiss was reputed to have been one of the few Oxford men of his day who had a knowledge of German (*Dictionary of National Biography* [London: Smith, Elder, & Co., 1898–99], 19:1320), he confined his history of German political economy to a mention of List, Osiander, and Rau.

A review in the *Journal des économistes* (19 [1847]: 394–95) criticized his history for being bibliographic and chronological, rather than doctrinal and philosophical, and concluded that there was "encore place pour l'histoire future des doctrines économiques."

Twiss led a busy life.[27] Some early side current of interest took him into the history of political economy. It first appeared with his appointment for a term (1842–47) as Drummond Professor of Political Economy, to fulfill the requirements of which he lectured on the history of political economy and published these lectures. In the following fifty years he never again wrote on the subject of political economy.

101* Grieb, Christoph Friedrich
    Populäre Gesellschafts-Oekonomie, enthaltend eine gedrängte Darstellung 1) der Geschichte der politischen Oekonomie, 2) der politischen Oekonomie der Adam Smith'schen Schule, und 3) der Arbeiten der Socialisten. Aus der "Neuen Encyklopädie der Wissenschaften und Künste," Band V besonders abgedruckt. Stuttgart: Verlag der Franckh'schen Buchhandlung, 1848. 346 p. 24 cm.

A standard history that allotted much space to Smith. It was probably written on order for the *Neuen Encyklopädie.* Grieb did not write anything else on political economy.[28]

First history to include a separate bibliography of the histories of political economy. It listed the histories of Blanqui, Villeneuve-Bargemont, Pecchio, Say, McCulloch, Rau, Schön, Hermann, Storch, and Twiss.

102* Hildebrand, Bruno (1812–78)
    Die Nationalökonomie der Gegenwart und Zukunft. Erster Band. Frankfurt am Main: Literarische Anstalt (J. Rütten), 1848 (reprinted, in "Sammlung sozialwissenschaftlicher Meister," 1922). xii, 329 p. 19 cm.

Hildebrand began with the Mercantilists, turned to the Physiocrats, and then concentrated on Smith before ending the first chapter with Ricardo. He gave a chapter each to Mueller and to List, and the last two-thirds of the book to the socialists, giving most attention to St. Simon, Engels, and Proudhon.

103* Ferrara, Francesco (1810–1900; professor at Turin), ed.
    Biblioteca dell'economista. Prima serie: *Trattati complessivi.* Torino: Cugini Pomba e Comp., 1850–55. Seconda serie: *Trattati speciali.* Torino, 1856–68. 26 v. 23 cm.

The first series had consisted principally of translations into Italian of the writings of noted foreign economists. The second series, arranged by subject, was less historical in purpose. Most volumes of the first series, and some of the second, had interpretative introductions by Ferrara. Frequent references to the *Biblioteca* showed its wide use. These translations and introductions encouraged consideration of the history of political economy in Italy. Ferrara's prefaces to the first series were published separately in 1889.

104* Blanqui, Jérôme Adolphe (1798–1854)
    Geschiedenis der staathuishoudkunde, van de vroegste tijden tot op onze dagen. Naar de derde uitgave uit het fransch . . . door . . . J. Versfelt.

's Hertogenbosch: Gebr. Muller, 1851–52. 2 v. (384, 452 p.) 17 cm.
See entry for first (1837–[1838]) French edition.

105 Molster, Johannes Adriaan (1827–89)
De geschiedenis der staathuishoudkunde van de vroegste tijden tot heden.
Amsterdam: Gebroeders Kraay, 1851 (also a second edition in same
year). x, 264 p. 18 cm.
In Columbia University Library.

Molster was influenced by Blanqui. He included a brief history of Dutch political
economy.

Written while Molster was studying at the University of Utrecht (1847–50).
Subsequently he wrote only on jurisprudence.

106 Rooy, Evert Willem de (1816–66)
Geschiedenis der staathuishoudkunde in Europa, van de vroegste tijden
tot heden. Met eene voorrede van D. A. Walraven. Amsterdam:
L. F. J. Hassels, 1851–52. viii, 617 p. 8°.
In Yale University Library.

The proportion of history of events to history of political economy was perhaps
as high as five to one.

The author included Dutch economists. He mentioned Blanqui, McCulloch,
and Twiss, but supplied little other bibliography.

107* Coquelin, Charles (1803–52), and Guillaumin, Urbain Gilbert (1801–64)
Dictionnaire de l'économie politique, contenant l'exposition des principes
de la science, l'opinion des écrivains qui ont le plus contribué à sa
fondation et à ses progrès, la bibliographie générale de l'économie
politique par noms d'auteurs et par ordre de matières, avec des notices
biographiques, et une appréciation raisonnée des principaux ouvrages.
Paris: Guillaumin et Cie, 1852–53. 2 v. (971, xxvii, 896 p.) 25 cm.
Later editions: 1854, 1864, 1873 (reprinted, Aalen, 1973).

The introduction announced that "c'est pour la première fois que l'Économie
politique aura une bibliographie complète." Block, who competently compiled
most of the bibliographies, was the first to use the national bibliographies of
Quérard, J. F. & L. G. Michaud, Ersch & Gruber, Kayser, and Heinsius in the
preparation of lists of books on political economy.

Cossa called it "a scientific monument such as no other nation can boast of"
(*Guide to the Study of Political Economy* [no. 136 infra], p. 182).

108* Knies, Karl Gustav Adolf (1821–98; professor at Freiburg im Breisgau)
"Die Volkswirtschaftslehre in geschichtlicher Bewegung und im Zusam-
menhange mit der Periode ihre Entstehung" [pp. 168–206 in his] *Die*
politische Oekonomie vom Standpunkte der geschichtlichen Methode.
Braunschweig: C. A. Schwetschke und Sohn, 1853.
Later editions: 1883, 1930 (reprinted, 1964).

An explicit attempt to turn the history of economics into an investigation of the dependence of the history of economic theory on the political and economic history of the time.

109* Trinchera, Francesco (1810–74; later a professor at Modena, Bologna, and Naples)
    "Sommario storico della scienza economica" [2:245–665 in his] *Corso di economia politica*. Torino: Tipografia degli Artisti A. Pons e Comp., 1854. 21.5 cm.
    Later histories: 1873 (2 entries).

Began with the Greeks and Romans, turned to the Middle Ages, and then to Mercantilism, where it treated Italian, English, French, Dutch, Spanish, and German writers. After the Physiocrats and Smith, it looked at eighteenth-century writers in all languages, especially Italian. The last 100 pages covered the nineteenth century up to 1842.

Cossa accurately characterized Trinchera as a follower of Bianchini (*An Introduction to the Study of Political Economy* [no. 169 infra], pp. 117, 490). The main outlines of the two histories coincided. Bianchini's influence was clearest in the long lists of writers that Trinchera copied. Not only did Trinchera organize his lists following Bianchini, but he also usually used Bianchini's Italian translation of foreign titles. Trinchera's "Sommario storico" might be thought of as an abbreviated later version of Bianchini's history.

Published when Trinchera held a position with the Neapolitan government.

110* Bianchini, Lodovico (1803–71)
    Della scienza del ben vivere sociale e della economia pubblica e degli stati. Parte storica e di preliminari dottrine. Seconda edizione riveduta ed accresciuta. Napoli: Dalla Stamperia Reale, 1857. xix, 547 p. 27 cm.
    See entry for first (1845) edition.

111* Hamilton, Gustaf Axel Knut, Greve (1831–1913)
    Om politiska ekonomiens utveckling och begrepp. Akademisk Afhandling. Upsala: C. A. Leffler, 1858. 94 p. 22.5 cm.

A university dissertation, with acknowledgements to Blanqui and Twiss, that presented a history of political economy beginning with the Medes and the Persians, and ending with Bastiat.

In 1820 Maslov had published the first university dissertation that was a general history of political economy.

112* Mohl, Robert von (1799–1875; professor at Tübingen [1824–46] and at Heidelberg [1847–61])
    "Die Schriften über die Geschichte der politischen Oekonomie" [3:293–338 in his] *Die Geschichte und Literatur der Staatswissenschaften.* Erlangen: Verlag von Ferdinand Enke, 1858 (reprinted, Graz, 1960). 24 cm.

A diligent bibliographer's review of all social sciences, which incidentally contained the first critical survey of histories of political economy. Mohl presented a methodical discussion of the topics proper to histories of political economy: the general histories, the supplementary or specialized publications, and the bibliographies that supported the writing of histories.

Mohl appraised the past histories of political economy. For example, he credited Blanqui's history with an extended coverage and with being readable; blamed it for not differentiating sharply between the history of facts and the history of political economy, for being excessively nationalistic by giving Say too much attention and treating non-French, especially German, writers superficially, and for not containing a bibliography arranged by subjects. Extensive serious criticisms in this vein foreshadowed the next development, in which histories dealt only with political economy, became international, and incorporated recent scholarship.

Mohl served for eight years as *Oberbibliothekar* of the Tübingen Library, an institution which he reformed (see Karl Geiger, "Robert von Mohl als Vorstand der Tübinger Universitätsbibliothek, 1836–1844," *Centralblatt für Bibliothekswesen* 7 [1900]: 161–91). His interest in and knowledge of the literature on the social sciences was shown by his personal library of over 10,000 volumes, part of which he sold to Yale for 7,500 gulden.

113   Vernadskiĭ, Ivan Vasil'evich (1821–84)
       Ocherki istorii politicheskoi economii. St. Petersburg, 1858. viii, 272, vi p. 21 cm.
       In Yudin Collection at the Library of Congress.

The first history in the Russian language. It mentioned Gossen and Jennings in the same sentence.[29]

Vernadskii's dissertation (1849) had been a study on Italian political economy made possible by Custodi's *Scrittori classici.*

The author taught at the University of Moscow (1851–56). He was employed at the Ministry of the Interior in 1858, and spent his later years in the State Bank of Kharkov. After 1858 he never wrote on the history of political economy.

114*   Blanqui, Jérôme Adolphe (1798–1854)
       Histoire de l'économie politique en Europe, depuis les anciens jusqu'à nos jours, suivie d'une bibliographie raisonnée des principaux ouvrages d'économie politique. Quatrième édition, revue et annotée. Paris: Guillaumin et Cie, 1860. 2 v. (384, 412 p.) 17.5 cm.
       See entry for first (1837–[1838]) edition.

115*   Kautz, Gyula (1829–1909; professor in the Polyteknikum at Ofen [Buda] and a docent in the University at Pest in 1860)
       Die geschichtliche Entwickelung der National-Oekonomik und ihrer Literatur [Zweiter Theil in] *Theorie und Geschichte der National-Oekonomik.* Propyläen zum volks- und staatswirthschaftlichen Studium. Wien: Druck und Verlag von Carl Gerold's Sohn, 1860 (reprinted, Frankfurt, 1968). 792 p. 23 cm.

A longer, and more studious, survey of the literature than that found in any previous history. It had greater bibliographic accuracy than was then common, and it presented a better guide to the literature on political economy, of all times and countries, than could be found elsewhere.

The summaries that it contained saved time for the reader who sought to know the works of earlier writers. Ott recognized that these summaries added to the merits of the history (*Journal des économistes,* 2d ser. 33 [1862]: 435–42). It did not contain extensive criticism, perhaps less than an optimum amount, and it had a common kind of absolutism which showed in the discussion of the Mercantilists, where the standards were those of Smith.

Kautz wrote his book for the specialist, rather than for the general student. Since few could use this kind of history, it never had a second edition, or a translation. Ott provided its initial praise in the *Journal des économistes* in 1862 (2d ser. 33: 435–42), where he called it the first history of political economy that was not adulterated with a history of events, and he also pointed to "les recherches consciencieuses, le désir d'être exact et complet, les indications littéraires et bibliographiques" of its author. Later, others concurred. Cossa, in 1879, said that it was "immeasurably superior to all those preceding" (*Guide to the Study of Political Economy* [no. 136 infra], p. 80) and added, in 1892, "and in some ways even than those that followed it" (*An Introduction to the Study of Political Economy* [no. 169 infra], p. 119). Alfred Marshall, in 1891, recommended it as "profound, just and suggestive" (*Principles of Economics,* 2d ed. [London: Macmillan & Co.], p. 53 n). Haney called it "the best of the older works" in 1911 and said that it "may still be consulted with profit" (*History of Economic Thought* [no. 234 infra], p. 553). In a 1922 survey of the histories, Theo Surányi-Unger characterized his countryman's history as a first-rank work, regarded its publication as a turning point, and concluded that it had not so far been surpassed in excellence (*Die Dogmengeschichte der Nationalökonomie als selbständige Wissenschaft* [Budapest: Verlag "Internationaler Donau Lloyd"], pp. 48–49).

Kautz has been credited with some originality. Marshall said that he "was the first to recognize the importance of Cantillon's work" (*Principles of Economics,* 3d ed. [London: Macmillan & Co., 1898], p. 58). For the most part, however, Kautz conventionally interpreted the past, a course that Surányi-Unger summarized by saying that Kautz "was stronger in comprehensive, synthetic research than in analysis and creativeness" and that he was "narrative rather than critical" (Kautz, Guyla," *Encyclopaedia of the Social Sciences* [New York: Macmillan Company, 1932], 8:551).

116* Du Puynode, Michel Gustave Partounau (1817–76; lawyer, political economist, writer)
        "Études sur les divers systèmes d'économie politique et sur les principaux économistes" [2e série: 45:343–60, 46:187–203, 47:341–68; 3e série: 2:5–29, 3:12–33, 4:39–60, in] *Journal des économistes.* Paris, 1865–66.
Appeared in 1868 as part of the author's *Études sur les principaux économistes.* Included studies of Turgot, Smith, and Ricardo.

117* Hertz, H. S.
Einleitung in die Geschichte der Volkswirthschaftslehre. Hamburg & Leipzig: J. P. F. E. Richter, 1867. 18 p. 38 cm.

"Vorträge, gehalten in 1863 in der technischen Section der hamburgischen Gesellschaft zur Beförderung der Kunste und Gewerbe."

Centered in a long discussion of Adam Smith. Only two Germans were mentioned, and then in the last paragraph.

Hertz also wrote a few short works, all of which were published in Hamburg: *Die Lehre von Arbeit und Capital* (1855), *Volkswirtschaftslehre* (1855), and *Die deutschen Zettelbanken* (1856).

118* Du Puynode, Michel Gustave Partounau (1817–76)
Études sur les principaux économistes: Turgot, Adam Smith, Ricardo, Malthus, J. B. Say, Rossi. Paris: Guillaumin et Cie, 1868. xiv, 493 p. 22 cm.

The chapters on Turgot, Smith, Ricardo, and Rossi had appeared earlier in the *Journal des économistes* (1865–67).

119 Balchen, Alexander Rosencrantz
Grunddragen af den politiska ekonomiens historia från äldsta till närvarande tid. Stockholm: Albert Bonnier, 1869. 174 p. 8°.
In uncatalogued portion of Seligman Collection at Columbia.

It was mentioned by Cossa (no. 164 infra).

120* Cadet, Félix (1827–88; "philosophe, moraliste et économiste français")
Histoire de l'économie politique: Les Précurseurs, Boisguilbert, Vauban, Quesnay, Turgot. Société industrielle de Reims, Conférences de 1867–1868. Reims: H. Gérard, 1869; Paris: E. Lacroix, 1869 (reprinted, New York, 1970). 249 p. 23.5 cm.

It was to have been completed by a second course of lectures on Smith, Franklin, Say, Cobden, and Bastiat, of which only those on Smith and Franklin were published.

121 Fiore-Goria, Ferdinando Maria
Ricerche sul concetto e sullo svolgimento delle scienze economiche. Torino: Vecco, 1869. 114 p. 8°.
Listed in *Catalogo generale della libreria italiana.*

122* Dühring, Eugen Karl (1833–1921)
Kritische Geschichte der Nationalökonomie und des Socialismus. Berlin: Theobald Grieben, 1871. xii, 591 p. 21.5 cm.
Later editions: 1875, 1879, 1900.

Followed lines of Blanqui and Kautz since the structure of the received history of political economy held a place sufficiently prominent to compel an academic writer to take it into account. Dühring used secondary sources to save time:

on the subject of Mercantilism, Marx wrote that it "would be better to read Herr Dühring's chapter . . . in the 'original,' that is, in F. List's *National System*."[30]

It was shorter (had less detail and fewer bibliographies) than Kautz's *Literatur-Geschichte;* omitted nineteenth-century developments except those of Thünen, List, and Carey; gave more space to socialism and less to the ancient world; and was less concerned with Smith's "Systems" than earlier histories had been.

Dühring had intended it, as the title indicated, to be a "critical" history. Its "critical" aim was to deny the view, supported by earlier histories, that present doctrine followed from the ideas of the political economists of the past who had *not* erred. It concluded that, on the contrary, present political economy was incorrect because it had clung to past error. This use of "critical" judgment, in part, led Ewald Schams to call it the first "scientific" history ("Die Anfänge lehrgeschichtlicher Betrachtungsweise in der Nationalökonomie," *Zeitschrift für Nationalökonomie* 3 [1932]: 49). No doubt Dühring exercised critical judgment or, at least, had a different canon. As a result, his history differed enough from others to ensure that it had no following.

Dühring was a controversial nineteenth-century thinker. His biographer, Gerhard Albrecht, regarded him as an outstanding figure of his time ("Dühring, Eugen Karl," *Encyclopaedia of the Social Sciences*, 5:272–73). Engels and Marx condemned him in a long book, the so-called *Anti-Dühring*. Schumpeter has recounted Dühring's accomplishments (*A History of Economic Analysis* [no. 574 infra], pp. 509–10). Dühring wrote on many subjects ranging from political economy to physical science, giving only a fraction of his lifetime to political economy and only a minor part of that fraction to its history. He wrote about political economy during the busiest period of his life. At the age of thirty, blindness led him to quit his law practice and to begin to lecture on political science and philosophy at the University of Berlin. It also made it necessary for him to be a cogitator rather than a bookish scholar. During the five years after 1864, he published seven books in the fields on which he lectured: *Capital und Arbeit* (1865), *Carey's Umwälzung der Volkswirtschaftslehre und Socialwissenschaft* (1865), *Natürliche Dialektik* (1865), *Kritische Grundlegung der Volkswirtschaftslehre* (1866), *Die Verkleinerer Carey's und die Krisis der Nationalökonomie* (1867), *Die Schicksale meiner socialen Denkschrift für das Preussische Staatsministerium* (1868), and *Kritische Geschichte der Philosophie* (1869). Two years later (1871), he added his history of political economy. In 1873 he published his last book on political economy, *Cursus der National- und Socialökonomie einschliesslich der Hauptpunkte der Finanzpolitik,* although he lived almost fifty years longer and continued to write.

123*   Trinchera, Francesco (1810–74)
   Schema di una storia dell'economia politica. Napoli: Stamperia della R. Università, 1873. 39 p.
   Other histories by Trinchera: 1854 and next below.

"Estratto dal Vol. IX degli Atti dell' Accademia di Scienze Morali e Politiche."
   Contained mainly precepts for the historiography of economics and only incidentally a short history of economics.

Storia critica dell'economia politica. Vol. 1: *Epoca antica.* Napoli: Tipografia dell' Università, 1873. xxix, 384 p. 8°.
Other histories by Trinchera: 1854 and next above.
Listed in *Catalogo generale della libreria italiana.*

125* Martello, Tullio (1841–1918; professor at Venice)
Quadro storico della economia civile. Lettura tenuta all'Accademia dei Concordi il 30 giugno 1872. Milano: Fratelli Treves, Editori della Biblioteca Utile, 1874. 60 p. 15 cm.
A popularization.

126* Dühring, Eugen Karl (1833–1921)
Kritische Geschichte der Nationalökonomie und des Socialismus. Zweite, theilweise umgearbeitete Auflage. Berlin: Theobald Grieben, 1875. 595 p. 22 cm.
Other editions: 1871, 1879, 1900.

127* Mariotti, Francesco
Delle origini e dei progressi della scienza economica in Europa. Imola: Ignazio Galeati, 1875. ix, 106 p. 20 cm.
Composed of lectures, given at the Università di Sassari, which covered all countries and all times. Mariotti mentioned the histories of Blanqui, Pecchio, Roscher, Custodi, Bianchini, and Kautz.

128* Contzen, Karl Wilhelm Heinrich (1835–88)
Geschichte, Literatur und Bedeutung der Nationalökonomie oder Volkswirtschaftslehre. Cassel und Leipzig: Carl Maurer, 1876. xiv, 208 p. 23 cm.
Second edition: 1881.

Contzen lectured at several German universities, edited at one time the *Pommerschen Reichpost* in Stettin, and wrote many books, none of which were well received. Best known was his *Geschichte der volkswirtschaftlichen Literatur im Mittelalter* (1869), which Cossa called "somewhat superficially and hastily written" (*Guide to the Study of Political Economy* [no. 136 infra], p. 99). His *Einleitung in das staats- und volkswirtschaftliche Studium* (1870) had a section "Zur Geschichte der socialen und ökonomischen Theorien."

129* Cossa, Luigi (1831–96)
Guida allo studio dell'economia politica. Milano: Ulrico Hoepli, 1876. vii, 261 p. 19 cm.
Later editions: 1878, 1892 (with title changed to *Introduzione allo studio dell'economia politica*). Translations: Spanish, 1878, 1884, 1892; British, 1880, 1893; German, 1880; French, 1899.
Cossa appraised the earlier histories. He treated Twiss's *View* somewhat unjustly

(*Guide to the Study of Political Economy* [no. 136 infra], p. 80) and misrepresented Colmeiro's *Historia de la economía política en España* (ibid., p. 83). Blanqui and Villeneuve-Bargemont were said to have confused "the history of theories and that of facts" and to have relied on "superficial" investigations (ibid., pp. 79–80). "Immeasurably superior to all those preceding" was his comment on Kautz's *Literatur-Geschichte* (ibid., p. 80). He judged that the defects outweighed the merit of Duhring's *Kritische Geschichte*, pointing to the ignorance "of the principal materials for his subject" and the "tone of presumptuous depreciation" which turned "a great part of his history into a vulgar libel" (ibid., p. 81).

Cossa treated the Mercantile and Agricultural systems as an introduction to the Industrial System of Smith. He changed Kautz's allocation of space, giving only half as much to antiquity and none to the socialists, and showed a much increased use of secondary literature and a polyglot viewpoint.

This history, especially the enlarged third edition, was well received. The influential English versions contained a preface by Jevons that recommended the book strongly. Rabbeno said that it "surpasses most of the existing works of its kind" (*Political Science Quarterly* 8 [1893]: 356). Edgeworth called it "an extensive, yet accurate, chart by which a stranger may be assisted in finding his way about the economic world" (*Economic Journal* 2 [1892]: 686). "Il est à souhaiter," Gide wrote, "qu'il soit traduit dans toutes les langues et qu'il devienne le vade-mecum de tout professeur d'économie politique" (*Revue d'économie politique* 6 [1892]: 1252). Böhm-Bawerk concluded that it was "ein unentbehrliches Requisit für jeden Nationalökonomen" (*Zeitschrift für Volkswirtschaft, Sozialpolitik und Verwaltung* 1 [1892]: 662). There were also more qualified reviews.[31]

After receiving a doctorate (1853) at Pavia, Cossa studied at Vienna and Leipzig. At Leipzig, Roscher provided the impulse to pursue the "studi storicobibliografici che furono una speciale predilizione della sua vita" (G. Ricca Salerno, "Luigi Cossa," in Institut International de Statistique, Rome, *Bulletin* 7 [1895/96]). This predilection led Cossa to become the nearest thing to a full-time historian of political economy that there had been. He settled in Pavia, became a professor in 1860, acquired a library (now part of the Biblioteca Civica in Bergamo) (Rouzel, *Journal des économistes,* 5th ser. 27 [1896]: 112), read widely, taught successfully (Schumpeter, *A History of Economic Analysis* [no. 574 infra], p. 856 n),[32] and eventually published four books between 1875 and 1878, one of which contained a history of political economy.[33] Cossa compiled and published bibliographies of political economy. A collection of these bibliographies has been published under the title *Saggi bibliografici di economia politica* (Bologna: Arnaldo Forni Editore, 1963).

130*   Malon, Benoit (1841–93)
    La Question sociale: histoire critique de l'économie politique. Lugano: Ajani et Berra, 1876. 320 p. 18 cm.
    Shorter published version: 1883.

Proposed to show how the governing class had used political economy to justify human misery.

131 Cossa, Luigi (1831–96)
Guia para el estudio de la economía política. Traducción de Jorge María de Ledesma y Palacios. Valladolid: Imp. Librería Nacional y Extranjera de Hijos de Rodriguez, 1878.
Listed in Palau.
See entry for first (1876) Italian edition.

132 ———
Guida allo studio dell'economia politica. 2ª edizione, corretta ed aumentata. Milano: Ulrico Hoepli, 1878. vii, 270 p. 18 cm.
In Northwestern University Library.
See entry for first (1876) edition.
Cossa rewrote parts, added several pages on Spain and Portugal, and appended an index prepared by Nicolini.

133* Dühring, Eugen Karl (1833–1921)
Kritische Geschichte der Nationalökonomie und des Socialismus. Dritte, theilweise umgearbeitete Auflage. Leipzig, Fues's Verlag (R. Reisland), 1879. xiv, 574 p. 22 cm.
Other editions: 1871, 1875, 1900.

134* Blanqui, Jérôme Adolphe (1798–1854)
History of Political Economy in Europe. Translated from the fourth French edition by Emily J. Leonard. With a preface by David A. Wells. New York: G. P. Putnam's Sons, 1880 (also dated 1882 and 1885; reprinted, New York, 1968); London: G. Bell & Sons, 1880. xxxviii, 590 p. 23.5 cm.
See entry for first (1837–[1838]) French edition.

135 Cossa, Luigi (1831–96)
Einleitung in das Studium der Wirtschaftslehre. Aus dem Italienischen nach der 2. Aufl. des Orig. übertr. und hrsg. von Ed. Moormeister. Freiburg im Breisgau: Herder, 1880. 240 p. 8°.
Listed in Kayser.
See entry for first (1876) Italian edition.

136* ———
Guide to the Study of Political Economy. Translated from the second Italian edition. With a preface by W. Stanley Jevons. London: Macmillan and Co., 1880. xvi, 237 p. 18.5 cm.
See entry for first (1876) Italian edition.

137 Fiorese, Sabino (professor at the Scuola Superiore di Commercio, Bari)
Breve svolgimento storico dell'economia sociale: prelezione. Bari: Petruzelli e Figli, 1880. 31 p. 8°.
Listed in *Catalogo generale della libreria italiana.*

138* Périn, Charles (1815–1905; professor at Lyons)
Les Doctrines économiques depuis un siècle. Paris-Lyon: V. Lecoffre,
1880. viii, 350 p. 18.5 cm.
German translation: 1882.
The first 157 pages served as a history of political economy from the Physiocrats
to Mill.

139* Contzen, Karl Wilhelm Heinrich (1835–88)
Geschichte, Literatur und Bedeutung der Nationalökonomie oder Volks-
wirtschaftslehre. 2te bis auf die Jetztzeit verbesserte Auflage. Berlin:
F. & P. Lehmann, 1881. xiv, 207 p. 23 cm.
First edition: 1876.
Had an author index, lacking in the first edition.

140* Eisenhart, Hugo (1811–93)
Geschichte der Nationalökonomik. Jena: Gustav Fischer, 1881. v, 2,
243 p. 22.5 cm.
Second edition: 1891 (also dated 1901, 1910, 1916).
This history, which was mainly a treatment of ideas, mentioned few authors or
book titles and had almost no bibliography.

It lasted a long while. Both Leser (*Jahrbücher für Nationalökonomie und*
Statistik, new ser. 4 [1882]: 540) and Roscher (ibid., 3d ser. 2 [1891]: 778–80)
praised it in reviews, and later historians also thought well of it. Ingram called
it "a vigorous and original sketch" (*A History of Political Economy* [no. 217
infra], p. ix). Spann mentioned it, along with the history by Contzen, as one
of the "earlier works on the history of our science" (*The History of Economics*
[no. 325 infra], p. 301). Haney quoted Ingram's estimate but added, "The
writer has not found it so useful or readable as might be inferred" (*History of*
Economic Thought [no. 262 infra], p. 664).

Eisenhart had lectured in the University at Halle from 1840 to the year of
his death. He was the first to teach the history of political economy at Halle
(Otto Lehmann, *Die Nationalökonomie an der Universität Halle im 19. Jahr-*
hundert [Halle: Eduard Klinz, 1935], p. 188). By the mid seventies he lectured
regularly on this subject and continued to do so each winter semester until
1887/88 (*Deutscher Universitäts-Kalender* [Leipzig: J. A. Barth], 1877 to 1888).
His book resulted from these lectures. It influenced Ely and James, for both
studied at Halle in 1877, and each interested himself in the history of political
economy on returning to the United States.

141* Geigel, Martin
Die wichtigsten volkswirtschaftlichen Theorien verbunden zu einem
Grundriss der Geschichte der Nationalökonomie. Würzburg: Stahel'sche
Buch- und Kunsthandlung, 1881. 32 p. 22.5 cm.
An outline for the use of students.

Geigel had been a student of Lexis's at the University of Freiburg im
Breisgau.

142* Blanqui, Jérôme Adolphe (1798–1854)
Histoire de l'économie politique en Europe, depuis les anciens jusqu'à nos jours, suivie d'une bibliographie raisonnée des principaux ouvrages d'économie politique. Cinquième édition. Paris: Guillaumin et Cie, 1882. xvi, 511 p. 22 cm.
See entry for first (1837–[1838]) edition.
This was the first edition in one volume. It omitted the "Bibliographie."

143* Périn, Charles (1815–1905)
Die Lehren der Nationalökonomie seit einem Jahrhunderte. Autorisirte Uebersetzung. Freiburg im Breisgau: Herder, 1882. 19, 358 p. 21 cm.
French edition: 1880.

144* Malon, Benoit (1841–93)
"Historique de l'économie politique, depuis les Athéniens jusqu'à nos jours" [pp. 1–159 in his] *Manuel d'économie sociale.* Paris: Derveaux, 1883. 19 cm.
A longer version was published in 1876.

145 Cossa, Luigi (1831–96)
Guia para el estudio de la economía política. Trad. de Jorge María de Ledesma y Palacios. Valladolid, 1884. 8°.
Listed in Palau.
See entry for first (1876) Italian edition.

146* James, Edmund Janes (1855–1925)
"Political Economy, History of" [3:237–57 in] *Cyclopaedia of Political Science, Political Economy, and of the Political History of the United States.* By the Best American and European Writers. Edited by John J. Lalor. Chicago: M. B. Cary & Company, 1884. 25 cm.
Last edition: 1904.
Acknowledged indebtedness to Kautz, Eisenhart, Blanqui, and particularly Cossa, whose *Guide* was called "a very convenient summary of the most valuable works on political economy in all languages."
  James, a professor at the University of Pennsylvania, wrote a preface to Ingram's *History* (1888) and to Cohn's *History* (1894).

147* Walcker, Karl (1839–1909)
Geschichte der Nationalökonomie, insbesondere der neueren und neuesten [Band 5 in his] *Handbuch der Nationalökonomie für Studirende, Landwirthe, Industrielle, Kaufleute und andere Gebildete.* Leipzig: Rossberg'sche Buchhandlung, 1884. xviii, 324 p. 21 cm.
Later editions: 1888, 1895, 1899, 1902.
Began with a survey of earlier histories, which mentioned Blanqui and Villeneuve-Bargemont, concluded that Kautz was valuable despite his errors, and that the works of Dühring, Contzen, and Eisenhart were more or less worthless. Cossa

was never mentioned. It briefly treated political economy through the Physiocrats, afterwards dividing the account nationally into ten different sections, of which the longest concerned German political economy. It was a long-lived history: a sixth edition, never published, was in process at the time of Walcker's death (*Kürschners Deutscher Literatur-Kalender* 31 [1909]: 1767). The second edition (1878) was drastically reduced to a 79-page summary; editions thereafter (1895, 1899, 1902) remained in this popular shortened form.

Walcker studied at Dorpat and Berlin from 1857 to 1863 and became, in 1877, a *Privatdozent* at Leipzig, where he first lectured on the history of political economy and socialism in the winter semester of 1878/79. From 1885 to 1898 he lectured annually on the subject.

148* Cohn, Gustav (1840–1919; professor at Göttingen)
"Geschichte der Nationalökonomie" [1:90–180 in his] *System der Nationalökonomie*. Stuttgart: Ferdinand Enke, 1885. 23.5 cm.
Translation: American, 1894.

The last two-thirds, which covered the period since J. S. Mill, treated socialism and political economy in Germany.

149* Ingram, John Kells (1823–1907)
"Political Economy" [19:346–430 in] *Encyclopaedia Britannica*. 9th edition. Edinburgh: Adam and Charles Black, 1885; New York: Charles Scribner's Sons, 1885. 28 cm.
See entries for 1886 and 1888 editions.

This was the first presentation of Ingram's *History of Political Economy*, which ranks among the six most popular textbooks on its subject of all times.[34]

The author had only recently won repute as a political economist by his presidential address (1878) to Section F of the British Association for the Advancement of Science.[35] He was elected because he had apparent presidential qualities,[36] was well-known in Dublin (where the meeting was held),[37] and had had a long, if not active, connection with the British Association.[38]

The extraordinary nature of Ingram's address established him as a political economist. In it, he replied to the arguments underlying the movement within the association to drop "Economic Science and Statistics" on the ground that it did not stand on a scientific footing with the other sciences. His defense of political economy was probably influenced by a recent article by Cliffe Leslie.[39] Ingram found the strongest support in Comte, who had put economic science on a par with the physical sciences, perhaps Comte's most substantial contribution to economic science.[40]

Ingram more than upheld the status of political economy in his address, for he followed Comte and Leslie in an attack on the old political economy, and he outlined an appealing program of reform. Ingram's attack and program resembled those of the German Historical School.[41] This address contained nothing relating to the history of political economy except the view that political economy had taken the wrong course since Smith.

Ingram's address created a stir.[42] With slight revision it appeared as a pamphlet.[43] At Professor Conrad's suggestion it was translated into German (*Die notwendige Reform der Volkswirtschaftslehre* [Jena: Gustav Fischer, 1879]).[44] Petersen prepared a Danish translation with notes in 1879 (*Nationaløkonomiens: Nuvaerende stilling og udsigter* [Copenhagen: Andr. Fred. Høst & Sons, 1879]).

In order to be asked to write the article on "Political Economy," Ingram needed an editor of the *Britannica* who appreciated the flavor of his "Address." An editor with this qualification appeared when William Robertson Smith became editor-in-chief.[45]

Ingram listed the histories of Blanqui, Villeneuve-Bargemont, Twiss, Kautz, Dühring, Cossa, Eisenhart, and Scheel and specified that "all . . . have been more or less, and some very largely, used in the preparation of the foregoing outline" (p. 401). He also cited the collections of Custodi and of Daire, the dictionary of Coquelin and Guillaumin, the bibliography of McCulloch, and the special histories of Pecchio, Colmeiro, Roscher, and Myer. He left no mystery as to how he had composed the article. Using the talents that had led him to be called "well-nigh the most perfectly educated man of his age"[46] and the bibliographic taste and skill that enabled him to serve as the Librarian of Trinity College (Dublin) from 1879 to 1887, he assembled the best of the histories and had a dictionary of political economy at hand, along with several special histories. From these materials he shaped history around the positivistic creed in which he had come to believe.

It was not a history based on extensive study or prolonged thought, nor was it one developed in the classroom. Schumpeter said: "He can hardly be said to have done any economic research at all. His *History of Political Economy* . . . is conclusive proof both of his wide philosophical (especially Comtist) and historical erudition and his inadequate command of technical economics. The later fact made it easier of course for him than it would otherwise have been to talk glibly about the New Economics to which the future belonged" (*A History of Economic Analysis* [no. 574 infra], p. 823 n.23).

150* ———

  A History of Political Economy. Reprinted from the *Encyclopaedia Britannica*.[47] Edinburgh: Adam and Charles Black, 1886. 346–401 p. 37 cm.

  See entry for 1885 and 1888 editions.

In May 1886, Taussig at Harvard wrote to Seligman at Columbia: "Have you seen Ingram's article in the volume of the *Britannica,* recently issued, on 'Political Economy'? It is an excellent sketch of the history of political economy, —the best in our language, by all odds. It is just what I want, as a book of general reference for the students in one of next year's courses. Now Messrs. Scribner offer to reprint it, that is, strike off (and bind) from the original *Britannica* plates, provided as many as 100 copies are taken. They do not want to put such reprints on the general market, but are willing to furnish blocks of this kind for college uses. My section . . . here is not likely to absorb 100 copies for a couple of years. It occurred to me that some of your students would possibly find the article useful . . . . Tell me whether you can engage any number of copies, or see a probability (without committing yourself) of using any" (Seligman correspondence, Columbia University Library).[48]

This reprint was also probably used by Ely, who already had taught the history of political economy at Johns Hopkins for several years.[49]

151* ———

> *A History of Political Economy.* Edinburgh (also London): Adam & Charles Black, 1888 (also dated 1893); New York: Macmillan and Co., 1888 (also dated 1893, 1894, 1897, 1902, 1905). xv, 250 p. 21 cm.
>
> The New York edition incorporated a preface by Professor James of the University of Pennsylvania. Otherwise, both editions were identical and followed the text of the *Britannica* article (1885).
>
> Other British and American editions: 1885, 1886, 1907, 1915 (with a new preface by Ely and an updating supplementary chapter by Scott [also dated 1919, 1923, 1967]). Translations: German, 1890, 1905; Russian, 1891, 1897; Polish, 1891; Italian, 1892; Swedish, 1892; French, 1893, 1907; Spanish, circa 1895; Czechoslovak, 1895; Japanese, 1896; Yugoslav, 1901; Indian (Urdu), 1932; Chinese, 1932.

Both Kirkup in the *Academy* and Seligman in the *Political Science Quarterly* noted Ingram's dependence on German sources. Kirkup declared the dependence inevitable: "For, on the whole, it is only in the highly organised universities of Germany that we have the leisure, division of labour, and love of hard work necessary for the production of elaborate histories" (26 May 1888, p. 353). Seligman complained that Ingram's interpretation of Ricardo agreed too closely with von Held's "ridiculously one-sided" account in *Zwei Bücher zur socialen Geschichte Englands* (3 [1888]: 695).[50]

Kirkup also judged that Ingram's allegiance to Comte had led him to forget that "what is best in the historical method had been put in practice long before Comte's time." An unsigned review in the *Journal of the Royal Statistical Society* warned that Ingram's *History* was "pervaded with Comtist ideas," which had led Ingram "to clothe simple ideas in unnecessarily difficult language" and to mistrust Malthus and Ricardo (51 [1888]: 654–56).

Two French reviews had dissimilar evaluations. In the orthodox *Journal des économistes,* S. R. (Sophie Raffalovich) regretted that the book had been written, since she thought that Ingram considered political economy "morte et bien morte" and that his history was an "oraison funèbre" (4th ser. 42 [1888]: 458–59). St. Marc defended Ingram from this criticism in the newly founded *Revue d'économie politique* (2 [1888]: 433–38) with a tongue-in-cheek reply that forecast the triumph of the Historical School and interpreted Ingram's *History* as showing the reasonableness of this change.

Both an opponent and an advocate of the Historical School prepared German reviews. Böhm-Bawerk, an Austrian opponent, conceded that it was a worthwhile and thorough *Tendenzschrift* (*Jahrbücher für Nationalökonomie und Statistik,* new ser. 18 [1889]: 673). However, he objected to its division into periods based on events in economic history rather than on changes in economic theory, likening these to the separation of physical science into periods identified with the steam engine, the railroad, etc. Schmoller, representing the German Historical School, spoke of the book's English common sense (*Jahrbüch für Gesetzgebung, Verwaltung und Volkswirtschaft im Deutschen Reich* 14 [1890]: 994–96). He noted its clarity and the sound, clear judgments on most important authors. He said that although Germans would not find Ingram's argument novel, they would be grateful to hear it expounded, with vigor and skill, by an Englishman. Schmoller criticized Ingram for following Roscher's example in including names of authors whose ideas were not evaluated, for not considering socialist theories, for not exploring the deeper philosophical principles of the relation of the writings to their times, and for treating Smith too leniently.

"Whatever critics may say," Ely wrote in the 1915 edition, "it is apparent that he had a message for the world at large" (p. xi). In a short time, students could read Ingram's *History* in eleven languages.

During his lifetime, and afterwards, Ingram enjoyed an excellent reputation. The American Economic Association made him an honorary member in 1891. Palgrave's *Dictionary* called him "an economist of considerable ability" (1908 ed., 3:750). Falkiner spoke of him as "the most distinguished authority on economics who had ever adorned the roll of the Statistical and Social Inquiry Society of Ireland" ("A Memoir of the Late John Kells Ingram, LLD., Sometime President of the Society," *Journal of the Statistical and Social Inquiry Society of Ireland* 12 [1908]: 105). His *History,* on occasion, aroused the opposition that his speech in 1878 had provoked. The elder Keynes wrote: "The more extreme members of the school are arrogant and exclusive in their pretensions . . . . The old doctrines, and the old ways of teaching them, are to be put on one side and seen no more. Professor Schmoller and Dr. Ingram may be taken as examples of this advanced wing of the new school" (John Neville Keynes, *The Scope and Method of Political Economy* [London: Macmillan and Co., 1891], p. 26). But resentment eventually died down. Edgeworth said so, pointing out that Ingram had "accepted a place on the Council of the British Economic Association, and did not rebel against the sort of *Pax Britannica* which its leading members have maintained with respect to controversies about economic method. All that was worth fighting for might seem to Ingram to have been won when in a treatise commanding the universal assent of the rising generation it was taught that there is no scope in economics for long chains of reasoning, that some of Ricardo's conclusions are liable to be dangerously misapplied, that the work which the Germans and their fellow-workers in other countries have done in tracing and explaining the history of economic institutions is one of the great achievements of our age. To have presented the work of the Germans in an English form was one of Ingram's great achievements. His economic mission was accomplished" (Francis Ysidro Edgeworth, "Obituary: John Kells Ingram," *Economic Journal* 17 [1907]: 301).

152   Walcker, Karl (1839–1909)
    Geschichte der Nationalökonomie und des Socialismus [Band 5 in his] *Handbuch der Nationalökonomie.* 2., verb. Aufl. Leipzig: Rossberg'sche

Buchhandlung, 1888. x, 79 p. 8°.
Listed in Kayser.
See entry for first (1884) edition.

153 Werunsky, Albert
"Der Entwicklungsgang der Volkswirtschaftslehre" [pp. 3–35 in] *Zwei-unddreissigster Jahres-Bericht über die Prager Handelsakademie*. Prag: A. Haase, 1888. 25 cm.
In Columbia University Library.
Later edition: 1894 (under a different title).

Based on standard German sources. Its promise of later treatment of communism and socialism was not fulfilled.

154* Ferrara, Francesco (1810–1900)
Esame storico-critico di economisti e dottrine economiche del secolo XVIII e prima metà del XIX. Raccolta delle prefazioni dettate dal Professore Francesco Ferrara alla 1ª e 2ª Serie della Biblioteca degli economisti. Volume primo. Parte prima—Prefazioni dei volumi I a VII. Parte seconda—Prefazioni dei volumi VIII a XIII. Prima serie. Torino: Unione Tipografico, 1889 (reprinted, 1955–56). 25 cm.
Originally published in the *Biblioteca dell'economista* (1850–68).

155* Block, Maurice (1816–1901)
Les Progrès de la science économique depuis Adam Smith. Revision des doctrines économiques. Paris: Guillaumin et Cie, 1890. 2 v. (vii, 557; vi, 598 p.) 22.5 cm.
Later edition: 1897 (considerably augmented).

Not intended as a usual history. It was the first long history to be topically arranged: each chapter stated the views on a topic of different economists, mostly recent, but often going back before Smith, not in order to represent the historical evolution of the subject, but to find the *best* view. It expressly sought to determine how Smith's views could be brought up-to-date.

This history received laudatory reviews. Seligman called it "a work of the first importance and of enduring value," a "veritable compend of economic science," and "a godsend to many whose library or linguistic attainments are limited" (*Political Science Quarterly* 5 [1890]: 534–36). Another American reviewer acclaimed it as "a work that only a tireless scholar would have undertaken, and which, being done, puts every working economist under enduring obligation to its author" (*Annals of the American Academy of Political and Social Science* 1 [1890/91]: 680–81). Molinari said, "Le style en est clair, la lecture facile" (*Journal des économistes,* 5th ser. 1 [1890]: 442). A second French reviewer concluded that it was "une oeuvre d'érudition remarquable, bien conçue et bien écrite. Il garde ainsi un haut caractère de mérite et d'utilité" (Paris, École libre des sciences politiques, *Annales des sciences politiques* 5 [1890]: 551).

Block's talent and wide acquaintance with political economy enabled him to write an outstanding history. His biographer, Émile Cheysson, said that from the first he was "un travailleur acharné et un liseur infatigable" ("Notice sur la vie et les travaux de M. Maurice Block . . . ," in Académie des sciences morales et politiques [Paris], *Memoires* 26 [1909]: 415). Block was born in Berlin and was educated in Germany and France, and he regularly read and reviewed books on political economy in French, German, and English. He began as a French government statistician, then became a well-known writer on political economy and a member of the Académie des sciences morales et politiques. While writing, he lived on a deserted street in a small house behind a garden, where he collected a library that was rich in works on political economy. Near his seventieth birthday, he published *Les Progrès,* which his biographer called his principal work (ibid.).

156* Ingram, John Kells (1823–1907)
    Geschichte der Volkswirtschaftslehre. Autorisierte Übersetzung von E.
    Roschlau. Tübingen: H. Laupp, 1890. viii, 344 p. 20 cm.
    See entry for 1888 British edition.

157* Eisenhart, Hugo (1811–93)
    Geschichte der Nationalökonomik. Zweite, vermehrte Auflage. Jena:
    G. Fischer, 1891 (also dated 1901, 1910, 1916). viii, 278 p. 23 cm.
    First edition: 1881.
Contained an added section on Malthus.

158* Espinas, Alfred Victor (1844–1922)
    Histoire des doctrines économiques. Paris: Armand Colin et Cie, 1891.
    359 p. 18 cm.
Mentioned only one recent history of political economy. "Nous avons mis à profit la belle *'Histoire de l'économie politique'* de M. Ingram," the author wrote, "mais nous espérons qui le présent livre ne fera pas double emploi avec le sien" (p. 4). In his review, Seligman, who thought this hope unjustified for English readers, said, "There will be very little not already contained in the works of Ingram and others" (*Political Science Quarterly* 7 [1892]: 741). Seligman later characterized the book as "only a slight sketch" and noted that "considerable attention is paid to the philosophical bases of the various doctrines" (ibid., 14 [1899]: 539).

Espinas, a professor at Douai, Bordeaux, and Paris, was not a political economist.[51] Chailly-Bert (1854–1928) had asked Espinas to help prepare historical notices for a proposed collection of extracts from the best known eighteenth- and nineteenth-century political economists. Since only a few of the volumes had appeared, Chailly-Bert published Espinas's notices as a separate volume.

159 Ingram, John Kells (1823–1907)
    Historya ekonomii politycznej. Przełożyła z angielskiego Zafia Daszynska.
    Warszawa: Wydawnictwo Przeglądu Tygodniowego, 1891. 8, 322,
    5 p. 8°.

Listed in Lyster.
See entry for 1888 British edition.

160 ———

Istoriia politicheskoĭ ekonomii. Perevod s'angliĭskago I. I. Ianzhula. Izdanie K. T. Soldatenkova. Moskva: Tipografiia M. P. Shtepkina, 1891. xii, 322, iv p. 24.5 cm.
In Library of Congress.
See entry for 1888 British edition.

161 Price, Langford Lovell Frederick Rice (1862–1950)
A Short History of Political Economy in England, from Adam Smith to Arnold Toynbee. London: Methuen, 1891. ii, 201 p. 17.5 cm.
In New York Public Library.

Had 15 editions, some issued with several dates, of which only the 14th (1931), which was revised and enlarged, and the 15th (1937), are included in this bibliography.

Confined to England but, nonetheless, included as general history, since it contained a good part of the material in other general histories, and since Bonar, in his review, considered it a substitute for Ingram's *History* (*Economic Journal* 1 [1891]: 608).

162 Chuprov, Aleksandr Ivanovich (1842–1908)
Istoriia politicheskoĭ ekonomii. Moskva: 1892. 231, ii p. 8°.
Listed in Chuprov.
Later editions: 1904, 1906, 1907, 1908, 1911, 1913.
Other history by Chuprov: 1900.

Taken from Chuprov's university lecture notes on the history of political economy, which had first been mimeographed. According to Normano, it "remained [in Russia] for almost three decades *the* textbook" (*The Spirit of Russian Economics* [New York: John Day Company, 1905], p. 24).

Studied under Roscher at Leipzig and lectured on political economy and statistics at Moscow (1874–99).

163 Cossa, Luigi (1831–96)
Introducción al estudio de la economía política. Trad. por Jorge María de Ledesma y Palacios. Valladolid, 1892. xii, 639 p. 8°.
Listed in Palau.
See entry for first (1876) Italian edition.

164* ———

Introduzione allo studio dell'economia politica. 3.ª edizione interamente rifatta della Guida allo Studio dell'Economia politica. Milano: Ulrico Hoepli, 1892. xii, 594 p. 22.5 cm.
See entry for first (1876) edition.

165   Ingram, John Kells (1823–1907)
       Nationalekonomiens historia. Öfversatt af Reinhold Rudbeck. Stock-
       holm: C. E. Fritze's K. Hofbokhandel, 1892. viii, 258 p. 8°.
       Listed in *Svensk Bok-katalog.*
       See entry for 1888 British edition.

166*   ——
       Storia della economia politica. Prima traduzione italiana dell'Avv. Rodolfo
       Debarbieri. Torino-Roma: L. Roux e C.-Editori, 1892. 6, 243 p. 22 cm.
       See entry for 1888 British edition.

167*   Quarta, Alberto
       Prolegomeni alla storia dell'economia politica. Volume primo [no more
       published]. Roma: Tipografia Elzeviriana, 1892. vi, 457 p. 24 cm.
Only the last 130 pages are wholly on the history of political economy, beginning
with Colbert and ending with the German Historical School.

168*   Bonar, James (1852–1941)
       Philosophy and Political Economy in Some of Their Historical Relations.
       London: Swann Sonnenschein & Co., 1893; New York: Macmillan
       & Co., 1893. xvi, 410 p. 24 cm.
       Later editions: 1909, 1922.
Most general of Bonar's many excellent publications on the history of economics.

169*   Cossa, Luigi (1831–96)
       An Introduction to the Study of Political Economy. Revised by the Author
       and translated from the Italian by Louis Dyer, M.A. Balliol College.
       London: Macmillan and Co., 1893. x, 587 p. 18.5 cm.
       See entry for first (1876) Italian edition.

170   Ingram, John Kells (1823–1907)
       Histoire de l'économie politique. Traduction par MM. Henry de Varigny
       et E. Bonnemaison. Paris: L. Larose et Forcel, 1893. 359 p. 12mo.
       In Harvard University Library.
       See entry for 1888 British Edition.

171   Nathusius, Martin von (1843–1906; theologian)
       "Geschichtliche Entwickelung der Volkswirtschaftslehre" [1:76–194 in his]
       Die Mitarbeit der Kirche an der Lösung der socialen Frage. Leipzig:
       Hinrich, 1893–94. 8°.
       In Oberlin College Library.
Emphasized the ethical standpoint.

172*   Cohn, Gustav (1840–1919)
       A History of Political Economy. Translated by Dr. Joseph Adna Hill.
       With an Introductory Note by Edmund J. James. Philadelphia: Amer-

ican Academy of Political and Social Science, 1894. 142 p. 23.5 cm. (*Supplement to the Annals of the American Academy of Political and Social Science,* March 1894.) German edition: 1885.

Intended as a textbook.

173 Werunsky, Albert
Grundzüge des Entwicklungsganges der Volkswirtschaftslehre in übersichtlicher Darstellung, zugleich eine Einführung in das Studium der Nationalökonomie überhaupt. Zittau, 1894. 38 p. 8°.
Listed in Kayser.
First edition: 1888.

174* Blanqui, Jérôme Adolphe (1798–1854)
Istoriia politicheskoĭ ekonomii. 2. ed. [1st ed. said to have been published in 1869.] St. Petersburg: 1895.
See entry for first (1837–[1838]) French edition.

175 Bunge, Nikolaĭ Khristianovich (1823–95; professor at Kiev, 1850–80)
Ocherki politiko-ekonomicheskoĭ literatury. St. Petersburg, 1895. vi, 465 p. 25.5 cm.
In Columbia University Library.
Translation: French, 1898.

An extension of an original sketch which, Bunge said, was published in 1868. I was not able to identify the original publication.

176 Farini, Luigi
Sunto storico della scienza economica. Forlì: Bordandini, 1895. 73 p. 8°.
Listed in *Catalogo generale della libreria italiana.*

177 Ingram, John Kells (1823–1907)
Dějiny vědy národohospodářské. Autorisovaný překlad dle vydáni z roku 1893 od Jos. Pelcla. V Praze a Chrudimi, 1895. 208 p. 8°.
In Syracuse University Library.
See entry for 1888 British edition.

Translation of chapters 1–4 of the *History of Political Economy.*

178 ⸻
Historia de la economía política. Traducida del inglés por Miguel de Unamuno. Madrid: La España Moderna, [1895?]. 328 p. 22 cm.
In University of Illinois Library.
See entry for 1888 British edition.

179* Walcker, Karl (1839–1909)
Geschichte der Nationalökonomie und des Sozialismus. Dritte, völlig

umgearbeitete Auflage. Leipzig: Verlag der Rossberg'schen Hofbuch-handlung, 1895. x, 113 p. 21 cm.
See entry for first (1884) edition.

180 Ingram, John Kells (1823–1907)
Tetsu ri kei sei gaku shi. Abe Tora no suke, yaku. Tokyo, 1896.
Listed in Lyster.
See entry for 1888 British edition.
First general history of political economy available in Japanese.

181* Macleod, Henry Dunning (1821–1902)
The History of Economics. London: Bliss, Sands and Co., 1896; New York: G. P. Putnam's Sons, 1896. xv, 690 p. 23 cm.
Not strictly a history of economics. Miller commented: "The book is misnamed; it is not what an intelligent reader expects to find under the title of 'History of Economics.' It is historical only so far as it is Mr. Macleod repeating himself. Of its 690 pages, but 130 deal with the history of economics, and these are largely autobiographical . . . . Smith, Ricardo, and Mill 'butchered' the science and . . . the author 'originated' it in its modern form" (*Journal of Political Economy* 5 [1896/97]: 355).

Seligman said of it, "Those who expect to find in Mr. Macleod's latest book a veritable history of the science of economics will be grievously disappointed" (*Political Science Quarterly* 12 [1897]: 350).

The first use of the title "The History of Economics" had occurred in his *The Elements of Economics* (1881).

182* Block, Maurice (1816–1901)
Les Progrès de la science économique depuis Adam Smith. Revision des doctrines économiques. 2e édition, considérablement augmentée. Paris: Guillaumin et Cie, 1897. 2 v. (xi, 679; vi, 871 p.) 23 cm.
First edition: 1890.
Liesse called it "une seconde édition revue avec un soin minutieux et une science très éclairée" (*Journal des économistes,* 5th ser. 30 [1897]: 270).

183* Denis, Hector (1842–1913)
Histoire des systèmes économiques et socialistes. Bruxelles: Charles Rozez, 1897. 275 p. 18.5 cm.
New enlarged edition: 1904–7.
Contained more than the orthodox view of the history of political economy required of students. Denis considered that political economy began with Physi-ocracy, in which it was unified with sociology; that Smith separated political economy and sociology; that socialism was an attempt to recombine them; and that, in the end, the two streams would merge into "sociologie économique," a concept that had its base in "la relativité universelle." "J'avoue humblement," Bouet wrote in a review, "que je ne comprends pas cette relativité universelle" (*Journal des économistes,* 6th ser. 4 [1904]: 496).

Denis, who taught the history of economic doctrines at the Université libre de Bruxelles, proposed to expand this initial work, and lived to publish two of the planned volumes (1904, 1907). Gide conjectured that there would be five or six volumes (*Economic Journal* 17 [1907]: 564). The manuscript of an incomplete third volume was found at the time of Denis's death (Louis Bertrand, "Denis, Hector," *Encyclopedia of the Social Sciences,* 5:90).

184   Ghio, Paolo Arnaldo [later Paul] (b. 1865)
      Della economia politica nell'età nostra e nella evoluzione della storia. Due conferenze pubblicate a cura dell'Idea Liberale di Milano. Milano: Tipo-Litografia Agraria, 1897. 90 p. 12°.
      In New York Public Library.
      Later histories by same author: 1908, 1923.

185   Ingram, John Kells (1823–1907)
      Istoriia politicheskoĭ ekonomii. Perevod s'angliĭskago Aleksandra Miklashevskago. Izdanie K. T. Soldatenkova. Moskva: Tipo-litografiia V. Richter, 1897. viii, 352, viii p. 8°.
      Listed in Lyster.
      See entry for 1888 British edition.

186* Andrade, Abel Pereira de (1866–1958; on the faculty at Coimbra in 1898)
      Synthese histórica das doutrinas económicas (resumo de trabalho do Exmo Sr. Dr. Frederico Laranjo). Coimbra: Minerva Central, 1898. 195 p. 21 cm.
Included Portuguese economists.

187* Bunge, Nikolaĭ Khristianovich (1823–95)
      Esquisses de littérature politico-économique. Basle: George & Cie, 1898 (reprinted, 1971). xliii, 455 p. 25.5 cm. Author's portrait.
      Russian edition: 1895.

188* Cossa, Luigi (1831–96)
      Histoire des doctrines économiques. Avec une préface de A. Deschamps. Traduit par Alfred Bonnet. Traduction faite sur le manuscrit de la 3e édition révise par L. Cossa postérieurement à sa publication. Paris: V. Giard & Brière, 1899. xii, 574 p. 22.5 cm.
      See entry for first (1876) Italian edition.

189* Rambaud, Joseph (1849–1919; professor on Faculté catholique de droit de Lyon)
      Histoire des doctrines économiques. Paris: L. Larose, 1899. 512 p. 21.5 cm.
      Later editions: 1902, 1909.
Prepared for use by candidates for a new degree, established in 1895 at the French universities, which necessitated teaching the history of economic doc-

trines. It contained the kind of history that came down to Mill, then looked at the historical school, and finally at socialism.

Seligman said that it is "on the whole, a solid and respectable performance: it is not only the best of its kind in France, but also possesses some advantages in the way of arrangement and contents over anything that we yet have in English or German" (*Political Science Quarterly* 14 [1899]: 541).

190   Walcker, Karl (1839–1909)
      Geschichte der Nationalökonomie und des Sozialismus. Vierte, völlig umgearbeitete Auflage. Leipzig: Rossberg'sche Hof-Buchhandlung, 1899. vii, 132 p. 8°.
      In Columbia University Library.
      See entry for first (1884) edition.

In the preface Walcker wrote: "Es ist möglich, dass im 20. Jahrhundert ein mehrbändiges Sammelwerk über die Geschichte der Nationalökonomie erscheinen wird. Heutzutage ist aber, meines Erachtens, ein grosses, von einem Manne verfasstes Werk über den in Rede stehenden Gegenstand kein Bedürfnis" (p. iii).

191   Chuprov, Aleksandr Ivanovich (1842–1908)
      Ocherki istorii politicheskoĭ ekonomii. Moskva, 1900. 117 p. 26 cm. Lithographed.
      In Columbia University Library.
      Later editions: 1904, 1906, 1908.
      Another history by Chuprov: 1892.

192* Costa, Affonso Augusto da (1871–1937; professor at Coimba)
      Lições de sciencia económica. Coimbra: Minerva Central, 1900. 80 p. 21 cm.
      Arranged by Schools.

193* Dühring, Eugen Karl (1833–1921)
      Kritische Geschichte der Nationalökonomie und des Socialismus von ihren Anfängen bis zur Gegenwart. Vierte, neubearbeitete und stark vermehrte Auflage. Leipzig: Druck und Verlag von C. G. Naumann, 1900. xxii, 653 p. 21.5 cm.
      Earlier editions: 1871, 1875, 1879.

194   Ingram, John Kells (1823–1907)
      Istorija političke ekonomije. Preveo Milič J. Radovanović. Beograd: Milosa Velikog Štamparija Bojoviča i Mičića, 1901. xxv, 275 p.
      Listed in Lyster.
      See entry for 1888 British edition.

195   Tugan-Baranovskiĭ, Mikhail Ivanovich (1865–1919; professor at St. Petersburg and Kiev)

"Ocherki iz istorii politicheskoĭ ekonomii" [January 1901 to October 1902 in] *Mir Bozhii*. St. Petersburg.
In New York Public Library.
Later editions: 1903, 1906, 1907.

196* Oncken, August (1844–1911; professor at Bern)
Geschichte der Nationalökonomie. In zwei Teilen. Erster Teil: *Die Zeit vor Adam Smith* [no more published]. Leipzig: C. L. Hirschfeld, 1902. x, 516 p. 25 cm.
Later edition: "2. unveränderte anastatische Auflage," 1922. Translation: Russian, 1908.

Higgs called this first volume of a projected general history "a very important contribution" in its attention to the Physiocrats, which was its principal subject, although he found it "less satisfying" in other fields (*Economic Journal* 13 [1903]: 614). Plehn said that "anyone who hereafter undertakes to write a history of political economy will have to defend his view of what that history should include against the strong views set forth in this volume" (*Journal of Political Economy* 12 [1903/4]: 421).

Oncken started with an interest in agriculture, which led him to Physiocracy, on which he became an authority.

197* Rambaud, Joseph (1849–1919)
Histoire des doctrines économiques. Deuxième édition, revue et considérablement augmentée. Paris: L. Larose, 1902. 738 p. 22.5 cm.
Other editions: 1899, 1909.

198* Walcker, Karl (1839–1909)
Geschichte der Nationalökonomie und des Sozialismus. Fünfte, völlig umgearbeitete Auflage. Leipzig: Rossberg & Berger, 1902. vii, 124 p. 20 cm.
See entry for first (1884) edition.

199* Dubois, Auguste (1866–1935; professor at Lille, then at Poitiers)
Précis de l'histoire des doctrines économiques dans leurs rapports avec les faits et avec les institutions. Tome premier [no more published]: *L'Époque antérieure aux Physiocrates*. Paris: Arthur Rousseau, 1903 (reprinted, Genève, 1970). 342 p. 23 cm.

Surveyed the literature before the Physiocrats. This history aimed to relate objectively the development of political economy, both to the social-economic milieu and to the general intellectual milieu. It also sought to estimate the separate discernible influence of the individuality of the political economist and to value subjectively the leading characteristics of the political economy in different periods, in terms of the present.

"Parmi les traités généraux de langue française," Truchy wrote, "cet ouvrage prendra sans peine une des meilleures places par la sûreté et l'étendue de sa documentation" (*Revue d'économie politique* 18 [1904]: 89).

Professor first at Lille and then at Poitiers, where he remained for the rest of his life teaching the history of economic doctrines. Together with August Deschamps, he founded the *Revue d'histoire des doctrines économiques et sociales* (1908) and edited the *Collection des économistes et des réformateurs sociaux de la France* (1910–38).

200* Schweizer, Franz August (1870–1908)
  Geschichte der Nationalökonomik in vier Monographien über Colbert, Turgot, Smith, Marx nebst einer philosoph[ischen] Systematik der Nationalökonomie. Vol. 1: *Merkantilismus von Colbert.* Ravensburg: Dorn'sche Verlagsbuchhandlung (F. Alber), 1903. x, 63 p. 21 cm. Vol. 2: *Physiokratismus von Turgot.* Ravensburg: Friedrich Alber, 1904. x, 149 p. 21 cm. Vol. 3: *Individualismus von Smith.* Ravensburg: Friedrich Alber, 1905. xiv, 257 p. 21 cm.

Hoped to show the development of political economy by examining the works of four writers. The final volume (on Marx) was never published.

201 Tugan-Baranovskiĭ, Mikhail Ivanovich (1865–1919)
  Ocherki iz noveĭsheĭ istorii politicheskoĭ ekonomii. St. Petersburg, 1903. x, 434 p. 25 cm.
  In Columbia University Library.
  Other editions: 1901–2, 1906, 1907.

202 Chuprov, Aleksandr Ivanovich (1842–1908)
  Istoriia politicheskoĭ ekonomii. 2. izd. Moskva, 1904. 231 p. 8°.
  Listed in Chuprov.
  See entry for first (1892) edition.

203 ———
  Ocherki istorii politicheskoĭ ekonomii. Moskva, 1904. 79 p. 8°.
  Listed in Chuprov.
  See entry for first (1900) edition.

204* Denis, Hector (1842–1913)
  Histoire des systèmes économiques et socialistes. Paris: V. Giard & E. Brière, 1904–7. 2 v. (365, 515 p.) 23 cm.
  First edition: 1897.

Extended the coverage to Malthus, Ricardo, Sismondi, Owen, and Thompson.

Gide, soon to publish a history himself, praised Denis's volumes. "One might," he said, "even call it a final pronouncement. I at least do not very well see how one could add to it, either by way of exhaustive and well attested records, or in the conscientious reading of every subject which is discussed, or in the consummate knowledge of all the economic problems which are met on the way, or in the impartiality and—to speak quite without exaggeration—the benevolence with which men and systems are judged, even where personal sympathies are not enlisted" (*Economic Journal* 17 [1907]: 561).

205   Damaschke, Adolf Wilhelm Ferdinand (1865–1935)
       Geschichte der Nationalökonomie. Eine erste Einführung. Jena: Gustav
       Fischer, 1905. viii, 231 p. 21 cm.
       In New York Public Library.
       Other editions: 1905 (next below), 1909, 1910, 1911, 1912, 1913, 1916,
       1918, 1919, 1920, 1922, 1929.

A successful history which grew from a short first edition to a long, two-
volume fourteenth edition, meanwhile selling 100,000 copies.
       Intended for readers with little knowledge of political economy.
       Damaschke edited a journal on land reform.

206*   ———

       Geschichte der Nationalökonomie. Eine erste Einführung. Zweite,
       durchgesehene Auflage. Jena: Gustav Fischer, 1905. viii, 244 p. 21 cm.
       See entry next above.

207*   Ingram, John Kells (1823–1907)
       Geschichte der Volkswirtschaftslehre. Autorisierte Übersetzung von E.
       Roschlau. Zweite Auflage. Tübingen: H. Laupp, 1905. vii, 326 p.
       22 cm.
       See entry for 1888 British edition.

208*   Marx, Heinrich Karl (1818–83)
       *Theorien über den Mehrwert; aus dem nachgelassenen Manuskript "Zur
       Kritik der politischen Ökonomie" von Karl Marx, herausgegeben von
       Karl Kautsky.* Stuttgart: J. H. W. Dietz Nachf., 1905–10 (also with
       numbered "unveränderte Aufl.," not separately listed in this bibliogra-
       phy, in 1910, 1919, 1921, 1923). 3 v. in 4. 20 cm.
       Translations: Russian, 1906 (vol. 1 only), 1923–25; French, 1924–25;
       Japanese, 1936 (vols. 1 and 2 only), 1953–54; Mexican, 1944–45; Chinese,
       1949, 1975; Yugoslav, 1953–56; Italian, 1954–58, 1974; Spanish, 1974.
       Translations of selected parts: Italian, 1906; British, 1951; American,
       1952.
       A new interpretation of the original manuscript: Russian, 1954–61; Ger-
       man, 1956–62, 1965–72, 1968; Japanese, 1957–58, 1963–70; Polish, 1959–
       66; British, 1963 (Moscow; pt. 1 only), 1969–72 (London and Moscow);
       Italian, 1971–73, 1974; French, 1974.

Not usually considered to be a history of political economy, partly because it
supported unpopular views, and partly because it was over forty years old when
first published. It was, however, a history of political economy to the extent that
it gave a chronological discussion of the same writers that earlier historians of
political economy had selected. Marx picked out "surplus value" as the central
thread, a thread that touched many parts of the history of political economy.
His history consisted of about 50 percent quotations from the authors discussed,
thus serving as a combined history and source book.
       It was part of the "enormous manuscript" that Marx wrote before 1866

(Franz Mehring, *Karl Marx: The Story of His Life* [New York: Covici, Friede, 1935], p. 383). By 1867 Marx had organized from this manuscript the first volume of *Das Kapital,* the preface of which stated his plans for three additional volumes. He intended the last to contain the "history of the theory." He took notes for this planned last volume in the British Museum, where he found "material on the history of political economy" (*A Contribution to the Critique of Political Economy* [Chicago: Charles H. Kerr, 1918], p. 14). After Marx's death in 1883, the "enormous manuscript" passed to Engels, who turned out the second volume of *Das Kapital* in 1885 and the third in 1894. In the third volume, Engels said: "I am going to start on the fourth volume—the history of the theory of surplus value—as soon as it is in any way possible." He did not live to do so (*Capital* [New York: International Publishers, 1967], 3:8). Kautsky received the manuscript after Engels's death in 1895. It took him ten years to abandon the idea of adding a fourth volume and instead to piece together the first three volumes of a history, which, following Engels's suggestion, he called the *Theorien über der Mehrwerth.* He described it as a "companion piece" of *Das Kapital.* Five years later (1910), he published the final volume, which completed the history that Marx had begun almost fifty years earlier. This unusual delay resulted from the character of Marx's manuscript; from the continual involvement of Marx, Engels, and Kautsky in revolutionary politics; and from the advanced age of both Marx and Engels when they undertook the task. The character of the notes led to editorial decisions that made the final result in some part the work of Kautsky.

It might be expected that a new publication largely by Karl Marx on an important subject would be received with great interest, especially when many had known of it and speculated on its contents for two generations. There seems, however, to have been little interest anywhere. The volumes that Kautsky had labored over received no reviews in economic journals, although a few recorded that they had received copies.[52] The socialist press likewise gave no good account of it.

Karl Marx's posthumously published history of political economy later came to life as a consequence of the translations that were then made. In three cases the translations bore titles that designated them as histories of political economy (*Histoire des doctrines économiques* [no. 289 infra], *A History of Economic Theories: From the Physiocrats to Adam Smith* [no. 538 infra], and *Storia delle teorie economiche* [no. 568 infra]).

A new version—based on the original manuscript and sharply critical of the Kautsky edition—was published, beginning in 1954, in Russian, German, Japanese, Polish, English, and Italian (for the criticisms, see its Preface). It placed the history where Marx had intended, as Book 4 of *Das Kapital.*

209 Chuprov, Aleksandr Ivanovich (1842–1908)
 Istoriia politicheskoĭ ekonomii. 3. izd. Moskva, 1906. 193 p. 4°.
 Listed in Chuprov.
 See entry for first (1892) edition.

210 ——
Ocherki istorii politicheskoĭ ekonomii. Moskva, 1906. 64 p. 4°.
Listed in Chuprov.
See entry for first (1900) edition.

211 Marx, Karl (1818–83)
[A partial translation into Italian of *Theorien über den Mehrwerth* in]
*Divenire sociale, rivista di socialismo scientifico, diretta da Enrico Leone
e Paolo Mantica.* Roma: Tip. Industria e Lavoro, 1906.
In New York Public Library.
See entry for first (1905–10) German edition.

212 ——
*Teorii pribavochnoĭ stoimosti: Iz neizdannoĭ rukopisi k kritike politi-
cheskoĭ ekonomii Karla Marksa.* Vol. 1: *Zachatki teorii pribavochnoĭ
stoimosti do Adama Smita vkliuchitel'no* [no more published]. St.
Petersburg: Tip. T-va Obshchestvennaia, 1906. viii, x, ii, 333 p. 26 cm.
In New York Public Library.
See entry for first (1905–10) German edition.

213* Miller, Adolph Caspar (1866–1953; professor at University of California
in 1904)
"Economic Science in the Nineteenth Century" [7:21–44 in] *International
Congress of Arts and Sciences, Universal Exposition, St. Louis, 1904.*
Edited by Howard Jason Rogers. Boston: Houghton Mifflin, 1906.
Summarized the history of political economy from the Physiocrats to the His-
torical School.

214 Tugan-Baranovskiĭ, Mikhail Ivanovich (1865–1919)
Ocherki iz noveĭsheĭ istorii politicheskoĭ ekonomii i sotsializma. 3. izd.
St. Petersburg, 1906. 270 p.
In Columbia University Library.
Other editions: 1901–2, 1903, 1907.

215 Chuprov, Aleksandr Ivanovich (1842–1908)
Istoriia politicheskoĭ ekonomii. 4. izd. Moskva, 1907. 224 p. 8°.
Listed in Chuprov.
See entry for first (1892) edition.

216* Ingram, John Kells (1823–1907)
Esquisse d'une histoire de l'économie politique. Traduite de l'anglais par
V. E. Pépin. Paris: Revue Positiviste Internationale, 1907. 286 p. 23 cm.
See entry for 1888 British edition.

217* ——
A History of Political Economy. 2d edition. London: A. and C. Black,

1907 (also dated 1910, 1914); New York: Macmillan Company, 1907 (also dated 1908, 1909). xi, 249 p. 19.5 cm.
See entry for 1888 edition.

218   Levitskiĭ, Vladimir Favstovich (b. 1855)
       Istoriia politicheskoĭ ekonomii. Kharkov, 1907. 126 p. 25 cm.
       In Columbia University Library.
       Later edition: 1914 (augmented).
Lectured on the history of political economy at a higher commercial school in Kharkov.

219*   Tugan-Baranoviskiĭ, Mikhail Ivanovich (1865–1919)
       Ocherki iz novieĭsheĭ istorii politicheskoĭ ekonomii i sotsializma. 4. izd.
       St. Petersburg: M. A. Alexandrov, 1907. 284 p. 26 cm.
       Earlier editions: 1901–2, 1903, 1906.

220*   Chuprov, Aleksandr Ivanovich (1842–1908)
       Istoriia politicheskoĭ ekonomii. 3. izd. Moskva, 1908. 216 p. 23 cm.
       See entry for first (1892) edition.

221   ———
       Ocherki istorii politicheskoĭ ekonomii. Moskva, 1908. 72 p. 8°.
       Listed in Chuprov.
       See entry for first (1900) edition.

222*   Ghio, Paul (b. 1865; "Professor à l'Université nouvelle de Bruxelles et au
       Collège libre des sciences sociales de Paris")
       Cours d'économie politique. Tome 1 [no more published]: *Les Origines.*
       Paris: Marcel Rivière, 1908. 121 p. 18.5 cm.
       Other histories by Ghio: 1897, 1923.
Covered the period before Smith. First of three planned volumes.

223   Oncken, August (1844–1911)
       Istoriia politicheskoĭ ekonomii: do Adama Smita. [Edited by] M. V.
       Bernatskii. [Foreword by] A. S. Posnikov. St. Petersburg, 1908.
       Listed in 1922 German edition.
       German editions: 1902, 1922.

224   Bonar, James (1852–1941)
       Philosophy and Political Economy in Some of Their Historical Relations.
       2d edition. London: Swann Sonnenschein & Co., 1909; New York:
       Macmillan & Co., 1909. 410 p. 8°.
       In New York Public Library.
       Other editions: 1893, 1922.
Contained no change of importance from first edition.

225* Damaschke, Adolf Wilhelm Ferdinand (1865–1935)
Geschichte der Nationalökonomie. Eine erste Einführung. Dritte um-
gearbeitete Auflage. Jena: Gustav Fischer, 1909. vii, 428 p. 21.5 cm.
See entry for 1905 edition.

226* Gide, Paul Henri Charles (1847–1932), and Rist, Charles (1874–1955)
*Histoire des doctrines économiques depuis les physiocrates jusqu'à nos
jours.* Paris: L. Larose et L. Tenin, 1909. xix, 766 p. 22 cm.
Later editions: 1913, 1920, 1922, 1926, 1944, 1947. Translations: German,
1913, 1921, 1923; Russian, 1914; British and American, 1915, 1948;
Czechoslovak, 1920; Polish, 1920; Yugoslav, 1921; Romanian, 1926;
Spanish, 1927, 1947, 1953, 1973; Greek, 1930–31, 1959; Portuguese,
1938; Japanese, 1943; Israeli, 1951–52; Argentine, 1949, [1964]; Chinese,
1956–58; Cuban (selections), 1960.

The first outstanding durable twentieth-century history. It was used as a textbook in many countries, with new editions in several languages as late as the
1940s and 1950s. It was still in print in England in 1973. It was the first history
to incorporate successfully the rise of the Marginal Utility School (R. S. Howey,
The Rise of the Marginal Utility School [Lawrence: University of Kansas Press,
1960], p. 220).

The reviewers appreciated the book. "We do not think," Price wrote, "that
by any different avenue of learning a student could possibly make a more agree-
able or satisfactory approach to this important region of economic study" (*Economic Journal* 19 [1909]: 419). Johnson said that it was "not only the fairest
book in its field, but the most readable and instructive as well" (*Journal of
Political Economy* 19 [1911]: 243). Bonar compared it favorably with the available histories in English (*American Economic Review* 1 [1911]: 309). A French
reviewer called it "à la fois lucide, précis, bien documenté et complet," adding
that it appeared destined "a devenir classique" (*Le Musée social,* 1910, p. 43).
Brocard noted that, as a textbook, it concentrated on a small number of names
and ideas; that the authors presented their history in the guise of a struggle,
with the Classical School as the main participant; and that the book "est composé
et écrit avec un art consommé" (*Revue d'histoire des doctrines économiques et
sociales* 3 [1910]: 217–22). Walras's last publication was a complimentary review of Gide and Rist's book (*Gazette de Lausanne,* 6 January 1910). This
high esteem continued. In 1932 Garnsey concluded: "It still stands preëminent
in its field, and forms an indispensable part of the library of every student of
economics" (*American Economic Review* 22 [1932]: 693).

Charles Gide had followed his older brother Paul through the law course
of the University of Paris, but he developed no taste for law. In 1874 an inclina-
tion toward study led him to an appointment at the University of Bordeaux to
one of the few professorships of political economy in France that had been
established before an 1877 decree required the teaching of that subject in all
French universities. Up to this time, Gide had never studied political economy.
His brother gave him a set of Bastiat's *Oeuvres complètes* as an introduction to
the subject. This was as ample a preparation as that of the other French pro-

fessors appointed immediately after 1877, who were required to be graduates of the French law schools, where no political economy had been taught (Charles Gide, "Comment est née la Revue d'économie politique," *Revue d'économie politique* 45 [1931]: 1350–53).

In the next twenty years, Gide established his reputation.[53] He moved in 1881 to the University of Montpellier, where, from 1896 to 1898, he taught the history of economic doctrines, a course that an 1895 decree had made a required subject in French universities. In 1898 he began to lecture on comparative social economics at the University of Paris. He never lectured at Paris on the history of economic doctrines, since Auguste Deschamps was already established there as the lecturer on that subject.

During his first years in Paris, Gide decided to add a textbook on the history of doctrines to the publications that he then had in process. It would make use of the materials he had prepared at Montpellier. He put his *Histoire* together between 1902 and 1909. As Lavondès said, "Charles Gide n'était pas spécialement historien, son esprit était plutôt tourné vers l'avenir que vers le passé" (A. Lavondès, *Charles Gide: un apôtre de la coopération entre les hommes, un précurseur de l'Europe unie et de l'O.N.U.* [Uzès: La Capitelle, 1953 (copyright)], p. 124).

Gide sought a collaborator to help with German economics. He found one in Rist, his young replacement at the University of Montpellier, who was lecturing there on the history of economic doctrines. Rist eventually supplied more than a history of German economics, contributing about half the chapters.

227   Miklashevskiĭ, Aleksandr Nikolaevich (1864–1911; professor at Dorpat)
      Istoriia politicheskoĭ ekonomii. Iar'ev [also] Moskva: K. Mattisen, 1909.
      viii, 638 p. 23.5 cm.
      In Columbia University Library.

A mixture of economic history with some economic thought, largely socialist economic thought.

228* Rambaud, Joseph (1849–1919)
      Histoire des doctrines économiques. Troisième édition, revue, mise à jour et augmentée. Paris: L. Larose, 1909. 816 p. 23 cm.
      Earlier editions: 1899, 1902.

229* Damaschke, Adolf Wilhelm Ferdinand (1865–1935)
      Geschichte der Nationalökonomie. Eine erste Einführung. Vierte, erweiterte Auflage. 8.–10. Tausend. Jena: Gustav Fischer, 1910. viii, 514 p. 21.5 cm.
      See entry for first (1905) edition.

230   Diepenhorst, Pieter Arie (1879–1953; professor at Free University of Amsterdam)
      Voorlezingen over de geschiedenis der economie. Utrecht: G. J. A. Ruys, 1910. viii, 336 p. 8°.

Listed in *Brinkman's Catalogus van boeken.*
Later editions: 1912, 1920, 1934, 1946.

The first half of this long-lived history took the account up to the Historical School; the last half treated mainly socialism and anarchism.

231   Svialovskii, Vladimir Vladimirovich (b. 1871; docent at St. Petersburg in 1910, lecturing on the history of political economy)
      Ocherki po istorii politicheskoĭ ekonomii. St. Petersburg: 1910. viii, 534 p. 23.5 cm.
      In Library of Congress.

232   Chuprov, Aleksandr Ivanovich (1842–1908)
      Istoriia politicheskoĭ ekonomii [3:1–231 in] *Uchenye trudy v izdanii Imperatorskago moskovskago universiteta.* Moskva, 1911. 25.5 cm.
      In Columbia University Library.
      See entry for first (1892) edition.

233* Damaschke, Adolf Wilhelm Ferdinand (1865–1935)
      Geschichte der Nationalökonomie. Eine erste Einführung. Fünfte, durchgesehene Auflage. 11.–14. Tausend. Jena: Gustav Fischer, 1911. xii, 574 p. 21.5 cm.
      See entry for first (1905) edition.

234* Haney, Lewis Henry (1882–1969)
      History of Economic Thought: A Critical Account of the Origin and Development of the Economic Theories of the Leading Thinkers in the Leading Nations. New York: Macmillan Company, 1911 (also dated 1912, 1913, 1915, 1916, 1917). xvii, 567 p. 20.5 cm.
      Later editions: 1920, 1936, 1949. Translations: Chinese, 1930, 1969.

The first textbook on the subject written in the United States. It had no rival for ten years after publication, and only one after twenty years. It was the second history (Gide and Rist's was the first) to include the developments after 1870 and thus to mark the change from "political economy" to "economics." This history played a part in the teaching of the subject to the rapidly growing number of students in the universities of the United States.

It resulted from the university teaching not only of Haney but also of Ely. In his early years, Haney had begun his study of economics by reading the article "Political Economy" in the *Encyclopaedia Britannica* that became Ingram's *History.* He reread Ingram in 1901, when he was a student of Wicker's at Dartmouth. During his years (1904–6) as a graduate student at Wisconsin, the university *Catalogue* listed courses in history of economics taught by both Ely and Scott (who had been Ely's student at Johns Hopkins). At this time, Ely was one of the experienced teachers of the history of economics in the United States. Ely's acquaintance with Haney lead to Haney's *History.* Haney first taught at the University of Iowa, offering a course in which the "rise and development of the Classical School of economics will first be considered" (*Cata-*

logue of the State University of Iowa [Iowa City, Iowa, 1906/7]). The history of political economy had been taught at Iowa since 1895 by Loos (ibid., 1895/96). While at Iowa, Haney accepted Ely's suggestion that he use Ely's notes on the history of economics to prepare a book under their joint authorship. The notes consisted of a stack of typed half-sheets. Ely had worked by accumulating materials of this kind, to which, from time to time, he had made small additions. Haney intermingled Ely's notes with his own, used them in his teaching, and began to prepare the book. Haney left Iowa in 1908 for the University of Michigan, where, along with other subjects, he taught the history of economics and where he continued to prepare the manuscript. He completed it, however, only after he had moved to the University of Texas in 1910. Haney took the finished manuscript to Madison, where he went over it with Ely, noting a reticence which he attributed to Ely's characteristic avoidance of enthusiasm. Ely finally stopped the discussion with the observation that the manuscript differed so greatly from his notes that he could not consider it as a joint venture.[54] Consequently, Haney published the volume under his own name but with a Preface that expressed his obligations to Ely.

Of the principal reviews, Johnson's was the most thorough. He noted the frequent complaints that the earlier textbooks were unsatisfactory, and he concluded that Haney's book put economists in a "far better position than formerly to conduct undergraduate courses in the history of economics" (*Journal of Political Economy* 19 [1911]: 711). Price thought that it "superseded all previous English treatises" (*Journal of the Royal Statistical Society* 76 [1912/13]: 230). Schumpeter concluded that "der Autor hat sehr nützliche Arbeit galeistet und das Buch verdient sicher eine Empfehlung" (*Zeitschrift für Volkswirtschaft, Sozialpolitik und Verwaltung* 21 [1912]: 289). Seligman, who had planned to write a general history himself, thought that Haney's book was only an inadequate sketch (*Political Science Quarterly* 27 [1912]: 156–58). Seligman deplored "the lack of correlation between the particular theory and the institutions of economic life which were responsible for it." He thought it doubtful that "the history of economic science could be successfully written by a comparatively young man." As had Seligman, Fay lectured Haney on the importance of "the influence of specific events on the emergence of particular economic generalisations" (*Economic Journal* 21 [1911]: 603–7). He ended by saying: "What we should like to know from him is why there was such a slump in Economics, and such a hatred of Economists, from the death of Ricardo right down to the last generation. History might tell us. Dr. Haney does not." Hollander thought that it failed to interrelate "life and thought" and that more work should be spent on it (*American Economic Review* 2 [1912]: 877–79).

Reviews of later editions were fewer and concentrated on additions that had been made. The principal later reviews were those by Ferguson (*American Economic Review* 26 [1936]: 487–88) and by Hayek (*Jahrbücher für National-ökonomie und Statistik* 144 [1936]: 743).

235* Karmin, Otto Maurice Adalbert (1882–1920; professor of social psychology
      at Geneva)

Tableaux chronologiques pour servir à l'étude de l'histoire des systèmes économiques et socialistes de 1500 à 1886. Préface de M. H. Fazy. Paris: Marcel Rivière & Co., 1911. 8, xxiii p. 23.5 cm.

236   Spann, Othmar (1878–1950)
      Die Haupttheorien der Volkswirtschaftslehre auf dogmengeschichtlicher Grundlage. Leipzig: Quelle & Meyer, 1911. viii, 132 p. 19 cm.
      In Harvard University Library.
      Other editions included in this bibliography: 1916, 1920, 1923, 1930, 1936, 1949, 1967. Translations: Swedish, 1927, 1932; American, 1930 (reprinted, 1972); Chinese, 1934; Spanish, 1934; Italian, 1936, 1945; Yugoslav, 1944.

The seed from which Spann's "Universalism" grew (see Edgar Salin, "Romantic and Universalist Economics," *Encyclopedia of the Social Sciences,* vol. 5 [1931], pp. 385–87). Doubtless "Universalism," rather than "history," explained the book's long life.

It intended to link "economic doctrine with the great fundamental outlooks on society and life" (Spann, *The History of Economics* [no. 325 infra], p. 13), placing the universe of society, rather than the individual, at the top in importance. This social universe remained vague. "The student of economics," Spann wrote, "must discover in himself, must experience in his own being, what society and economics are; and this knowledge must keep him company in all his experience, observation, analysis, and research" (ibid., p. 10).

Spann's loose ideas had some influence on Schumpeter, who thought Spann was possibly more important than any high-powered technician of economic theory (*A History of Economic Analysis* [no. 574 infra], pp. 1139–40) and that he was "difficult to characterize from a professional standpoint" (ibid., p. 854). Schumpeter reviewed Spann's *Haupttheorien* in 1912 (*Zeitschrift für Volkswirtschaft, Sozialpolitik und Verwaltung* 21 [1912]: 289–91). At that time he did not detect the beginning of the Universalist School, treating Spann's history as a good book for the lay public and mainly finding fault only with the materials that it included and excluded.[55] While Elster recognized the *Haupttheorien* as a different kind of book in his review of the second edition in 1921 (*Jahrbücher für Nationalökonomie und Statistik,* 3d ser. 61 [1921]: 364–66), he did not elaborate on the difference.

Spann's later editions and translation received many reviews, which were often more appreciative than might be expected.[56] For example, Knight wrote that "every teacher of economics should enthusiastically welcome this translation." He went on to explain that "for a really understanding presentation and criticism of the classical position, it goes without saying that no one should be directed to Spann," but that the "educable student of Anglo-Saxon background who reads Spann should be helped in grasping the idea that there is another psychology, another sociology, and another ethic than those traditional in his own culture, in terms of which the relations of buying and selling, hiring and firing, leasing, lending, etc., of which economics treats, looks very, very different."

The manuscript of Spann's history dated from 1903, the year that Spann received, summa cum laude, his *Doktor der Staatswissenschaft* from Tübingen (Spann, *Die Haupttheorien der Volkswirtschaftslehre,* 23d ed. [Leipzig: Quelle & Meyer, 1933], pp. v–vi). He wrote it as an entry in a prize competition for the best "Introduction to Economics." He composed his entry on historical lines, because he had been interested in ascertaining the truth that could be found in the principles of the old masters who were discussed in the histories of political economy. He had looked for a critical history but had found none that suited him. Spann submitted his manuscript in the summer of 1904. It received no prize. In the summer of 1905, while traveling, his small trunk containing the manuscript was mistakenly picked up by a party of seven monks on their way to Chile as missionaries. A half year later, after Spann had given up hope, the badly damaged trunk was returned with the manuscript intact.

While a professor at the Technischen Hochschule in Brünn, he revised his manuscript, adding the section on Adam Mueller. Several publishers rejected the volume.

"Universalism" made Spann a sharp critic both of Marxism and of liberal democracy. This led him, after 1934, into the National Socialism of Dolfuss. After the Anschluss he lost his professorship and did not receive it back after 1945.

237* Damaschke, Adolf Wilhelm Ferdinand (1865–1935)
    Geschichte der Nationalökonomie. Eine erste Einführung. Sechste, durchgesehene Auflage. 15.–18. Tausend. Jena: Gustav Fischer, 1912. xxii, 606 p. 22 cm.
    See entry for first (1905) edition.

238 Diepenhorst, Pieter Arie (1879–1953)
    "Geschiedenis" [vol. 1 of his] *Voorlezingen over de economie.* Tweede, herziene druk. Utrecht: G. J. A. Ruys, 1912. 21 cm.
    In Columbia University Library.
    Other editions: 1910, 1920, 1934, 1946.

239* Fridrichowiéz, Eugen (b. 1864)
    Grundriss einer Geschichte der Volkswirtschaftslehre. München und Leipzig: Duncker & Humblot, 1912. vii, 267 p. 26 cm.

240* Chuprov, Aleksandr Ivanovich (1842–1908)
    Istoriia politicheskoĭ ekonomii. 7. izd. Moskva, 1913. 224 p. 21.5 cm.
    See entry for first (1892) edition.

241* Damaschke, Adolf Wilhelm Ferdinand (1865–1935)
    Geschichte der Nationalökonomie. Eine erste Einführung. Siebente Auflage. 19.–21. Tausend. Jena: Gustav Fischer, 1913. xii, 606 p. 22 cm.
    See entry for first (1905) edition.

242* Gide, Paul Henri Charles (1847–1932), and Rist, Charles (1874–1955)

Geschichte der volkswirtschaftlichen Lehrmeinungen. Nach der zweiten durchgesehenen und verbesserten Ausgabe, herausgegeben von Franz Oppenheimer. Deutsch von R. W. Horn. Jena: Gustav Fischer, 1913. xxii, 828 p. 24.5 cm.
See entry for first (1909) French edition.

243* ⸻

Histoire des doctrines économiques depuis les physiocrates jusqu'à nos jours. Deuxième édition, revue et augmentée. Paris: Sirey, 1913. xviii, 786 p. 22 cm.
See entry for first (1909) edition.

244 ⸻

Istoriia ekonomicheskikh uchenii. [Translation by] Viktor Serezhnikov. [Edited by] V. F. Totomiants. Moskva: Trud, 1914 (Rist's bibliography gave the date of the Russian translation as 1910). x, 496 p. 8°.
In New York Public Library.
See entry for first (1909) edition.

245 Levitskiĭ, Vladimir Favstovich (b. 1855)
Istoriia politicheskoĭ ekonomii. Kharkov: "Adolf Darre," 1914. 493 p. 26 cm.
In Library of Congress.
First edition: 1907.

246 [Lifschitz, Feitel] (b. 1875; Privatdocent at Bern)
Repetitorium der Geschichte der Nationalökonomie von Dr. Bernhard Siegfried [pseud.]. Bern: Akad. Buchh. v. M. Drechsel, 1914. 104 p. 8°.
In New York Public Library.
Later edition: 1922.

247* Schumpeter, Joseph Alois (1883–1950; professor at Graz in 1914)
"Epochen der Dogmen- und Methodengeschichte" [Abteilung 1:19–124, in] *Grundriss der Socialökonomik.* Tübingen: J. C. B. Mohr, 1914. 28.5 cm.
Second edition: 1924. Translations: Italian, 1953; British, 1954; Japanese, 1957; Swedish, 1957; French, 1962, 1971; Spanish, 1964; Korean, 1965.
Other histories by Schumpeter: 1951, 1954.

248* Gide, Paul Henri Charles (1847–1932), and Rist, Charles (1874–1955)
A History of Economic Doctrines from the Time of the Physiocrats to the Present Day. Authorised translation from the second revised and augmented edition of 1913, under the direction of the late Professor William Smart, by R. Richards. London: G. G. Harrap, 1915; Boston: D. C. Heath and Company, 1915 (both the London and the Boston editions were also issued with later dates). xxiii, 672 p. 22.5 cm.
See entry for first (1909) French edition.

249* Ingram, John Kells (1823–1907)
A History of Political Economy. New and enlarged edition, with a sup-
plementary chapter by William A. Scott . . . and an introduction by
Richard T. Ely. London: A. & C. Black, 1915 (also dated 1919, 1923,
and reprinted, New York, 1967). xix, 315 p. 21.5 cm.
See entry for 1888 edition.

250 Damaschke, Adolf Wilhelm Ferdinand (1865–1935)
Geschichte der Nationalökonomie. Eine erste Einführung. 8., durch-
gesehene Auflage. Jena: Gustav Fischer, 1916. x, 607 p. 8°.
Listed in *Deutsches Bücherverzeichnis.*
See entry for first (1905) edition.

251 Spann, Othmar (1878–1950)
*Die Haupttheorien der Volkswirtschaftslehre auf dogmengeschichtlicher
Grundlage.* 2., verm. Aufl. Leipzig: Quelle & Meyer, 1916. 156 p. 8°.
In Syracuse University Library.
See entry for first (1911) edition.

252* Schelle, Gustave (1845–1927; member [1919] of the Académie des sciences
morales et politiques)
*L'Économie politique et les économistes avec une introduction sur l'écono-
mique et la guerre.* Paris: Octabe Doin et Fils, 1917. xviii, 396 p.
18.5 cm.

253* Damaschke, Adolf Wilhelm Ferdinand (1865–1935)
Geschichte der Nationalökonomie. Eine erste Einführung. Neunte,
erweiterte Auflage (10th edition of same year was identical). 40. bis 42.
Tausend. Jena: Gustav Fischer, 1918. 2 v. (xiv, 400; xvi, 399 p.)
22 cm.
See entry for first (1905) edition.

254* ———
Geschichte der Nationalökonomie. Eine erste Einführung. Elfte, durchgesehene Auflage. 50.–60. Tausend. Jena: Gustav Fischer, 1919. 2 v.
(xvi, 402; iv, 415 p.) 21 cm.
See entry for first (1905) edition.

255* Polak, Siegfried
Beknopte geschiedenis der staathuishoudkunde in theorie en praktijk.
Amsterdam: Maatschappij voor Goede en Goedkoope Lectuur, 1919.
2 v. (266, 270 p.) 19 cm.
Second edition: 1928.

256 Liaschenko, Petr Ivanovich (1876–1955)
Istoriia ekonomicheskikh uchenii. Leningrad, 192–? 270 p.
In Columbia University Library.

257* Damaschke, Adolf Wilhelm Ferdinand (1865–1935)
Geschichte der Nationalökonomie. Eine erste Einführung. Zwölfte,
durchgesehene Auflage. 61.–70. Tausend. Jena: Gustav Fischer, 1920.
2 v. (xii, 402; iv, 415 p.) 21.5 cm.
See entry for first (1905) edition.

258* Diepenhorst, Pieter Arie (1879–1953)
"Geschiedenis" [vol. 1 in his] *Voorlezingen over de economie.* Derde,
herziene druk. Utrecht: G. J. A. Ruys, 1920. 22 cm.
Other editions: 1910, 1912, 1934, 1946.

259 Gide, Paul Henri Charles (1847–1932), and Rist, Charles (1874–1955)
[Czechoslovak translation of *Histoire des doctrines économiques*], 1920.
Listed in Flamant.
See entry for first (1909) French edition.

260* ———
*Histoire des doctrines économiques depuis les physiocrates jusqu'à nos
jours.* Troisième édition, revue et corrigée. Paris: Recueil Sirey, 1920.
xx, 806 p. 23 cm.
See entry for first (1909) edition.

261 ———
Historja doktryn ekonomicznych od fizjokratów do czasów najnowszych.
Warszawa: Nakładem Gebethnera i Wolffa, 1920. 2 v. 20.5 cm.
In Columbia University Library.
See entry for first (1909) French edition.

262* Haney, Lewis Henry (1882–1969)
*History of Economic Thought: A Critical Account of the Origin and
Development of the Economic Theories of the Leading Thinkers in the
Leading Nations.* Revised edition. New York: Macmillan Company,
1920 (also dated 1926). xix, 677 p. 20.5 cm.
See entry for first (1911) edition.
Preface listed additions made to this edition.

263* Kawakami, Hajime (1879–1946)
Kinsei keizai shiso shi ron. Tokyo: 1920 (also dated 1921, 1922, 1949).
357 p. 19 cm.
Another history by Kawakami: 1923.
This history started with Smith; had chapters on Malthus, Ricardo, and Marx;
ended with chapters on Capitalism and Social Democracy. It was the earliest
publication that might be called a general history written by a Japanese.
Kawakami was "a well-known Marxist who taught economics at Kyoto
University . . . known for his political activities as a member of the Communist
Party during the later years of his life" (Charles F. Remer and Saburo Kawai,

Japanese Economics: A Guide to Japanese Reference and Research Materials
[Ann Arbor: University of Michigan Press, 1956], p. 21).

264* Seligman, Edwin Robert Anderson (1861–1939; professor at Columbia
       University)
       *Curiosities of Early Economic Literature: An Address to His Fellow
       Members of the Hobby Club of New York.* San Francisco: Privately
       Printed by J. H. Nash, 1920. xxvi p. 40 cm.
       One hundred copies printed.
       Another history by Seligman: 1931.
An unusual history: told in terms of "curiosities." Seligman read it at the
quarterly dinner of the Hobby Club, November 1914. Perhaps it was the best
printed of all general histories of economics.

265   Spann, Othmar (1878–1950)
       *Die Haupttheorien der Volkswirtschaftslehre auf dogmengeschichtlicher
       Grundlage.* Mit einem Anhang: "Wie studiert man Volkswirtschafts-
       lehre?" Sechste Auflage. 26.–30. Tausend. Leipzig: Quelle & Meyer,
       1920. 176 p. 18.5 cm.
       In Columbia University Library.
       See entry for first (1911) edition.

266* Tyszka, Carl von (b. 1873; professor at Hamburg)
       *Volkswirtschaftliche Theorien: Merkantilismus, Individualismus, Sozial-
       ismus, Bolschewismus, Imperialismus.* Jena: Gustav Fischer, 1920. iv,
       136 p. 24 cm.
An attempt to connect past theories with the economic conditions leading to them.

267* Boucke, Oswald Fred (1881–1935; professor at Pennsylvania State Uni-
       versity)
       The Development of Economics, 1750–1900. New York: Macmillan
       Company, 1921. vi, 348 p. 19.5 cm.
Described this period under four headings: Naturalism, Utilitarianism, His-
torism, and Marginism.

268   Gide, Paul Henri Charles (1847–1932), and Rist, Charles (1874–1955)
       Geschichte der volkswirtschaftlichen Lehrmeinungen. Zweite Auflage,
       nach der dritten französischen Ausgabe, herausgegeben von Franz
       Oppenheimer. Deutsch von R. W. Horn. Jena: Gustav Fischer, 1921
       (also dated 1923). xx, 804 p. 23.5 cm.
       In Columbia University Library.
       See entry for first (1909) French edition.

269   ———
       Istorija ekonomiskih doktrina: od fiziokrata do naših dana. [Translation
       by] S. Savić. Beograd: Mirotočivi, 1921.

Listed in Flamant.
See first (1909) French edition.

270*   Gonnard, Charles René (1874–1966; professor at Lyons)
         Histoire des doctrines économiques. Paris: Nouvelle Librairie Nationale,
         1921–22. 3 v. (293, 320, 356 p.) 21 cm.
         Later French editions: 1924–27, 1930, 1941. Translations: Spanish, 1931,
         1938, 1944, 1952, 1956; Portuguese, 1942; Mexican, 1948.
Spengler said, of a later edition, that despite revisions "and despite Professor
Gonnard's three decades of work on historical movements in doctrine, the present
work is a distinct disappointment. . . . Most serious . . . is the disproportionate
distribution of space among ideas and writers" (*American Economic Review*
21 [1931]: 288).

271   Totomiants, Vakhan Fomich (b. 1875)
         Istoriia ekonomicheskikh i sotsial' nykh uchenĭ. [Moskva], 1921. 283 p.
         In Columbia University.
         Translations: French, 1922; Italian, 1922, 1943; Czechoslovak, 1923;
         German, 1925, 1929; Yugoslav, 1928; Spanish, 1934; Cuban, 1960.
Lectures given at the University of Moscow in 1916/17 and at the Polytechnic
Institute of Tiflis in 1919/20.

272   Bonar, James (1852–1941)
         Philosophy and Political Economy in Some of Their Historical Relations.
         3d edition. London: G. Allen & Unwin, 1922 (also dated 1927; re-
         printed, New York, 1966). vii–xvii, 424 p. 22 cm.
         In Library of Congress.
         Other editions: 1893, 1909.

273*   Damaschke, Adolf Wilhelm Ferdinand (1865–1935)
         Geschichte der Nationalökonomie. Eine erste Einführung. Dreizehnte,
         durchgesehene Auflage. 71.–85. Tausend. Jena: Gustav Fischer, 1922.
         2 v. (xii, 409; iv, 442 p.) 22 cm.
         See entry for first (1905) edition.

274*   Gide, Paul Henri Charles (1847–1932), and Rist, Charles (1874–1955)
         *Histoire des doctrines économiques depuis les physiocrates jusqu'à nos
         jours.* Quatrième édition, revue et corrigée. Paris: Recueil Sirey, 1922.
         832 p. 24 cm.
         See entry for first (1909) edition.

275   [Lifschitz, Feitel] (b. 1875)
         *Repetitorium der Geschichte der Nationalökonomie, von Dr. Bernhard
         Siegfried* [pseud.]. Zweite Auflage. Bern: Paul Haupt, 1922. 104 p.
         20 cm.
         In Library of Congress.
         First edition: 1914.

276   Oncken, August (1844–1911)
       Geschichte der Nationalökonomie. In zwei Teilen. Erster Teil: *Die*
       Zeit vor Adam Smith [no more published]. Dritte, unveränderte
       Auflage. Leipzig: C. L. Hirschfeld, 1922. ix, 516 p. 25 cm.
       In Columbia University Library.
       First edition: 1902. Translation: Russian, 1908.

277*   Totomiants, Vakhan Fomich (b. 1875)
       Histoire des doctrines économiques et sociales. Préface de C. Rist. Paris:
       Marcel Giard, 1922. x, 238 p. 19 cm.
       See entry for Russian (1921) edition.

278*   ———
       Storia delle dottrine economiche e sociali. Prefazione di Achille Loria.
       Torino: Fratelli Bocca, 1922. xii, 216 p. 21 cm.
       See entry for Russian (1921) edition.

279   Ghio, Paul (b. 1865)
       La Formation historique de l'économie politique. Paris: Marcel Rivière,
       1923. xi, 177 p. 23 cm.
       In New York Public Library.
       Second edition: 1926.
       Other histories by Ghio: 1897, 1908.
A borderline general history that looked at the early development of moral,
political, and economic liberty; then at Smith, Ricardo, and Marx; and ended
with a discussion of economic laws.

280   Gide, Paul Henri Charles (1847–1932), and Rist, Charles (1874–1955)
       Geschichte der volkswirtschaftlichen Lehrmeinungen. Dritte Auflage,
       nach der vierten durchgesehenen und verbesserten französischen
       Ausgabe, herausgegeben von Franz Oppenheimer. Deutsch von R. W.
       Horn. Jena: Gustav Fischer, 1923. xx, 811 p. 23.5 cm.
       In Library of Congress.
       See entry for first (1909) French edition.

281   Kawakami, Hajime (1879–1946)
       Shihonshugi keizaigaku no shiteki hatten. Tokyo, 1923. 16, 625 p. 22 cm.
       In Hoover Institution at Stanford.
       Another history by Kawakami: 1920.
A history of economic theory from a Marxist point of view.

282   Marx, Karl (1818–83)
       Teorii pribavochnoĭ tsennosti: iz neĭzdannoĭ rukopisi. K Kritiki politi-
       cheskoĭ ekonomii Karla Marksa. Petrograd: Kommunisticheskii Univ.
       Zinov'eva, 1923–25. 3 v.
       In Harvard University Library.
       See entry for first (1905–10) German edition.

283* Salin, Edgar (b. 1892; privatdocent at Heidelberg, later professor at Basel)
Geschichte der Volkswirtschaftslehre. Berlin: Julius Springer, 1923.
42 p. 25 cm.
Later editions: 1929, 1944, 1951, 1967. Translations: Japanese, 1935;
Argentine, 1948; Italian, 1973.

284 Spann, Othmar (1878–1950)
*Die Haupttheorien der Volkswirtschaftslehre auf lehrgeschichtlicher
Grundlage.* Mit einem Anhang: *Wie studiert man Volkswirtschafts-
lehre?* 12., 13., 14., 15., abermals vermehrte Auflage. 56.–75. Tausend.
Leipzig: Quelle & Meyer, 1923. viii, 207 p. 18.5 cm.
In Columbia University Library.
See entry for first (1911) edition.

285* Surányi-Unger, Theo Victor (b. 1898; professor at Szeged, Pécs, and
Syracuse, N.Y.)
*Philosophie in der Volkswirtschaftslehre: Ein Beitrag zur Geschichte der
Volkswirtschaftslehre.* Jena: Gustav Fischer, 1923–26. 2 v. (viii, 400;
viii, 547 p.) 24 cm.
A chronological arrangement emphasizing philosophical implications.

286 Totomiants, Vakhan Fomich (b. 1875)
Dejiny narodohospodárských a sociálních nauk. V. Praze: Otto, 1923.
171 p. 19 cm.
In Columbia University Library.
See entry for Russian (1921) edition.

287* Gonnard, Charles René (1874–1966)
Histoire des doctrines économiques. Deuxième édition, revue et corrigée.
Paris: Nouvelle Librairie Nationale, 1924–27. 3 v. (292, 319, 364 p.)
See entry for first (1921–22) edition.

288 Heller, Farkas Heinrich (1877–1955; professor in the Technischen Hoch-
schule at Budapest)
Die Entwicklung der Grundprobleme der volkswirtschaftlichen Theorie.
Zweite, umgearbeitete und stark vermehrte Auflage. Leipzig: Quelle
& Meyer, 1924. viii, 144 p. 18.5 cm.
In Columbia University Library.
First edition (1921), with title *Die Grundprobleme der theoretischen
Volkswirtschaftslehre,* was not a history.
Later editions: 1928, 1931.

289* Marx, Karl (1818–83)
Histoire des doctrines économiques, publiée par Karl Kautsky. Traduit
par J. Molitor. Paris: Alfred Costes, 1924–25 (also with later dates).
8 v. (xix plus 319, 215, 364, 320, 178, 256, 266, 256 p.) 18 cm.
See entry for first (1905–10) German edition.

290 Schumpeter, Joseph Alois (1883–1950)
"Epochen der Dogmen- und Methodengeschichte" [Abteilung 1, Teil 1, in] *Grundriss der Socialökonomik*. 2., erw. Aufl. Tübingen: J. C. B. Mohr, 1924. 4°.
In *Deutsches Bücherverzeichnis*.
See entry for first (1914) edition.

291 Thörnberg, Ernst Herman (b. 1873)
Nationalekonomiens historia. En framställning av det ekonomiska tänkandets utveckling. Första delen. Stockholm: Tidens Förlag, 1924. 262 p. 8°.
In New York Public Library.
Covered the period from the Greeks to Mill.

292* Wilbrandt, Robert (1875–1945; professor at Tübingen)
Die Entwicklung der Volkswirtschaftslehre [vol. 1 of his] *Einführung in die Volkswirtschaftslehre*. Stuttgart: Ernst Heinrich Moritz, 1924. xi, 133 p. 19 cm.
Devoted the last two-thirds to the Romantics, the Socialists, and the Historical School.

293* Bigelow, Karl Worth (b. 1898; tutor at Harvard and Radcliffe in 1925)
"Economics" [pp. 333–95 in] Henry Elmer Barnes, ed., *The History and Prospects of the Social Sciences*. New York: Alfred A. Knopf, 1925. 24 cm.
Summarized economics from Plato to Institutional Economics. It was contained, for comparison, along with the histories of eight other social sciences, in a volume with Barnes's introduction to this particular kind of history.

294 Gëmahling, Paul (b. 1883; professor at Strasbourg)
Les Grands économistes: textes et commentaires. Paris: Recueil Sirey, 1925. xii, 330 p. 23.5 cm.
In New York Public Library.
Second edition: 1933.
A text composed of readings, with commentaries, arranged chronologically from Aristotle to Walras.

295* Totomiants, Vakhan Fomich (b. 1875)
Geschichte der Nationalökonomie und des Sozialismus, im Zusammenhang mit der Wirtschaftsgeschichte. Mit einem Vorwort von Heinrich Herkner. Jena: Thüringer Verlagsanstalt und Druckerei, 1925. 192 p. 21 cm.
See entry for Russian (1921) edition.

296* Ghio, Paul (b. 1865)

La Formation historique de l'économie politique. Deuxième édition revue. Paris: Marcel Rivière, 1926. xii, 173 p. 23 cm.

Earlier edition: 1923.

Other histories by Ghio: 1897, 1908.

297   Gide, Paul Henri Charles (1847–1932), and Rist, Charles (1874–1955)
Histoire des doctrines économiques depuis les physiocrates jusqu'à nos jours. 5ᵉ éd., rev. et cor. Paris: Recueil Sirey, 1926 (also dated 1929). xvi, 814 p. 23.5 cm.

In Columbia University Library.

See entry for first (1909) edition.

298   ———

Istoria doctrinelor economice de la fiziocraţi până azi. Traducere cu aprobarea autorilor de Georg Alexianu. După ed. Bucureşti: Editura Cassei Scoalelor, 1926. 942 p. 24.5 cm.

In Columbia University Library.

See entry for first (1909) edition.

299*   Bousquet, Georges Henri ("Chargé de cours à Alger")
Essai sur l'évolution de la pensée économique. Paris: Marcel Giard, 1927 (also dated 1935 and 1943). xv, 314 p. 23 cm.

A later synthesis in translation: Mexican, 1938.

Looked at the "aim" rather than the "results" of the economists. It determined that the aim was to formulate a system of equations expressing the competitive system and that this goal had already been reached or passed.

Knight said that "the work has . . . remarkable lucidity, wit and charm, without too much depth or consistency . . . it is a very stimulating book, and also contains much historical information put in a way to suggest fresh viewpoints" (*American Economic Review* 18 [1928]: 278–79).

300   Budge, Siegfried (b. 1869; professor at Frankfurt am Main)
Geschichte der volkswirtschaftlichen Ideen und Theorien [pp. 200–350 in] *Die Beamten-Hochschule.* Lehr- und Handbuch zur hochschulmässigen Fortbildung der deutschen Beamten. Zweiter Teil. Wirtschafts- und Sozialwissenschaften. 3. Band. Volkswirtschaftslehre, Statistik und Soziologie. Berlin: Industrieverlag, Spaeth & Linde, 1927. 27 cm.

In Harvard University Library.

Covered history from Mercantilism to 1914.

301*   Gide, Paul Henri Charles (1847–1932), and Rist, Charles (1874–1955)
Historia de las doctrinas económicas desde los fisiócratas hasta nuestros días. Vertida al español de la cuarta edición francesa por C. Martínez Peñalver. Con unas palabras de dedicatoria para los lectores de lengua española de Carlos Gide. Madrid (also Barcelona): Editorial Reus, 1927. xxiv, 1011 p. 23 cm.

See entry for first (1909) French edition.

302* Junker, Paul
Geschichte der Volkswirtschaftslehre. Dessau: C. Dünnhaupt Verlag, 1927. 83 p. 19.5 cm.
Presented a discussion of Mercantilism, Physiocracy, and the Classical School, as a preface to Utopian Socialism, German Universalism, and Scientific Socialism.

303* Kerschagl, Richard (b. 1896; professor at Vienna)
Volkswirtschaftslehre: eine Darstellung ihrer wichtigsten Lehrmeinungen. Wien: Manz, 1927. vi, 150 p. 22 cm.
Later editions: 1946, 1947, 1952.

304 Kobayashi, Ushisaburo (1866–1930)
Keizai shiso oyobi gakusetsu shi. Tokyo: Nihon Hyoron-sha, 1927. 2, 4, 487 p. 23 cm.
In Library of Congress.
Translation: Chinese, 1938.

305* Mombert, Paul (1876–1935; professor at Giessen)
Geschichte der Nationalökonomie. Jena: Gustav Fischer, 1927. ix, 557 p. 23.5 cm.

306 Spann, Othmar (1878–1950)
Huvudteorierna uti nationalekonomien. Övers., och bearb. av Malte Welin. Stockholm: Wahlström & Widstrand, 1927. 147 p. 8°.
Listed in *Svensk Bok-katalog.*
For *Andra Delen* see 1932 entry.
See entry for first (1911) edition.

307 Heller, Farkas Heinrich (1877–1955)
Die Entwicklung der Grundprobleme der volkswirtschaftlichen Theorie. Dritte, umgearbeitete und stark vermehrte Auflage. Leipzig: Quelle & Meyer, 1928. 164 p. 18 cm.
In Columbia University Library.
Other editions: 1924, 1931.

308* Polak, Siegfried
Beknopte geschiedenis der staathuishoudkunde in theorie en praktijk. Tweede, geheel herziene en uitgebreide druk. Amsterdam: Maatschappij voor Goede en Goedkoope Lectuur, 1928. 795 p. 19 cm.
First edition: 1919.

309 Rubin, Isaak Il'ich (b. 1886)
Istoriia ekonomicheskoĭ mysli. Moskva, 1928 (also dated 1929). 380 p. 24 cm.

In Columbia University Library.
By the author of *Klassiki politicheskoĭ economii* (Moskva, 1926).

310　Totomiants, Vakhan Fomich (b. 1875)
　　　Istorija ekonomskih i socijalnih doktrina. [Translation by] Milan F.
　　　Bartoš. Beograd, 1928.
　　　Listed in Blagojević.
　　　See entry for Russian (1921) edition.

311*　Cannan, Edwin (1861–1935; professor at the London School of Economics)
　　　A Review of Economic Theory. London: P. S. King and Son, Ltd., 1929.
　　　x, 448 p. 22.5 cm.
　　　Later edition: 1964. Translations: Italian, 1932; Mexican, 1940, 1946.
The substance of a course of about sixty lectures entitled "Principles of Economics, Including the History of Economic Theory."

　　　Cannan's *A History of the Theories of Production and Distribution in English Political Economy from 1776 to 1848* (London, 1894) had not been a general history. His *Review* was somewhat a general history, although much of the spirit and contents of the earlier book remained.

　　　Garver appraised Cannan's book thus: "It has the merits and the defects of lectures: it is compact, it moves swiftly, and positions are boldly taken; but it raises problems which are not always discussed exhaustively, and it seldom attempts complicated analysis" (*American Economic Review* 20 [1930]: 80).

312　Cassola, Carlo (1878–1931; professor at Naples)
　　　Appunti di storia delle dottrine economiche. [Litografato]. Napoli,
　　　1929–30.
　　　Listed in Morgenstern and Schams.

313*　Damaschke, Adolf Wilhelm Ferdinand (1865–1935)
　　　Geschichte der Nationalökonomie. Eine erste Einführung. Vierzehnte,
　　　durchgesehene und erweiterte Auflage. 86.–100. Tausend. Jena: Gustav
　　　Fischer, 1929. 2 v. (xii, 455; xxx, 445 p.) 21.5 cm.
　　　See entry for first (1905) edition.

314*　Kalitsounakēs, Dēmētrios Emmanouēl (b. 1888)
　　　*Historia tēs politikēs oikonomias. Historia oikonomikē kai tōn oikono-
　　　mikōn theōriōn.* Athēnai, 1929. xvi, 312 p. 24.5 cm.

315*　Salin, Edgar (b. 1892)
　　　Geschichte der Volkswirtschaftslehre. Zweite, neugestaltete Auflage. Ber-
　　　lin: Julius Springer, 1929. 3, 106 p. 26 cm.
　　　See entry for first (1923) edition.

316　Takahashi, Seiichiro (b. 1884; professor at Keio University)
　　　Keizaigaku shi. 1929. 2, 15, 464 p. 23 cm.

In University of California at Los Angeles Library.
Later edition: 1937.
Other histories by Takahashi: 1940, 1948, 1949.

317 Totomiants, Vakhan Fomich (b. 1875)
Geschichte der Nationalökonomie und des Sozialismus im Zusammenhang mit der Wirtschaftsgeschichte. Mit einem Vorwort von Heinrich Herkner. 2. verb. Auflage. 4. bis 6. Tausend. Berlin: C. Heymann, 1929. vii, 179 p. 22.5 cm.
In Library of Congress.
See entry for Russian (1921) edition.

318* Weiss, Franz Josef (b. 1898)
Grundlagen der Volkswirtschaftspolitik in ihrer geschichtlichen Entwicklung. Wien: Manzsche Verlags- und Universitäts-Buchhandlung, 1929. 215 p. 18.5 cm.
Overlaid with the "Universalist" viewpoint of Spann.

319 Fenoglio, Giulio (b. 1885; docent at Turin)
Lezioni di storia delle dottrine economiche, tenute nell'anno accadèmico 1929–1930. Torino: Società Tipographico-editrice Nazionale, 1930. 96 p. 8°.
Listed in *Catalogo cumulativo, 1886–1957, del bollettino delle pubblicazioni italiane.*
Another history by Fenoglio: 1931.

320 Gide, Paul Henri Charles (1847–1932), and Rist, Charles (1874–1955)
Istoria tōn oikonomikōn theōriōn. Athēnai, 1930–31. 2 v. 24.5 cm.
In Columbia University Library.
See entry for first (1909) French edition.

321 Gonnard, Charles René (1874–1966)
Histoire des doctrines économiques. Nouvelle édition. Paris: Librairie Valois, 1930. viii, 709 p. 22.5 cm.
In Columbia University Library.
See entry for first (1921–22) edition.

322 Haney, Lewis Henry (1882–1969)
Ching chi ssü hsiang shih. [Translation by] Ch'i-fang Tsang. Shanghai, 1930. 791 p. 22 cm.
In University of Chicago Library.
See entry for first (1911) American edition.

323* Myrdal, Gunnar (b. 1898; docent at Stockholm)
Vetenskap och politik i nationalekonomien. Stockholm: Norstedt, 1930 (issued with new title page and dust wrapper in 1937). 308 p. 22 cm.

Later edition: 1971. Translations: German, 1932, 1963; Japanese, 1942, 1967; Italian, 1943; British, 1953 (also later dates); Spanish, 1967; Greek, 1971.
Originally lectures given at the University of Stockholm in 1928.

324* Spann, Othmar (1878–1950)
Die Haupttheorien der Volkswirtschaftslehre auf lehrgeschichtlicher Grundlage. Mit einem Anhang: "Wie studiert man Volkswirtschafts-lehre?" 20., neuerdings durchges. Auflage, 96.–100. Tausend. Ju-belausgabe, mit sechs Bildnissen und dem Bildnisse des Verfassers. Leipzig: Quelle & Meyer, 1930 (identical with 21. Aufl., 1931). xvi, 232 p. 18.5 cm.
See entry for first (1911) edition.

325* ――――
The History of Economics. Translated from the nineteenth German edi-tion by Eden and Cedar Paul. New York: W. W. Norton & Co., 1930 (reprinted, New York, 1972). 328 p. 22 cm.
"Published in Great Britain under the title 'Types of Economic Theory.' "
See entry for first (1911) German edition.

326* Bordewijk, Hugo Willem Constantijn (1879–1939; professor at Groningen)
Theoretisch-historische inleiding tot de economie. Groningen: J. B. Wolters', 1931. 3, 652 p. 23.5 cm.

327* Fenoglio, Giulio (b. 1885; docent at Turin)
Corso di storia delle dottrine economiche. Vol. 1: *Antichità e medio evo* [no more published of this planned four-volume history]. Torino: So-cietà Tipographico-editrice Nazionale, 1931. 204 p. 27.5 cm.
Another history by Fenoglio: 1930.

328 Gonnard, Charles René (1874–1966)
Historia de las doctrinas económicas. Traducción de J. Campo Moreno. Madrid: M. Aguilar, 1931. 605 p. 22 cm.
In Pennsylvania State University Library.
See entry for first (1921–22) French edition.

329* Gray, Alexander (1882–1968; professor at Edinburgh)
The Development of Economic Doctrine: An Introductory Survey. Lon-don: Longmans, Green, and Co., 1931 (also dated 1933, 1934, 1935, 1937, 1941, 1947, 1948, 1961, 1963). 384 p. 19.5 cm.
Translation: Indian (Hindi), 1958.
Edwards said that "the book's best feature is its one failure to follow conven-tion—its refusal to collect names . . . . Mercantilists, Physiocrats, classicists and their critics, romantics, optimists, socialists, and Austrians are summarized in the work of twenty-nine men" (*American Economic Review* 22 [1932]: 88).

As its faults, Edwards mentioned that "once it reaches Adam Smith it slights all economic thought except the conceptual systems known as economic theory . . . ; it fails to connect past thought with a cultural environment. . . . Essentially he [Gray] regards the economic past as a preface to the works of Alfred Marshall."

330   Heller, Farkas Heinrich (1877–1955)
Die Entwicklung der Grundprobleme der volkswirtschaftlichen Theorie.
    4., umgearb. Auflage. Leipzig: Quelle & Meyer, 1931. 156 p. Sm. 8°.
In Bryn Mawr College Library.
Earlier editions: 1924, 1928.

331   Hori, Tsuneo (b. 1896)
Keizaigaku shi yoron. Tokyo: Kobundo, 1931–33 (vol. 1 republished in
    1963). 3 v.
Listed in Remer and Kawai.
Later histories by Hori: 1948, 1950.

332   Philippe, Charles Émile
Les Doctrines économiques. 1re partie: *Évolution historique de l'antiquité*
    grecque et romaine à nos jours. 2e partie: *Doctrines contemporaines.*
    Abrégé à l'usage des officiers de toutes armes et de tous services. Paris:
    Charles-Lavauzelle & Cie., Éditeurs militaires, 1931. 106 p. 18.5 cm.
In Columbia University Library.
Translation: Bolivian, 1939.
Ended with Mill and the Socialists.

333*   Pino-Branca, Alfredo (b. 1890; "professor")
Storia delle dottrine economiche. Padova: Cedam, 1931. 135 p. 26 cm.
"Appendice al corso di storia economica."

334   Price, Langford Lovell Frederick Rice (1862–1950)
A Short History of Political Economy in England, from Adam Smith to
    Alfred Marshall. 14th edition, revised and enlarged. London: Methuen,
    1931. xvi, 315 p. 19.5 cm.
In Library of Congress.
See entry for first (1891) edition.

335*   Seligman, Edwin Robert Anderson (1861–1939), and others (Weulersse,
    Diehl, Knight, Morgenstern, Dobb, Schumacher, Lederer, Brinkmann,
    Salin, and Homan)
"History of Economic Thought" [5:346–95 in] *Encyclopaedia of the*
    Social Sciences. New York: Macmillan Company, 1931 (also with later
    dates). 28 cm.
Seligman fathered the *Encyclopaedia of the Social Sciences,* which gave wide coverage to the history of economics. He also taught the history of economics at Columbia University for many years, and for a long time he expected to pub-

lish a full history himself. He illustrated the history of economics by collecting a large library, which eventually he sold to Columbia. The influence of this historical library was apparent in his *Curiosities* (see entry no. 264 supra) and in his studies on early economic literature.

His article in the *Encyclopaedia* on "The Discipline of Economics" also counted as a piece of historical writing.

336* Cannan, Edwin (1861–1935)
    Rassegna della teoria economica. Traduzione del Prof. Renzo Fubini.
    [1:xvii–xxiv, 1–401 in] *Nuova collana di economisti stranieri e italiani.*
    Torino: Unione Tipografico-editrice Torinese, 1932. 25 cm.
    See entry for first (1929) edition.

337* Gangemi, Lello (b. 1894; professor at Naples)
    Svolgimento del pensiero economico. 1: *Dalle origini alla scuola classica*
    [no more published]. Milano-Roma: Treves-Treccani-Tumminelli,
    1932. xii, 357 p. 19.5 cm.

Burtchett wrote that "American students of the history of economic thought will find this volume useful (1) because of the wealth of new bibliographical material dealing with . . . Italian economists, (2) because of the segregation of the discussion along nationalist lines, and (3) because of the emphasis given in the first three chapters upon the general development of scientific thought in economics" (*American Economic Review* 23 [1933]: 697).

338 Ingram, John Kells (1823–1907)
    Ching chi hsüeh shih. [Translation by] Tse Hu. Shanghai, 1932. 4, 1,
    16, 104, 120, 75 p. 19 cm.
    In University of Chicago Library.
    See entry for first (1888) British edition.

339 ———
    Tarikh-i ma 'ashiyat. [Translation of 1915 British edition into Urdu].
    Haidarabad, 1932. 478, 48, 2 p.
    In Columbia University Library.
    See entry for first (1888) British edition.

340 Myrdal, Gunnar (b. 1898)
    Das politische Element in der nationalökonomischen Doktrinbildung. Aus
    dem Schwedischen übersetzt von Gerhard Mackenroth. Berlin: Junker
    und Dünnhaupt, 1932. xi, 309 p. 24 cm.
    In Yale University Library.
    See entry for first (1930) Swedish edition.

341* Patterson, Samuel Howard (b. 1892)
    Readings in the History of Economic Thought. New York: McGraw-
    Hill, 1932. xi, 745 p. 23.5 cm.

A collection of readings for English-speaking students that omitted: early writers, since they were in Monroe's volume; and Smith, Ricardo, and Mill, since they were available in cheap editions. It aimed to come "down to Neo-classicism" and to stress "the minor rather than the major prophets, and perhaps economic heresies, rather than economic orthodoxies."
One-page biographical articles were included.

342* Spann, Othmar (1878–1950)
Den moderna nationalekonomiens historia och huvudteorier. Efter Jublileumsupplagan överflyttad till svenska och after 21:sta upplagan (T.O.M. 105:te tusendet) genomsedd och med förord av Dr. Malte Welin. Stockholm: Wahlström & Widstrand, 1932. 206 p. 18 cm.
See entry for first (1911) German edition.
For first volume see entry in 1927.
Welin's foreword is titled "Universalismen och Sverige."

343* Deschamps, Auguste (1863–1935)
Répétitions écrites de histoire des doctrines économiques, rédigées d'après le cours de M. Deschamps. 1932–33. Diplôme d'études supérieures économie politique. Faculté de Droit de Paris. [Reproduced from typescript]. Paris: Les Cours de Droit, 1933. 381 p. 25 cm.
Another history by Deschamps: 1933 (next below).

344* ———
Résumé de histoire des doctrines économiques. Diplôme d'études supérieures économie politique, 1932–33. Paris: Les Cours de Droit, 1933. 85 p. 25 cm.
Another history by Deschamps: 1933 (next above).

345* Gemähling, Paul (b. 1883)
Les Grands économistes: textes et commentaires. Deuxième édition, revue et augmentée. Paris: Recueil Sirey, 1933. 372 p. 23.5 cm.
First edition: 1925.

346 Okinaka, Tsuneyuki (b. 1895; professor at Chuo University, Tokyo)
Keizai shiso hattenshi. Tokyo, 1933.
Listed in Svendsen.
Another history by Okinaka: 1946.

347 Otsuka, Kinnosuke (b. 1892; professor at Hitotsubashi University, Tokyo)
Keizai shiso shi. Tokyo, 1933.
Listed in Svendsen.

348* Scott, William Amasa (1862–1944; professor at University of Wisconsin)
The Development of Economics. New York: Century Co., 1933 (also 1936 and 1945). xii, 540 p. 23 cm.
Translation: Chinese, 1960.

The preface said that the "present form and content of the book are the result of years of class and individual discussions with hundreds of students . . . and its publication is due chiefly to the frequently expressed desire of many of them, especially those in academic positions, to have the subject-matter of these discussions in a form available for their own and their students' use."

349 Tivaroni, Jacopo (b. 1877; professor at Genoa)
Compendio di storia delle istituzioni e delle dottrine economiche dal principio dell'epoca moderna ai nostri giorni. Bari: Laterza, 1933. xvi, 271 p. 16°.
Listed in *Catalogo generale della libreria italiana.*

350 Vogt, Johan (b. 1900; later, professor at Oslo)
Den økonomiske tenknings historie. 1: *Den politiske økonomi inntil Adam Smith.* 2: *Den klassiske engelske socialøkonomi.* [Mimeographed]. Oslo: Studentenes Centralkontor, 1933–34. 2 v. (iv, 59; iv, 51 p.) 29 cm.
In University of Chicago Library.
Later edition: 1942.

351* Wagenführ, Horst (b. 1903; professor at Erlangen)
"Die Entwicklung zur Einheit des Systems" [pp. 25–216 in his] *Der Systemgedanke in der Nationalökonomie, eine methodengeschichtliche Betrachtung.* Jena: Gustav Fischer, 1933. 24 cm.
Another history by Wagenführ: 1934.
Has long bibliographies.

352 Wang, Ya-nan
Ching chi hsüeh shih. Shanghai, 1933. 16, 20, 492 p. 22 cm.
In Hoover Institution at Stanford.

353 Capodaglio, Giulio (b. 1910; professor at Bari)
Breve compendio di storia delle dottrine economiche. Roma: Officine di Arti Grafiche, 1934. 80 p.
Listed in "Avvertenza alla prima edizione" of second (1941) edition.
A manual for the use of students at the University of Rome.
Later editions (with different titles): 1937, 1941, 1945, 1958, 1968.

354* Diepenhorst, Pieter Arie (1879–1953)
Geschiedenis der economie [vol. 1 of his] *Leerboek van de economie.* Zutphen: G. J. A. Ruys, 1934. 560 p. 22 cm.
Other editions: 1910, 1912, 1920, 1946.

355 Kitazawa, Shinjiro (b. 1887; professor at Waseda University)
Keizaigaku shi taiko. Tokyo, 1934.
Listed in Svendsen.
Second edition (title changed): 1940.

356 Koizumi, Shinzo (1888–1966), and Kada, Tetsuji (b. 1895)
     Keizaigaku shi. Tokyo, 1934.
     In Library of Congress.
     Another history by Koizumi: 1946.

357 Rozenberg, David Iokhelevich (1879–1950)
     Istoriia politicheskoĭ ekonomii. Moskva, 1934–36. 3 v. (303, 334, 276 p.)
     23.5 cm.
     In Columbia University Library.
     Second edition: 1940. Translations: Japanese, 1937, 1951–54; Yugoslav,
     1949; Polish, 1955; Chinese, 1959.

358 Spann, Othmar (1878–1950)
     Ching chi hsüeh shuo shih. Shanghai, 1934. 267 p. 23 cm.
     In Hoover Institution at Stanford.
     See entry for first (1911) German edition.

359* ———
     Historia de las doctrinas económicas. Traducción de José Ramón Pérez
     Bances. Revisado por Lorenzo de la Madrid. Madrid: Editorial Revista
     de Derecho Privado, 1934. 324 p. 20 cm.
     See entry for first (1911) German edition.

360 Totomiants, Vakhan Fomich (b. 1875)
     Historia de las doctrinas económicas y sociales. [Translation from the
     second German edition by] Vicente Gay. Barcelona: Gustavo Gili, 1934.
     278 p. 19 cm.
     In Library of Congress.
     See entry for Russian (1921) edition.

361 Wagenführ, Horst (b. 1903)
     *Geschichte der wirtschaftlichen Lehrmeinungen und der wirtschafts-
     politischen Systeme.* Ein Leitfaden. Leipzig: Verlag von Philipp
     Reclam jun., 1934. 79 p. 15.5 cm.
     In Columbia University Library.
     Another history by Wagenführ: 1933.
     Summarized the history from the Greeks to National Socialism.

362* Lluch y Capdevila, Pedro (professor in Escuela de Altos Estudios Mer-
     cantiles de Barcelona)
     História de las doctrinas económicas. Barcelona: Artes Gráficas, 1935.
     343 p. 22 cm.
     Later editions: 1941, 1947, 1952, 1954.

363* [Mitchell, Wesley Clair] (1874–1948)
     Lectures on Current Types of Economic Theory. Delivered by Wesley

C. Mitchell at Columbia University. Vol. 1, Winter Session. Vol. 2, Spring Session. [Mimeographed]. New York, 1935. (Baker Library at Harvard has a 1931 version). 2 v. (670 p.) 28 cm. Later versions: 1949, 1967–69. Translation: Japanese, 1971.

The original mimeographed version was prepared from stenographic notes made by John N. Meyer in the academic year 1926/27 (according to Dorfman's Introduction in the 1967 edition [1:vii]). The version preceding that of 1931 had 55 chapters. The 1931 version had 62 chapters. The last version, that of 1935, had 83 chapters. The added chapters were the result of Meyer's subsequent attendance of the course. Professor Mitchell had taught some version as early as 1913; after 1922 his lectures took the form found in Meyer's notes.

364 Ono, Shinzo (b. 1900)
  Keizaigaku shi taiko. Tokyo, 1935.
  Listed in Svendsen.
  Second edition: 1940.
  Another history by Ono: 1972.

365* Peck, Harvey Whitefield (b. 1879; professor at Syracuse University)
  Economic Thought and Its Institutional Background. New York: Farrar & Rhinehart, 1935 (also dated 1937); London: Allen, 1935. 379 p. 22.5 cm.

366 Rodríguez, Juan Carlos (1897–1944; professor at the Universidad del Litoral y de Buenos Aires)
  Una nueva clasificación de los sistemas económicos y sus escuelas. Buenos Aires: Imprenta Caporaletti Hnos, 1935. 69 p. 24 cm.
  In Library of Congress.

A comparison (partly historical) of the different systems and schools of economics.

367 Salin, Edgar (b. 1892)
  [Japanese translation of *Geschichte der Volkswirtschaftslehre*]. 1935.
  Listed in Popescu.
  See entry for first (1923) German edition.

368* Haney, Lewis Henry (1882–1969)
  History of Economic Thought: A Critical Account of the Origin and Development of the Economic Theories of the Leading Thinkers in the Leading Nations. Third and enlarged edition. New York: Macmillan Company, 1936. xx, 827 p. 20.5 cm.
  See entry for first (1911) edition.

369 Marx, Karl (1818–83)
  [Japanese translation by I. Sakisaka, Y. Omori, and T. Inomata of the first two volumes of *Theorien über den Mehrwert*]. Tokyo, 1936.
  Listed in Svendsen.

See entry for first (1905–10) German edition.

370 Spann, Othmar (1878–1950)
Breve storia delle teorie economiche. Con aggiunte di Giuseppe Bruguier.
Trad. dal tedesco di Ottone Degregorio. Firenze: G. C. Sansoni, 1936.
viii, 297 p. 18.5 cm.
Listed in *Catalogo generale della libreria italiana*.
Reviewed by Einaudi (*Rivista di storia economica* 1 [1936]: 258–63).
See entry for first (1911) German edition.

371 ———
*Die Haupttheorien der Volkswirtschaftslehre auf lehrgeschichtlicher
Grundlage*. Mit einem Anhang: "Wie studiert man Volkswirtschafts-
lehre?" 24., neuerdings durchgesehene Auflage. Leipzig: Quelle &
Meyer, 1936. xvi, 251 p. 8°.
In Columbia University Library.
See entry for first (1911) edition.

372 Sumiya, Etsuji (b. 1895; professor at Doshisha University)
Keizaigaku shi no kisogainen. Tokyo, 1936.
Listed in Svendsen.

373 Aizawa, S.
Reimeiki no shimin keizaigaku. 1937.
Listed in Svendsen.
Second edition: 1947.
Another history by Aizawa: 1948.

374 Capodaglio, Giulio (b. 1910)
Sommario di storia delle dottrine economiche. Bologna: N. Zanichelli,
1937. viii, 220 p. 21.5 cm.
In Columbia University Library.
Other editions: 1934, 1941, 1945, 1958, 1968.
Gagliardo's review said that it "represents a thorough revision and elaboration
of an earlier compendium based on lectures delivered at the University of Rome"
and that it "presents an excellent simple introduction to the subject, for the be-
ginning students in economics and for the general reader as well" (*American
Economic Review* 28 [1938]: 328).

375 Chin, T'ien-hsi
Ching chi ssü hsiang fa chan shih. Nanking, 1937. 3, 9, 7, 575, 37 p.
28 cm.
In Library of Congress.

376 Crobaugh, Mervyn
Economics for Everybody: From the Pyramids to the Sit-Down Strike.

New York: W. Morrow & Company, 1937. 293 p. 21 cm.
In Columbia University Library.
Second edition: 1942. Translation: Swedish, 1938.
A popular history, written in a light style. It included an unusual chapter on the relation of Schools of Commerce to Economics.

377 Maide, Chogoro (b. 1891)
Keizaigaku shi gaiyo. Vol. 1 [no more published]. Tokyo: Iwanami Shoten, 1937.
In Hoover Institution at Stanford.
Later history by Maide and Yokohama: 1959.
"The author is professor of economics in Tokyo University and one-time Dean of the College of Economics" (Remer and Kawai, *Japanese Economics,* p. 15).

378* Price, Langford Lovell Frederick Rice (1862–1950)
A Short History of Political Economy in England, from Adam Smith to Alfred Marshall. 15th edition. London: Methuen, 1937. xvi, 315 p. 19.5 cm.
See entry for first (1891) edition.

379 Rozenberg, David Iokhelevich (1879–1950)
[Japanese translation of *Istoriia politicheskoĭ ekonomii*]. Tokyo, 1937.
Listed in Popescu.
See entry for first (1934–36) Russian edition.

380* Shên, Chih-yüan (b. 1901)
Chin tai ching chi hsüeh shuo shih. Shanghai, 1937. 465 p. 21.5 cm.
Second edition: 1950.

381 Takahashi, Seiichiro (b. 1884)
Keizaigaku shi. Vol. 1 [no more published]. Tokyo, 1937.
Listed in Svendsen.
Earlier edition: 1929.
Other histories by Takahashi: 1940, 1948, 1949.

382 [Bousquet, Georges Henri]
Evolución del pensamiento económico; con una crítica científica de las ideas económicas de Carlos Marx. México: Editorial "Cosmos," 1938. 157 p. 20 cm.
In Library of Congress.
A synthesis of the ideas in Bousquet's *Essai sur l'évolution de la pensée économique* (1927), prepared by Eduardo Hornedo.

383 Crobaugh, Mervyn
Det ekonomiska tänkandet: från pyramiderna till "nya given." Övers.

av Leif Björck. Orig:s titel: *Economics for Everybody.* Stockholm: Tiden, 1938. 224, 4 p. 8°.
Listed in *Svensk Bok-katalog.*
American editions: 1937, 1942.

384 Fanfani, Amintore (b. 1908; professor at Milan, Venice, and Rome)
Storia delle dottrine economiche. Parte 1: *Il volontarismo.* Como: Cavalleri, 1938. 211 p. 8°.
Listed in *Catalogo generale della libreria italiana.*
Later editions: Pt. 1, 1939, 1942; pt. 2, 1945; pts. 1 and 2, 1955, 1971.

385* Ferguson, John Maxwell (b. 1890; professor at the University of Pittsburgh)
Landmarks of Economic Thought. New York: Longmans, Green and Co., 1938 (also dated 1941, 1943, 1946, 1947, 1948, 1950). xvi, 295 p. 21.5 cm.
Second edition: 1950. Translations: Mexican, 1948, 1958, 1963, 1966.
Hewett's review remarked that "within the limits of 256 average size pages of text material, Professor Ferguson attempts to compress the entire history of economic thought from the Code of Hammurabi to the published works of Frederick W. Taylor on scientific management. The index includes over five hundred names touched upon in the text . . . . I submit that this book comes closer to *An Abridged Encyclopedia of Economic Thought* than *Landmarks* . . . . Your reviewer would welcome a little controversial comment in this journal on the place of the history of economic thought in our literature and the proper method of presentation" (*American Economic Review* 29 [1939]: 352–53).

386* Gide, Paul Henri Charles (1847–1932), and Rist, Charles (1874–1955)
História das doutrinas econômicas desde os fisiocratas até aos nossos dias.
Tradução de Eduardo Salgueiro. Com um apêndice sôbre a economia, desde a antiguidade até aos fisiocratas. Lisboa: Editorial Inquerito, 1938. 862 p. 26 cm.
See entry for first (1909) French edition.

387 Gonnard, Charles René (1874–1966)
Historia de las doctrinas económicas. Traducción de J. Campo Moreno. 2ª ed. Madrid: M. Aguilar, 1938. 624 p. 20 cm.
Listed in *Catálogo general de la librería española.*
See entry for first (1921–22) French edition.

388* Kobayashi, Ushisaburo (1866–1930)
Ching chi ssü hsiang shih. Hong Kong: Chung-hua Shu Chu, 1938. 2, 366 p. 23 cm.
Japanese edition: 1927.

389* Roll, Erich (b. 1907)
A History of Economic Thought. London: Faber and Faber, 1938;

New York: Prentice-Hall, 1938. 430 p. 22.5 cm.
Other editions: 1942, 1954, 1973 (all editions have later dates). Translations: Mexican, 1942, 1955, 1962, 1975; Brazilian, 1948, 1962, 1971; Japanese, 1951–52, 1970; Italian, 1954, 1966; Yugoslav, 1956; Chinese, [1957]; Indian (Hindic), 1965; Israeli, 1966; Egyptian, 1968.
Moffat, in his review, noted that "the discussion of socialist criticism and the doctrine of Marx covers . . . one-sixth of the entire book. For purposes of comparison we may note that in Haney's history the discussion of socialist thought comprises less than one-seventeenth of the total space" (*American Economic Review* 30 [1940]: 131).

390*   Cracco, W.
       Schets eener geschiedenis der economie. Antwerpen: De Nederlandsche
       Boekhandel, 1939. 270 p. 22 cm.
       Second edition: 1943.

391   Fanfani, Amintore (b. 1908)
       Storia delle dottrine economiche. Parte 1: *Il volontarismo.* 2ª ed. Como:
       Cavalleri, 1939 (according to Fanfani, first issued in November 1938).
       xii, 256 p. 22 cm.
       In Yale University Library.
       See entry for first (1938) edition.

392   Głabinski, Stanisław (b. 1862)
       Historia ekonomiki. Vol. 1: *Historia ekonomiki powszechnej.* Vol. 2:
       Historia ekonomiki polskiej. Lwów, 1939. 2 v. 24 cm.
       In Columbia University Library.

393   Philippe, Charles Émile
       Las doctrinas económicas. Traducción del Capitán A. Ponce. Compendio
       destinado al uso de los oficiales de todas las armas y todos los servicios.
       [Cochabamba (Bolivia)]: Universidad Autónoma de Cochabamba, 1939.
       vii, 84 p. 19 cm.
       In University of Texas Library.
       French edition: 1931.

394   Cannan, Edwin (1861–1935)
       Repaso a la teoría económica. Versión española de Javier Márquez.
       México: Fondo de Cultura Económica, 1940. viii, 423 p. 24 cm.
       In Library of Congress.
       See entry for first (1929) British edition.

395   Chang, Yü-shan
       Ching chi ssü hsiang shih. Chang-sha, 1940. 4, 2, 274 p. 19 cm.
       In Library of Congress.

396 Kitazawa, Shinjiro (b. 1887)
Keizai gakusetsu shi. Tokyo, 1940.
Listed in Svendsen.
First edition: 1934.

397 Lanzillo, Agostino (1886–1951; professor at Venice)
Lezioni di storia delle dottrine economiche. Lezioni tenute nell'anno
accademico 1939/1940. Padova: Cedam, 1940. 181 p. 8°.
Listed in *Catalogo generale della libreria italiana.*

398 Ono, Shinzo (b. 1900)
Keizaigaku shi taiko. [Second edition]. Tokyo, 1940.
Listed in Svendsen.
First edition: 1935.
Another history by Ono: 1972.

399* Paulet, Pedro E.
Breve historia de las doctrinas económicas. Chorrillos (Peru): Escuela
Militar, 1940. 26 p. 23.5 cm.

400 Rozenberg, David Iokhelevich (1879–1950)
Istoriia politicheskoĭ ekonomii. 2. izd. Moskva, 1940. 23 cm.
In Yale University Library.
See entry for first (1934–36) edition.

401 Takahashi, Seiichiro (b. 1884)
Keizai shiso shi zuihitsu. Tokyo, 1940 (also dated 1950).
Listed in Svendsen.
Other histories by Takahashi: 1929, 1937, 1948, 1949.

402 Tanuma, T.
Keizaigaku shi. Tokyo, 1940.
Listed in Svendsen.

403* Whittaker, Edmund (1897–1956; professor at the University of Illinois)
A History of Economic Ideas. New York: Longmans, Green and Co.,
1940. xii, 766 p. 23.5 cm.
Translation: Mexican, 1948.
Another history by Whittaker: 1960.
Treated the history under 16 subject headings: population, production, value,
wages, money, etc.
　　Johnson in his review said: "Writing the history of economic thought is
almost as hard as unscrambling eggs and one must not be unreasonable. . . .
But I do feel that there is more lost than gained by fragmentizing the contribu-
tions of a writer or a school" (*American Economic Review* 31 [1941]: 114).

404* Baudin, Louis (1887–1964; professor at Paris)
Précis d'histoire des doctrines économiques, conforme au programme de la partie générale du Diplôme d'études supérieures d'économie politique de la Faculté de droit de Paris. Paris: Domat-Montchrestien, 1941. 284 p. 22 cm.
Later editions: 1942, 1943, 1947, 1949.

405* Capodaglio, Giulio (b. 1910)
Sommario di storia delle dottrine economiche. Seconda edizione. Milano: Dott. A. Giuffrè-Editore, 1941. x, 227 p. 21 cm.
Other editions: 1934, 1937, 1945, 1958, 1968.

406* Gonnard, Charles René (1874–1966)
Histoire des doctrines économiques. Paris: Librairie Générale de Droit et de Jurisprudence, 1941. x, 723 p. 24 cm.
See entry for first (1921–22) edition.

407* Lluch y Capdevila, Pedro
Historia de las doctrinas económicas. Segunda edición. Barcelona: Bosch, 1941. 290 p. 22 cm.
Other editions: 1935, 1947, 1952, 1954.

408 Mantilla Pérez de Ayala, José María
Apostillas sobre economía: una esquema de historia de la economía. Madrid, 1941. 68 p. 16 cm. Publicaciones de la Inspección General de Comercio y Política Arancelaria, Sección de Información y Propaganda, Serie "Divulgación, núm. 4."
In Library of Congress.

409 Baudin, Louis (1887–1964)
Précis d'histoire des doctrines économiques, conforme au programme de la partie générale du Diplôme d'études supérieures d'économie politique de la Faculté de droit de Paris. 2ᵉ éd. Paris: Domat-Montchrestien, 1942.
Listed in *"Biblio."*
See entry for first (1941) edition.

410 Crobaugh, Mervyn
Economics for Everybody: From the Pyramids to the Sit-Down Strike. Second Edition. New York: W. Morrow & Company, 1942. 293 p. 12°.
Listed in *Cumulative Book Index.*
First edition: 1937. Translation: Swedish, 1938.

411* Fanfani, Amintore (b. 1908)
Storia delle dottrine economiche. Parte 1: *Il volontarismo.* Terza edizione. Milano-Messina: Casa Editrice Giuseppe Principato, 1942 (according

to Fanfani, first issued in 1943). xi, 256 p. 21.5 cm.
See entry for first (1938) edition.

412* Gonnard, Charles René (1874–1966)
História das doutrinas econômicas. Tradução e prefácio de Moses Bensabat
Amzalak. Lisboa: Depósito, Livraria Sá da Costa, 1942. 3 v. (346, 435,
490 p.) 19 cm.
See entry for first (1921–22) French edition.

413* Hugon, Paul (b. 1902; professor at Sao Paulo)
Elementos de história das doutrinas econômicas. São Paulo: Caixa
Econômica Federal, 1942. 504 p. 24 cm.
Later editions: 1943, 1946, 1952, 1956, 1959, 1962, 1966, 1967. Translation:
Canadian (French), 1947.
Another history by Hugon: 1955.

414 Kubota, Akiteru (b. 1897; professor at Waseda University)
Kinsei keizaigaku no seiseikatei. Tokyo, 1942.
Listed in Popescu.

415 Myrdal, Gunnar (b. 1898)
Seiji gakusetsu to seijiteki yoso. [Translation by] Yuzo Yamada. Tokyo:
Nihon Hyoron-sha, 1942. 22, 412, 29, 14 p.
Listed in Bohrn.
See entry for first (1930) Swedish edition.

416 Roll, Erich (b. 1907)
Historia de las doctrinas económicas. Versión española de Daniel Cosío
Villegas y Javier Márquez. México: Fondo de Cultura Económica,
1942. 2 v. 20 cm.
In Library of Congress.
See entry for first (1938) British edition.

417* ———
A History of Economic Thought. Revised and enlarged edition. New
York: Prentice-Hall, 1942; London: Faber and Faber, 1945 (London
issue delayed by war; both New York and London issues also with later
dates). xxi, 585 p. 23.5 cm.
See entry for first (1938) edition.

418 Vogt, Johan (b. 1900; professor at Oslo)
Kortfattet oversikt over den sosialøkonomiske vitenskaps historie. 1: *Den
Merkantilistiske tidsalder.* 2: *Den industrielle revolusjon og den
klassiske sosialøkonomi.* Oslo: Skrivemaskinstua, 1942. 39, iv; 50,
v. p. 4°.
Listed in *Norsk bokfortegnelse.*
Earlier edition: 1933–34.

419   Alvarado, Carlos M.
      Doctrinas económicas; complemento al libro de Julio A. Decoud, Economía
      política y Argentina. Buenos Aires: Editorial Dovile, 1943. 129 p.
      24.5 cm.
      In University of Texas Library.
Designed to give the student a view of the history of economic doctrines sufficient to satisfy the requirements for the program of political economy. It concluded with a chapter on the "isms."

420* Baudin, Louis (1887–1964)
      Précis d'histoire des doctrines économiques, conforme au programme de
      la partie générale du Diplôme d'études supérieures d'économie politique
      de la Faculté de droit de Paris. 3ᵉ édition. Paris: Domat-Montchrestien,
      1943. 280 p. 23 cm.
      See entry for first (1941) edition.

421   Cracco, W.
      Schets eener geschiedenis der economie. 2. uitgave. Brussel: Bernaerts
      Uitgeverij "De Phalanx." 1943. 252 p. 23 cm.
      In Library of Congress.
      First edition: 1939.

422   Gay y Forner, Vicente (1876–1949; professor of political economy at the
      University of Valladolid and an honorary professor at the University of
      Santiago de Chile and the University of Buenos Aires)
      Artículos sobre historia de las doctrinas económicas y sociales [*separata*
      A, B, C, D, E, de] *Nueva economía nacional.* Madrid, 1943–44.
      In New York Public Library.
A careful history of 536 pages with a graphical representation of the course of
the history at the end.

423* Gide, Paul Henri Charles (1847–1932), and Rist, Charles (1874–1955)
      Keizai gakusetsu shi. [Translation by] T. Miyakawa. Tokyo: Tokyo-do,
      1943. 2 v. 22 cm.
      See entry for first (1909) French edition.

424   Hugon, Paul (b. 1902)
      Elementos de história das doutrinas econômicas. 2ª edição. São Paulo,
      1943.
      Listed in seventh edition.
      See entry for first (1942) edition.

425   López Gento, José
      El hombre y la riqueza: síntesis comparativa de doctrinas económicas.
      Prólogo del Prof. Luis Jiménez de Asúa. Buenos Aires: "El Ateneo,"
      1943. 192 p. 20.5 cm.
      In Library of Congress.

Written by an exile from Spain, whose account began with the English Classical School and ended with Socialism and Henry George.

426*   McConnell, John Wilkinson (b. 1907)
The Basic Teachings of the Great Economists. New York: New Home Library, 1943; and New York: Barnes and Noble, 1947. xiii, 367 p. 21 cm.
Translations: Turkish, 1949; Argentine, 1961.
"[For] the general reader with an interest in economics . . . The aim . . . is the enlightenment of the layman" (see Preface).

427   Myrdal, Gunnar (b. 1898)
L'elemento politico nella formazione delle dottrine dell'economia pura. Firenze: G. C. Sansoni, 1943. xiii, 340 p. 24 cm.
In University of Illinois Library.
See entry for first (1930) edition.

428*   Totomiants, Vakhan Fomich (b. 1875)
Storia delle dottrine economiche e sociali. Prefazione di Achille Loria. 2ª edizione. Milano: Fratelli Bocca, 1943. x, 198 p. 21 cm.
See entry for Russian (1921) edition.

429*   Gide, Paul Henri Charles (1847–1932), and Rist, Charles (1874–1955)
Histoire des doctrines économiques depuis les physiocrates jusqu'à nos jours. Sixième édition, revue et augmentée. Paris: Recueil Sirey, 1944. xx, 896 p. 26 cm.
See entry for first (1909) edition.

430   Gonnard, Charles René (1874–1966)
Historia de las doctrinas económicas. Editorial M. Aguilar. Madrid: Imp. Bolaños y Aguilar, 1944. xx, 554 p. 22 cm.
Listed in _Catálogo general de la librería española._
See entry for first (1921–22) French edition.

431   James, Émile (b. 1899)
Cours d'histoire des doctrines économiques. Diplôme d'études supérieures. Économie politique, 1943–1944. [Dactylographie]. Paris: Les Cours de Droit, 1944. 324 p. 25.5 cm.
Listed in _"Biblio."_
Later editions: 1955, 1959.
Other histories by James: 1950, 1955.

432   Marx, Karl (1818–83)
Historia crítica de la teoría de la plusvalía. Versión directa y prólogo de Wenceslao Roces. México: Fondo de Cultura Económica, 1944–45. 3 v. (1352 p.) 22 cm.

In Library of Congress.
See entry for first (1905–10) German edition.

433* Nogaro, Pierre Gabriel Bertrand (1880–1950)
Le Développement de la pensée économique. Paris: Librairie Générale de
Droit et de Jurisprudence, 1944. 345 p. 23 cm.

Began with Cantillon. The preface stated that it was not, in any sense, "une
oeuvre d'érudition" and that it examined "le développement, et non le 'progrès' "
(see Avant-propos).

Block, in a review, said: "This book, written in the darkness of the occupa-
tion, is symptomatic of the old, not the new, French economic approach. It is
perhaps the last of the histories of thought published by a member of the school
of writers made famous by Gide, Rist and Gonnard. Professor Nogaro makes
no claim to originality and does not specialize in historical background work in
which Gide and Rist, and more recently, Paul Hugon, a French professor in
Brazil, excelled. . . . Nogaro justifies omission of Marx by stating that dogmatic
tendencies are excluded from this book" (*American Economic Review* 36 [1946]:
396).

434* Salin, Edgar (b. 1892)
Geschichte der Volkswirtschaftslehre. Dritte erweiterte Auflage. Bern:
A. Francke, 1944. 224 p. 23.5 cm.
See entry for first (1923) edition.

435 Spann, Othmar (1878–1950)
Teorije društvenog gospodarstva. Zagreb, 1944.
Listed in Šoškić.
See entry for first (1911) German edition.

436* Stark, Werner (b. 1909)
The History of Economics in Its Relation to Social Development. London:
K. Paul, Trench, Trubner & Co., 1944 (also with later dates). viii, 80 p.
22.5 cm.
Translations: Italian, 1950; Dutch, 1960; Mexican, 1961.

437* Villey, Daniel (1911–68; professor at Poitiers, Rio de Janeiro, and Paris)
Petite histoire des grandes doctrines économiques. Paris: Presses Uni-
versitaires de France, 1944. xv, 230 p. 19 cm.
Later editions: 1946, 1954, 1958, 1973. Translation: Argentine, 1960.
Another history by Villey: 1967.

Concerned almost entirely with the period before 1871, it was written while the
author was a prisoner of war.

438 Capodaglio, Giulio (b. 1910)
Sommario di storia delle dottrine economiche. 3ª ed. Milano: A. Giuffrè,
1945. vi, 257 p. 22 cm.

In New York Public Library.
Other editions: 1934, 1937, 1941, 1958, 1968.

439* Chevalier, Jean (b. 1902; professor at Alger)
Doctrines économiques. Paris: Perspectives, 1945. vii–viii, 371 p. 25 cm.
Later editions: 1946, 1947.
Contained a history of economics mixed with other history and with a good deal of comment.

440 Fanfani, Amintore (b. 1908)
Storia delle dottrine economiche. Parte 2: *Il naturalismo.* Losanna, 1945 (also published at Milan in 1946). xvi, 358 p.
Listed in fourth edition.
See entry for first (1938) edition.

441* Godinho, António Maria (b. 1904)
Sintese da história das doutrinas económicas. Preleçcöes proferidas pelo Exmo. Professor, Doutor António Maria Godinho ao curso prático da 10ª Cadeira, Política econômica Internacional. [Mimeographed]. Lisboa: Instituto Superior de Ciências Econômicas e Financeiras, 1945. 127 p. 28 cm.

442* Heimann, Eduard (1889–1967; professor at New York School for Social Research and "Honorarprofessor" at Bonn [1966])
History of Economic Doctrines: An Introduction to Economic Theory. New York: Oxford University Press, 1945 (issued as a Galaxy Book in 1964). iv, 263 p. 22 cm.
Translations: German, 1949; Japanese, 1950; Argentine, 1954; Brazilian, 1965, 1971.
The author said that he had "concentrated rigorously" on the "inward logic, revealed in retrospect, of the development of modern economic thinking" and had avoided presenting "material of a merely antiquarian or anecdotal interest" (see Preface).

Dillard praised the work: "Considering the brevity of his book, Professor Heimann gives a remarkable presentation and interpretation of the leading ideas of economic theory from Aristotle to J. M. Keynes. . . . it can be read with profit by beginners . . . [and] . . . is also useful at a more advanced level because of numerous provocative insights and because of the self-conscious attempt to apply a distinctive approach to the history of economic thought. The point of view is modern in the sense that earlier theories are interpreted in the light of recent views of saving, investment, interest, money, and economic fluctuations" (*American Economic Review* 39 [1949]: 986).

443* Prato, Giuseppe (1873–1928)
Lezioni di storia delle dottrine economiche. Prima edizione a stampa,

con note e indici a cura di Antonio Fossati. Torino: G. Giappichelli, 1945 (also dated 1948). ix, 205 p. 25 cm.

A posthumous publication of lectures given by Professor Prato at the University of Turin in 1924/25.

444* Spann, Othmar (1878–1950)
    Breve storia delle teorie economiche. Con aggiunte di Giuseppe Bruguier. Traduzione dal tedesco di Ottone Degregario. Seconda edizione. Firenze: G. C. Sansoni, 1945. viii, 297 p. 20 cm.
    A reissue of the 1936 edition.
    See entry for first (1911) German edition.

445* Abbott, Leonard Dalton (1878–1953), ed.
    Masterworks of Economics: Digest of 10 Great Classics. Garden City, N.Y.: Doubleday & Company, 1946 (also dated 1947). ix, 754 p. 22 cm.

Covered Mun, Turgot, Smith, Malthus, Ricardo, Owen, Mill, Marx, George, and Veblen. It contained a general introduction and a three- to ten-page sketch for each writer. The digests were in the words of their authors.

446* Cannan, Edwin (1861–1935)
    Repaso a la teoría económica. Traducción de Javier Márquez. Segunda edición en español. México: Fondo de Cultura Económica, 1946. 406 p. 25 cm.
    See entry for first (1929) British edition.

447* Chevalier, Jean (b. 1902)
    Doctrines économiques. Deuxième édition. Paris: Perspectives, 1946. 401 p. 25 cm.
    Other editions: 1945, 1947.

448 Diepenhorst, Pieter Arie (1879–1953)
    Geschiedenis der economie [vol. 1 of his] *Leerboek van de economie.* 2e. dr. Zutphen: G. J. A. Ruys, 1946. 504 p. 20 cm.
    Listed in *Brinkman's Catalogus van boeken.*
    Earlier editions: 1910, 1912, 1920, 1934.

449* Hugon, Paul (b. 1902)
    História das doutrinas econômicas. Terceira ediçáo. Brasil: Editôra Atlas, 1946. 365 p. 24 cm.
    See entry for first (1942) edition.

450* *Istorija ekonomiskih doktrina (Skripta).* Beograd: Izdavčka Sekcija Akcionog Orbora Studenata Beogradskog Univerziteta, 1946. 165 p. 8°.

451 Kerschagl, Richard (b. 1896)
    Volkswirtschaftslehre: ein Abriss der wichtigsten Lehrmeinungen. Zweite

Auflage (also as 3. Auflage). Wien: Manzsche Verlagsbuchhandlung, 1946. xii, 202 p. 24 cm.
In Columbia University Library.
Other editions: 1927, 1947, 1952.

452   Koizumi, Shinzo (1888–1966; president of Keio University)
Kindai keizai shicho gaikan. 1946 (also dated 1949 and issued in 1952 with title *Kindai keizai shiso shi*). 3, 2, 226 p. 22 cm.
In Library of Congress.
Another history by Koizumi: 1934.

453   Ledermann, László (b. 1903; professor at Geneva), and Stalder, André
Histoire élémentaire des doctrines économiques. Bâle: Éditions de l'Union Suisse des Coopératives de Consummation, 1946. 188 p. 18 cm.
Listed in *"Biblio."*

454*   Neff, Frank Amandus (1879–1961; professor at University of Wichita)
Economic Doctrines. Wichita, Kans.: McGuin Publishing Company, 1946. xiii, 439 p. 22 cm.
Second edition: 1950.

455   Okinaka, Tsuneyuki (b. 1895)
Keizai gakusetsu shi. Tokyo, 1946.
Listed in Svendsen.
Another history by Okinaka: 1933.

456*   Roca, Raymond ("Directeur du Centre d'études du contrôle économique")
Résumé d'histoire des doctrines économiques. [Mimeographed]. Paris: Domat-Montchrestien, 1946 (also dated 1948). 101 p. 25 cm.
A French-type course that went from antiquity to the Socialists.

457*   Villey, Daniel (1911–68)
Petite histoire des grandes doctrines économiques. 2ᵉ édition. Paris: Presses Universitaires de France, 1946. xv, 236 p. 19 cm.
See entry for first (1944) edition.
Another history by Villey: 1967.

458   Aizawa, S.
Reimeiki no shimin keizaigaku. [2d ed.]. Tokyo, 1947.
Listed in Svendsen.
First edition: 1937.
Another history by Aizawa: 1948.

459*   Baudin, Louis (1887–1964)
Précis d'histoire des doctrines économiques, conforme au programme de la partie générale du Diplôme d'études supérieures d'économie politique

de la Faculté de droit de Paris. 4ᵉ édition. Paris: Domat-Montchrestien, 1947. 214 p. 23 cm.
See entry for first (1941) edition.

460 Chevalier, Jean (b. 1902)
Doctrines économiques. 3ᵉ édition. Paris: Perspectives, 1947. x, 401 p. 25.5 cm.
In Cornell University Library.
Other editions: 1945, 1946.

461* Gide, Paul Henri Charles (1847–1932), and Rist, Charles (1874–1955)
Histoire des doctrines économiques. Septième édition, revue et augmentée. Paris: Recueil Sirey, 1947 (also dated 1959). 2 v. (xx, 901 p.) 26 cm.
See entry for first (1909) edition.

462 ———
Historia de las doctrinas económicas desde los fisiócratas hasta nuestros días. Vertido al español por Carmelo Martínez Peñalver. Segunda edición. Madrid: Instituto Editorial Reus, 1947. xxi, 1083 p. 24 cm.
Listed in *Catálogo general de la librería española.*
See entry for first (1909) edition.

463* Hugon, Paul (b. 1902)
Les Doctrines économiques. Préface de Jean Désy. Montréal: Fides, 1947. 413 p. 21 cm.
See entry for first (1942) Portuguese edition.

464* Kerschagl, Richard (b. 1896)
Volkswirtschaftslehre: ein Abriss der wichtigsten Lehrmeinungen. Vierte Auflage. Wien: Manz, 1947. xii, 218 p. 23 cm.
Other editions: 1927, 1946, 1952.

465 Lluch y Capdevila, Pedro
Historia de las doctrinas económicas. Tercera edición. Barcelona: Bosch, 1947. 290 p. 22 cm.
In University of Texas Library.
Other editions: 1935, 1941, 1952, 1954.

466 Renwick, Cyril
Economists and Their Environment. Sydney: Economic Society of Australia and New Zealand, New South Wales Branch, 1947. 50 p. 22 cm.
In Columbia University Library.
A series of lectures that gave a popular approach centered on Ricardo, Marshall, and Keynes.

467 Yamada, Yuzo (b. 1902; professor at Hitotsubashi University, Tokyo)

Keizaigaku no shiteki hatten. Tokyo: Toyo Keizai Shimposha, 1947.
Listed in Remer and Kawai, *Japanese Economics.*
Other histories by Yamada: 1951, 1957.

468 Zimmerman, Louis Jacques (b. 1913)
Geschiedenis van het ekonomisch denken. Amsterdam: Uitgeverij Vrij
Nederland, 1947. 231 p. 24 cm.
In Library of Congress.
Later editions: 1950, 1953, 1955. Translation: German, 1954.

469 Aizawa, S.
Keizai gakusetsu shi. Tokyo, 1948.
Listed in Svendsen.
Another history by Aizawa: 1937.

470 Chao, Nai-po
Ou mai ching chi shuo shih. Taipei: Cheng-chung Publishing Co., 1948
(5th ed., 1969; 7th ed., 1970). 574 p. 21 cm.
Listed in an unpublished letter.

471* Ferguson, John Maxwell (b. 1890)
Historia de la economía. Traducción de Vicente Polo. México (also
Buenos Aires): Fondo de Cultura Económica, 1948. 319 p. 22 cm.
See entry for first (1938) American edition.

472* Gide, Paul Henri Charles (1847–1932), and Rist, Charles (1874–1955)
*A History of Economic Doctrines from the Time of the Physiocrats to
the Present Day.* Authorized translation by R. Richards. Second English
edition, with additional matter from the latest French editions translated by Ernest F. Row. London: George G. Harrap, 1948; Boston:
D. C. Heath and Company, 1948 (also with later dates). 800 p. 22 cm.
See entry for first (1909) French edition.

473 Gonnard, Charles René (1874–1966)
Historia de las doctrinas económicas. Traducción de J. Campo Moreno.
Rev. y ampliada con arreglo á la última ed. francesa, de 1947, por
Inocencia Rodríguez-Mellado. México, 1948. xxiv, 650 p.
Listed in *Index translationum.*
See entry for first (1921–22) French edition.

474 Hori, Tsuneo (b. 1896; professor at Osaka Commercial University)
Kinsei keizaigaku shi taiko. 1948. 178 p. 21 cm.
In Library of Congress.
Later published under title *Keizaigaku shi tsuron* in 1950.
Another history by Hori: 1931–33.
Hori also published a dictionary of the history of economics, *Keizai shiso shi
jiten* (1951, 1959).

475*   Kruse, Alfred (b. 1912; professor at Berlin)
Geschichte der volkswirtschaftlichen Theorien. München: Richard Pflaum, 1948. 208 p. 24 cm.
Later editions: 1953, 1959.
Another history by Kruse: 1960.

476   Liu, Chi-ch'ên
Chin tai tzŭ pên chu i ching chi ssŭ ch'ao. Shanghai, 1948. 6, 1, 338 p. 22 cm.
In Library of Congress.

477   Roll, Erich (b. 1907)
História das doutrinas econômicas. Tradução de Cid Silveira. São Paulo: Companhia Editôra Nacional, 1948. 526 p. 22 cm.
Listed in *Bibliografia brasileira.*
See entry for first (1938) British edition.

478   Salin, Edgar (b. 1892)
Historia de la doctrina económica. Traducción de la 3. ed., corr. y rev. por su autor, por C. de las Cuevas. Buenos Aires: Editorial Atalaya, 1948. 283 p. 24 cm.
In Library of Congress.
See entry for first (1923) German edition.

479   Stephanidēs, Dēmosthenēs Sophokleous (b. 1896)
Hē koinōnikē oikonomikē en tē historikē tēs exelixei. Athēnai, 1948–50. 3 v. (382, 415, 596 p.) 26 cm.
In New York Public Library.
Went from early economics to the Austrian School. It had an extensive bibliography.

480   Takahashi, Seiichiro (b. 1884)
Keizaigaku shi ryaku. Tokyo: Keio Shuppan-sha, 1948. 2, 6, 585 p. 22 cm.
In Library of Congress.
Other histories by Takahashi: 1929, 1940, 1949.

481*   Whittaker, Edmund (1897–1956)
Historia del pensamiento económico. Versión española de Cristóbal Lara Beautell. México (also Buenos Aires): Fondo de Cultura Económica, 1948. 862 p. 25 cm.
American edition: 1940.
Another history by Whittaker: 1960.

482*   Baudin, Louis (1887–1964)
Précis d'histoire des doctrines économiques, conforme au programme de la partie générale du Diplôme d'études supérieures d'économie politique

de la Faculté de droit de Paris. 5ᵉ édition. Paris: Domat-Montchrestien, 1949. 215 p. 22 cm.
See entry for first (1941) edition.

483   Gide, Paul Henri Charles (1847–1932), and Rist, Charles (1874–1955)
Historia de las doctrinas económicas. Traducción directa de la 7ª ed. francesa, ampliada y actualizada por Carlos M. Giuliani Fonrouge. Buenos Aires: Editorial Depalma, 1949. 2 v. (xxiv, 1103 p.) 24 cm.
In Library of Congress.
See entry for first (1909) French edition.

484*   Graziani, Augusto (1865–1938; professor at Siena and Naples)
Storia delle dottrine economiche: saggi. Napoli: A. Morano, 1949. x, 319 p. 24 cm.
Not a usual or textbook history. It touched the landmarks from medieval times to the times of Marshall.

485*   Griziotti Kretschmann, Jenny
Storia delle dottrine economiche. Torino: Unione Tipografico Editrice Torinese, 1949. xvi, 473 p. 22 cm.
Second edition: 1954. Translation: Argentine, 1951.

486   Gutsche, Heinz
Die Entwicklung der Volkswirtschaftslehre. Berlin: Colloquium Verlag, 1949. 252 p. 18 cm.
In University of Chicago Library.

487*   Haney, Lewis Henry (1882–1969)
History of Economic Thought: A Critical Account of the Origin and Development of the Economic Theories of the Leading Thinkers in the Leading Nations. Fourth and enlarged edition. New York: Macmillan, 1949 (also dated 1964). xii, 966 p. 21 cm.
See entry for first (1911) edition.

488*   Heimann, Eduard (1889–1967)
Geschichte der volkswirtschaftlichen Lehrmeinungen: eine Einführung in die nationalökonomische Theorie. Übersetzung von Stephan Skalweit. Frankfurt am Main: Vittorio Klostermann, 1949. 294 p. 21 cm.
See entry for first (1945) American edition.

489   Horie, Yasuzo (b. 1904; professor at Kyoto)
Seiyo keizai shi gaiyo. Tokyo, 1949. 275 p. 22 cm.
In Library of Congress.
Another history by Horie: 1958.

490*   Kapp, Karl William (b. 1910), and Kapp, Lore L.

Readings in Economics. New York: Barnes and Noble, 1949. vi, 444 p. 22 cm.

Reissued as *History of Economic Thought: A Book of Readings* (1962). Contained selections from principal economists, arranged chronologically and provided with introductions and bibliographies.

491* Lajugie, Joseph (b. 1914; professor at Bordeaux)
Les Doctrines économiques. Paris: Presses Universitaires de France, 1949. 136 p. 18 cm.
Later editions included in this bibliography: 1956 (4ᵉ éd.), 1967 (9ᵉ éd.). Translations: Spanish, 1952 (and Argentine), 1971; Brazilian, 1955, 1964; Greek, 1964; Turkish, 1971; Lebanese, 1970; Italian, 1974.

492 McConnell, John Wilkinson (b. 1907)
Büyük iktisat çilarin temel doktrinleri. [Translation by Hurçid Çalika]. Istanbul: Ismail Akgün Matbaasí, 1949. 389 p.
In Columbia University Library.
American edition: 1943. Other translation: Argentine, 1961.

493 Marx, Karl (1818–83)
Shêng yü chia chih hsüeh shuo shih. [Translation into Chinese by] Ta-li Kuo. [n.p.], 1949. 4 v. in 2. 21 cm.
In Hoover Institution at Stanford.
See entry for first (1905–10) German edition.

494* Mitchell, Wesley Clair (1874–1948)
Lecture Notes on Types of Economic Theory as Delivered by Professor Wesley C. Mitchell. New York: Augustus M. Kelley, 1949. 2 v. (261, 300 p.) 27 cm.
See entry for first (1935) edition.

495 Natan, Zhak
Istoriia na ikonomicheskite ucheniia. Sophiia: Narodna Kultura, 1949. 21 cm.
In Library of Congress.

496 Rozenberg, David Iokhelevich (1879–1950)
Istorija političke ekonomije. [Translation by] Radoš Stamenković [and] Dimitrije Stanisavljević. Beograd: Stručno Odeljenje Univerzitetskog Komiteta Narodne Omladine, 1949. 396 p.
Listed in *Index translationum.*
See entry for first (1934–36) Russian edition.

497* Spann, Othmar (1878–1950)
Die Haupttheorien der Volkswirtschaftslehre auf lehrgeschichtlicher Grundlage. Mit einem Anhang: "Wie studiert man Volkswirtschafts-

lehre?" 25., durchgesehene Auflage. 126.–130. Tausend. Heidelberg: Quelle & Meyer, 1949. xv, 259 p. 20 cm.
See entry for first (1911) edition.

498   Takahashi, Seiichiro (b. 1884)
Seiyo keizaigaku shi. Tokyo, 1949.
Listed in Svendsen.
Other histories by Takahashi: 1929, 1940, 1948.

499   Abe, Gen'ichi (b. 1904)
Keizaigaku shi gairon. [Tokyo?], 1950.
Listed in later editions.
Later editions: 1958, 1962.

500*   Ferguson, John Maxwell (b. 1890)
Landmarks of Economic Thought. Second edition. New York: Longmans, Green, and Co., 1950 (also with later dates). xvi, 320 p. 21 cm.
See entry for first (1938) edition.

501   Heimann, Eduard (1889–1967)
Keizai gakusetsu shi. [Translation by] Hiroshi Kitamura. Tokyo: Chuokoron-sha, 1950. 410 p.
Listed in *Index translationum.*
See entry for first (1945) American edition.

502   Hendricks, Henry George (b. 1892)
Masterpieces in Economics. El Paso, Tex.: Guynes Printing Co., 1950. 102 p. 23 cm.
In Library of Congress.
Contained selections from the writings of Smith, Malthus, Ricardo, Senior, Mill, Cairnes, Jevons, Walker, and George, arranged chronologically to give a historical view.

503   Hesse, Albert (b. 1876; professor at Halle and Breslau)
Volkswirtschaftliche Ideen und Theorien. Wiesbaden: Betriebswirtschaftlicher Verlag, 1950. 110 p. 8°.
Listed in *Deutsches Bücherverzeichnis.*

504   Hillebrecht, Arno (b. 1901)
Geschichte der volkswirtschaftlichen Lehrmeinungen. Stuttgart: W. Kohlhammer, 1950 (also dated 1955). 119 p. 23 cm.
In Harvard University Library.

505*   Hori, Tsuneo (b. 1896)
Keizaigaku shi tsuron. [Second edition]. Tokyo: Jikkyo Shuppan-sha, 1950 (also dated 1961). 447 p. 22 cm.

In Library of Congress.
First edition: 1948.
Another history by Hori: 1931–33.

506 Hsü, Ti-hsin
Ching chi ssü hsiang hsiao shih. Shanghai, 1950. 114 p. 19 cm.
In Library of Congress.

507* James, Émile (b. 1899; professor at Paris)
Histoire des théories économiques. Paris: Flammarion, 1950. 329 p.
20 cm.
Other histories by James: 1944, 1955.

Covered economic theory from Aristotle to Keynes. James had said that his
history was for the person who knew a little about political economy and was
beginning the study of economic theory. Silberner, in his review, called it an
"interesting volume" (*American Economic Review* 40 [1950]: 913–15). Kapp
said that James had followed Boucke, Bousquet, and Nogaro (as opposed to
Gide and Rist) in an attempt "to free the history of economic thought from
the normative and doctrinaire elements of thinking contained . . . in the Continental and English literature on the subject. To separate doctrine from theory,
evaluation from explanation, and controversial value judgments from systematic
analysis of reality—these are the aims which the author feels should guide the
writing of history of economic thought. . . . [T]he author has succeeded admirably in writing a new history of economic theory which is likely to preserve
its value for students and professional economists for a considerable period of
time" (*American Economic Review* 42 [1952]: 404).

508 Lipiński, Edward (b. 1888)
Historia myśli ekonomicznej. Warszawa, 1950. 133 p.
Listed in Svendsen.
Other histories by Lipiński: 1950 (next below), 1968.

509 ———
Rozwój myśli ekonomicznej: od merkantylizmu do socjalizmu utopijnego.
Warszawa, 1950. 375 p.
Listed in Svendsen.
Other editions: 1953, 1956.
Other histories by Lipiński: 1950 (next above), 1968.

510* Neff, Frank Amandus (1879–1961)
Economic Doctrines. 2d edition. New York: McGraw-Hill, 1950. xii,
532 p. 24.5 cm.
First edition: 1946.

Reviewed by Shaffer (*American Economic Review* 41 [1951]: 205–7).

511 Okochi, Kazuo (b. 1905; professor at Tokyo)

Keizai shiso shi. Tokyo: Keiso Shobo, 1950–58. 2 v. (287; 3, 256 p.)
22 cm.
In Library of Congress.
Another history by Okochi: 1970.

512 Shên, Chih-yüan (b. 1901)
Chin tai ching chi hsüeh shuo shih kang. [2d ed.] Peking, 1950. 316 p.
22 cm.
In Library of Congress.
First edition: 1937.

513* Stark, Werner (b. 1909)
La storia dell' economica in relazione allo sviluppo sociale. Milano:
L'Industria, 1950. 82 p. 25 cm.
See entry for English (1944) edition.

514 Suenaga, Shigeki (b. 1908; professor at Tohoku University)
Keizaigaku shi. Tokyo, 1950.
Listed in Svendsen.

515* Tautscher, Anton (b. 1906; professor at Graz)
Geschichte der Volkswirtschaftslehre. Wien: A. Sexl, 1950. xii, 279 p.
22 cm.

516* Zimmerman, Louis Jacques (b. 1913)
Geschiedenis van het ekonomisch denken. Tweede, herziene druk. Den
Haag: Uitgeverij Albani, 1950. 276 p. 25 cm.
Other editions: 1947, 1953, 1955. Translation: German, 1954.

517* Zweig, Ferdynand (b. 1896; professor at Cracow, then at Manchester)
Economic Ideas: A Study of Historical Perspectives. New York: Prentice-
Hall, 1950. 197 p. 23 cm.
Translation: Mexican, 1954.

518* Åkerman, Johan Henrik (b. 1896; professor at Lund)
Nationalekonomiens utveckling. Lund, Sweden: C. W. K. Gleerup, 1951.
180 p. 25 cm.
"After an explanation of the birth of economic theory two centuries ago the
development of economic doctrines and economic methods is analyzed under
four heads, constituting the fundamental categories: value, interdependence,
sequence and power. Thus one gets four flows of economic thought: from Locke
to welfare economics, from Quesnay to national budgeting and programming,
from Malthus to econometric analysis of time-series, and from mercantilism to
institutionalism" (from "English Summary," p. 181).
This history contained tables listing the principal events in (1) "Politik,"
(2) "Teknik," (3) "Ekonomi," and (4) "Samhällsvetenskap" (pp. 64–80), as
well as the portraits of twenty-four economists (pp. 82–87).

519   Gide, Paul Henri Charles (1847–1932), and Rist, Charles (1874–1955)
Toledot ha-mishnot ha-kalkaliyot. [Translation by] M. Atar. Tel-Aviv:
Am Oved, 1951–52. 742 p.
Listed in *Index translationum.*
See entry for first (1909) French edition.

520*   Griziotti Kretschmann, Jenny
Historia de las doctrinas económicas. Traducción del italiano por Irma
F. de Fierro y Dino Jarach. Cordoba (Argentina): Editorial Assandri,
1951. 493 p. 24 cm.
Italian editions: 1949, 1954.

521*   Marx, Karl (1818–83)
*Theories of Surplus Value: A Selection from the Volumes Published be-
tween 1905 and 1910 as "Theorien über den Mehrwert."* Edited by
Karl Kautsky. Translated from the German by G. A. Bonner and
Emile Burns. London: Lawrence & Wishart, 1951; New York: Inter-
national Publishers, 1952. 432 p. 23 cm.
See entry for first (1905–10) German edition.

522   Roll, Erich (b. 1907)
Keizai gakusetsu shi. [Translation by] Mikio Sumiya. Tokyo: Yuhikaku,
1951–52. 2 v. (327, 359 p.)
Listed in *Index translationum.*
See entry for first (1938) British edition.

523   Rozenberg, David Iokhelevich (1879–1950)
Keizaigaku shi. [Translation by] Sadayoshi Hiroshima & Koki Hashi-
moto. Tokyo: Aoki Shoten, 1951–54. 3 v.
Listed in *Index translationum.*
See entry for first (1934–36) Russian edition.

524   Salin, Edgar (b. 1892)
Geschichte der Volkswirtschaftslehre. 4. erweiterte Auflage. Bern: A.
Francke, 1951. 205 p. 24 cm.
In Library of Congress.
See entry for first (1923) German edition.

525*   Schumpeter, Joseph Alois (1883–1950; professor at Harvard University)
Ten Great Economists: From Marx to Keynes. New York: Oxford
University Press, 1951 (also dated 1952, 1962, 1965); London: Allen
and Unwin, 1952. xiv, 305 p. 22 cm.
Translations: Japanese, 1952; Italian, 1953; Swedish, 1953; Spanish, 1955,
1967; Brazilian, 1958, 1970; Egyptian, 1959; Indonesian, 1963.
Other histories by Schumpeter: 1914, 1954.

Although strictly speaking not a general history, this was included because of its
connections with Schumpeter's general histories of 1914 and 1954.

526 Stavenhagen, Gerhard
Geschichte der Wirtschaftstheorie. Göttingen: Vandenhoeck & Ruprecht, 1951. 320 p. 24 cm.
In Library of Congress.
Later editions: 1957, 1964, 1969. Translation: Argentine, 1960.
Two-thirds of its space given to the period after 1870.

527* Taylor, Arthur
As grandes doutrinas econômicas. Lisboa: Publicações Europa-América, 1951. 119 p. 18 cm.

528 Yamada, Yuzo (b. 1902)
Keizaigaku wa ikani shimpo shita ka. Tokyo: Shunvu-sha, 1951. 2, 4, 168, 3 p. 21 cm.
In Library of Congress.
Other histories by Yamada: 1947, 1957.

529 Blanqui, Jérôme Adolphe (1798–1854)
Oshu keizai shiso shi. [Translation by] Keiichi Yoshida. Tokyo: Sogen-sha, 1952 (also dated 1965). 2 v.
Listed in *Index translationum.*
See entry for first (1837–[1838]) French edition.

530* Bouvier-Ajam, Maurice Jean (b. 1914; "professeur à l'École nationale du génie rural, des eaux et des forêts")
"Histoire des doctrines économiques" [1:73–334 in his] *Traité d'économie politique et d'histoire des doctrines économiques.* Paris: Plon, 1952. 23 cm.

531* Braeuer, Walter (b. 1906; professor at Marburg)
Handbuch zur Geschichte der Volkswirtschaftslehre. Ein bibliographisches Nachschlagewerk. Frankfurt am Main: Vittorio Klostermann, 1952. 224 p. 25 cm.
Handy reference tool.
Chronologically arranged, it began with Hesiod, ended with Röpke, and included 242 economists; it gave short sketches of the lives and ideas of the main economists, a list of their principal works, and a list of writings about the economists.

532 Choumanidēs, Lazaros Th.
Historia tēs oikonomikēs skepseōs. Athēnai, 1952. 245 p. 24 cm.
In Columbia University Library.
Covered the period from the beginning to Keynes.

533 Gonnard, Charles René (1874–1966)
Historia de las doctrinas económicas. Traducción de J. Campo Moreno.

Revisada y ampliada con arreglo a la última edición francesca, de 1947, por Inocencia Rodríguez-Mellado. [4ª ed.] Madrid: Aguilar, 1952. 664 p. 20 cm.
In Library of Congress.
See entry for first (1921–22) French edition.

534   Hugon, Paul (b. 1902)
História das doutrinas econômicas. 4ª edição. São Paulo, 1952.
Listed in seventh edition.
See entry for first (1942) edition.

535   Kerschagl, Richard (b. 1896)
Volkswirtschaftslehre: ein Abriss der wichtigsten Lehrmeinungen. 5. Auflage. Wien: Manz, 1952. 293 p. 23 cm.
In Library of Congress.
Earlier editions: 1927, 1946, 1947.

536   Lajugie, Joseph (b. 1914)
Las doctrinas económicas. [Translation by] Sebastián Mantilla. Buenos Aires (also Barcelona): Salvat, 1952. 164 p.
Listed in *Index translationum.*
See entry for first (1949) French edition.

537   Lluch y Capdevila, Pedro
Historia de las doctrinas económicas. Cuarta edición. Barcelona: Editorial Lux, 1952.
Listed in fifth edition.
Other editions: 1935, 1941, 1947, 1954.

538*   Marx, Karl (1818–83)
A History of Economic Theories: From the Physiocrats to Adam Smith. Edited, with a Preface, by Karl Kautsky. Translated from the French, with an Introduction and Notes, by Terence McCarthy. New York: Langland Press, 1952. 337 p. 22 cm.
See entry for first (1905–10) German edition.

539*   Newman, Philip Charles (b. 1914; professor at Rutgers)
The Development of Economic Thought. New York: Prentice-Hall, 1952 (also with later dates). 456 p. 24 cm.
Translations: Swedish, 1953; Dutch, 1955; Spanish, 1963.
Another history by Newman: 1954.
"The imprint of Doctor Mitchell's celebrated course in Types of Economic Theory at Columbia on those portions of this book that cover the same ground will be readily apparent" (p. viii).
Reviewed by Whittaker (*Annals of the American Academy of Political and Social Science,* July 1952, pp. 150–51) and Blodgett (*Southern Economic Journal*

19 [1952]: 118). The latter said: "This is almost entirely a book *about* economic thought. It presents a description and analysis of what the various writers thought, and the description sometimes seems more adequate than the analysis."

540   Schumpeter, Joseph Alois (1883–1950)
      Ju dai keizaigakusha. [Translation by] Ichiro Nakayanna [and] Seiichi
          Tohata. Tokyo: Nihon Hyoron Shin-sha, 1952. 450 p.
      Listed in *Index translationum.*
      See entry for first (1951) American edition.

541* Soule, George Henry (1887–1970; professor at Bennington College)
      Ideas of the Great Economists. New York: Viking Press, 1952. 218 p.
          22 cm.
      Later edition: 1955. Translations: German, 1955; Iranian, 1955; Egyptian,
          1957; Pakistani [Urdu], 1957, 1960; Indonesian, 1958; Italian, 1960;
          Argentine, 1961; Japanese, 1962; French, 1963.

542* Spiegel, Henry William (b. 1911; professor at the Catholic University of
          America), ed.
      The Development of Economic Thought: Great Economists in Perspective.
          Foreword by Kenneth Boulding. New York: John Wiley & Son, 1952.
          811 p. 24 cm.
      Translation: Japanese, 1954–55.
      Another history by Spiegel: 1971.

A collection of 42 essays on economists from Plato to Pigou, written by authorities, and for the most part previously published. Some of the essays were translated into English for the first time.

In the Foreword, Boulding said that the book gave "a sense of the progress through time of a true science, a sense not always obtained even from formal histories." In a review, Patterson wrote that "the book contains many of the best statements about the most important figures in the history of economic thought . . . [it] supplements both texts and readings in its field by providing additional material of high quality in accessible form" (*American Economic Review* 43 [1953]: 406–7).

543   Weng, Ch'ing-p'ing
      Min chu chêng chih ti shê hui ching chi. Kaolan, 1952. 2, 1, 108 p. 18 cm.
      In Library of Congress.

544* Bell, John Fred (b. 1898; professor at the University of Illinois)
      A History of Economic Thought. New York: Ronald Press, 1953. 696 p.
          24 cm.
      Second edition: 1967. Translation: Brazilian, 1961.

"Designed primarily as a textbook for college courses, it seeks to give the student a proper understanding of the evolution of the significant economic doctrines, their content and methodology, their application and influence" (p. v).

Bell's first interests in the subject "were stimulated by . . . Professor . . . Weston (1868–1933), in whose seminars at the University of Illinois many hundreds of students had the thrill of association with a great classical mind" (p. vi).

545 Ch'oe, Ho-jin (b. 1914; professor at Yonsei University)
Kyŏngjesa. Seoul, 1953. 191 p. 19 cm.
In Library of Congress.

546 Deguchi, Yuzo (b. 1909; professor at Kyoto), ed.
Keizaigaku shi. Kyoto, 1953. 470 p.
Listed by Mizuta.
Third edition: 1958.
Another history by Deguchi: 1969.

547 Gide, Paul Henri Charles (1847–1932), and Rist, Charles (1874–1955)
Historia de las doctrinas económicas desde los fisiócratas hasta nuestros días. Versión española de C. Martínez Peñalver. 3ª edición. Madrid: Instituto Editorial Reus, 1953. 782 p. 23 cm.
Listed in *Libros españoles*.
See entry for first (1909) French edition.

548* Heilbroner, Robert Louis (b. 1919)
The Worldly Philosophers: The Lives, Times, and Ideas of the Great Economic Thinkers. New York: Simon and Schuster, 1953. 342 p. 23 cm.
Later editions: 1961, 1966 (large type), 1967, 1972. Translations: British, 1955; Dutch, 1955; French, 1957, 1971; Spanish, 1958, 1964, 1972; Korean, 1959, 1962; Swedish, 1959; German, 1960; Indian (Hindi), 1960; Egyptian, 1963; Danish, 1964; Japanese, 1964, 1970; Indian (Bengali), 1965, 1970; Brazilian, 1965; Indian (Marathi), 1969; Portuguese, 1972; Italian, 1975.

For the beginning reader in economics. It was praised as "an enchanting book about what was once described as the Dismal Science (Gerald A. Johnson, *New Republic* 129 [3 August 1953]: 19). Galbraith called it "a brilliant achievement" (*New York Herald Tribune Book Review,* 23 August 1953, p. 7).

549 Koshimura, Shinzaburo (b. 1907; professor at Yokohama)
Keizaigaku shi. Tokyo, 1953. 334 p.
Listed by Mizuta.
Later edition: 1962.

550* Kruse, Alfred (b. 1912)
Geschichte der volkswirtschaftlichen Theorien. 3., erweiterte Auflage. München: R. Pflaum, 1953. 319 p. 24 cm.
Other editions: 1948, 1959.
Another history by Kruse: 1960.

116

551 Lipiński, Edward (b. 1888)
Rozwój myśli ekonomicznej: od merkantylizmu do socjalizmu utopijnego.
[Mimeographed]. Wyd. 2. Warszawa: Nakładem Państwowego
Wydawnictwo Naukowego, 1953. 267 p. 30 cm.
In Library of Congress.
Other editions: 1950, 1956.
Other histories by Lipiński: 1950, 1968.

552 Marx, Karl (1818–83)
Joyo kachi gakusetsu shi. [Translation by] Kazuji Nagasu. Tokyo:
Kokumin Bunko-sha, 1953–54. 2 v. (265, 326 p.)
Listed in *Index translationum.*
See entry for first (1905–10) German edition.

553 ———
Teorije o višku vrednosti. Predgovor napisao Karl Kautsky. [Translation
by] Slavko Petrović [and] Mara Fran. Beograd: "Kultura," 1953–56.
3 v. (392, 636, 524 p.) 21 cm.
Listed in *Jugoslovenska retrospektivna bibliografska grada.*
See entry for first (1905–10) German edition.

554* Myrdal, Gunnar (b. 1898)
The Political Element in the Development of Economic Theory. Trans-
lated from the German by Paul Streeten. London: Routledge & Kegan
Paul, 1953 (also dated 1954, 1969, 1970, 1971, 1973). xvii, 248 p. 23 cm.
See entry for first (1930) Swedish edition.

555 Newman, Philip Charles (b. 1914)
De ekonomiska idéernas historia. [Translation by] Ulrich Herz. Stock-
holm: Kooperativa Förbundet, 1953. 367 p. 8°.
Listed in *Index translationum.*
See entry for American (1952) edition.
Another history by Newman: 1954.

556* Schumpeter, Joseph Alois (1883–1950)
Epoche di storia delle dottrine e dei methodi [and] *Dieci grandi economisti.*
Traduzione et presentazione di Giuseppe Bruguier Pacini. Torino:
Unione Tipografico Editrice Torinese, 1953 (also dated 1954, 1956,
1965). xii, 472 p. 25 cm.
See entries for first (1914) German and first (1951) American editions.

557 ———
Stora nationalekonomer. Övers. och red. av Anders Byttner. Stockholm:
Natur och Kultur, 1953. 353 p. 8°.
Listed in *Svensk Bok-katalog.*
See entry for first (1951) American edition.

558* Sidéris, Aristotéles, Dēmētriou (b. 1889)
Historia oikonomikōn theōriōn. Vol. 1 [no more published?]. Athēnai:
A. Papazēsēs, 1953. 388 p. 26 cm.
Volume 1 included value and distribution. Volume 2 was planned to include
money, international trade, and crises.

559 Takagi, Shinsuke (b. 1901)
Keizaigaku shi genron. Tokyo: Hitotsubashi Shobo, 1953. 22 cm.
In Library of Congress.

560 Toda, Masao
[*A History of Economic Doctrine* (in Japanese)]. Tokyo, 1953. 1, 2,
316, 13 p.
Listed by Mizuta.

561 Zimmerman, Louis Jacques (b. 1913)
Geschiedenis van het ekonomisch denken. Derke, herziene druk. Den
Haag: Albani, 1953. 310 p. 24 cm.
In British Museum.
Other editions: 1947, 1950, 1955. Translation: German, 1954.

562 Bhatnagar, Kalka Prasad (b. 1896), and Bahadur, Satish (professors at
D.A.V. College in Kanpur)
A History of Economic Thought. Kanpur: Kishore Publishing House,
1954.
Listed in fourth edition.
Later editions: 1955, 1957, 1963, 1965, 1969, 1974.
Covered "the history of economic thought for a first-reading for postgraduate
Indian Students." It included several chapters on Indian economic thought.

563* Griziotti Kretschmann, Jenny
Storia delle dottrine economiche. Seconda edizione, riveduta e completata.
Torino: Unione Tipografico Editrice Torinese, 1954. xii, 408 p. 25 cm.
First edition: 1949. Translations: Argentine, 1951.

564 Heimann, Eduard (1889–1967)
Historia de las doctrinas económicas. Buenos Aires: Arayú, 1954.
Listed in *Libros en venta.*
See entry for first (1945) American edition.

565* Kishimoto, Seijiro (b. 1902; professor at Kyoto)
Keizaigaku shi. Tokyo: Seirinshoin, 1954 (also dated 1962). 552 p.
21 cm.

566 Kuruma, Samezo (b. 1893; professor at Hosei University), and Tamanoi,
Yoshiro

Keizaigaku shi. Tokyo: Iwanami, 1954. 367 p. 17 cm.
In Library of Congress.

567* Lluch y Capdevila, Pedro
Historia de las doctrinas económicas. Quinta edición. Barcelona: Editorial Lux, 1954. 290 p. 23 cm.
Earlier editions: 1935, 1941, 1947, 1952.

568* Marx, Karl (1818–83)
Storia delle teorie economiche. 1: *La teoria del plusvalore da William Petty a Adam Smith.* 2: *David Ricardo.* 3: *Da Ricardo all'economia volgare.* Introduzione di Maurice Dobb. Traduzione di Elio Conti. Torino: Giulio Einaudi Editore, 1954–58 (facsimile edition, 1968 [also dated 1971]). 3 v. (xxviii, 339; ix, 645; x, 577 p.) 22 cm.
See entry for first (1905–10) German edition.

569 ———
Teorii pribavochnoĭ stoimosti (IV tom "Kapitala"). Moskva: Gos. Izl-vo Politicheskoĭ Lit-ry, 1954–61. 3 v. 22 cm.
In Columbia University Library.
See entry for first (1905–10) German edition.
A new interpretation of original manuscript earlier published as *Theorien über den Mehrwert.*

570* Newman, Philip Charles (b. 1914); Gayer, Arthur D. (1903–51); and Spencer, Milton H. (b. 1926), eds.
Source Readings in Economic Thought. New York: Norton, 1954. xii, 762 p. 25 cm.
Another history by Newman: 1952.

571* Roll, Erich (b. 1907)
A History of Economic Thought. 3d ed. London: Faber and Faber, 1954; Englewood Cliffs, N.J.: Prentice-Hall, 1954 (also dated 1956). 540 p. 23 cm.
See entry for first (1938) edition.

572 ———
Storia del pensiero economico. 2ª ed. Torino: G. Einaudi, 1954. xiii, 659 p. 8°.
Listed in *Catalogo cumulativo, 1886–1957, del bollettino delle pubblicazioni italiane.*
See entry for first (1938) British edition.

573* Schumpeter, Joseph Alois (1883–1950)
Economic Doctrine and Method: An Historical Sketch. English translation by R. Arias. London: George Allen & Unwin, 1954; New York:

Oxford University Press, 1954 (also dated 1966, 1967). 207 p. 23 cm. See entry for first (1914) German edition.

574* ———— (professor at Harvard)
  A History of Economic Analysis. Edited from manuscript by Elizabeth Boody Schumpeter. New York: Oxford University Press, 1954 (also dated 1955, 1966, 1969). xxv, 1260 p. 24 cm.
  Translations: Japanese, 1955–62; Italian, 1959–60, 1968; German, 1965; Brazilian, 1965; Mexican, 1971; Spanish, 1971.
  Other histories by Schumpeter: 1914, 1951.

An unintended and uncompleted outgrowth of Schumpeter's attempt to revise his *Epochen* (1914), using the Kress Library during World War II.

It received long reviews, generally laudatory, but critical of parts.

Knight wrote that "this volume suggests the expletive, *c'est formidable!*" that "practically every sentence will merit thoughtful attention," and that "both the learning and the penetrating reflections" are "truly 'stupendous'" (*Southern Economic Journal* 21 [1955]: 261). It was, Viner said, "by a wide margin, the most constructive, the most original, the most learned, and the most brilliant contribution to the history of the analytical phases of our discipline which has even been made" (*American Economic Review* 44 [1954]: 895). Stigler judged that "the quality of the performance is not rivaled by any other work of comparable scope" (*Journal of Political Economy* 62 [1954]: 344). In Taylor's view it was a "magnificent work" (*Review of Economics and Statistics* 37 [1955]: 12). Robbins held it to be "without serious rival" (*Quarterly Journal of Economics* 69 [1955]: 3). Richardson wrote that the "*History* will surely rank as one of the most important books on economics to be published in the last half-century" (*Oxford Economic Papers,* new ser. 7 [1955]: 136). Little declared that it was "the most important [history] there has yet been" (*Economic History Review* 8 [1955]: 91). Kuznets concluded that it was "a heroic attempt to do the impossible" (*Journal of Economic History* 15 [1955]: 325). Coats said that it "will long remain a classic" (*Economica,* new ser. 22 [1955]: 174). It was, Bladen announced, "a very great book which no economist . . . can afford to neglect" (*Canadian Journal of Economics and Political Science* 22 [1956]: 103). Singer thought that "there is no risk in predicting that the year 1954 will in the history of economics live on as the date of publication of one book" (*Economic Record* 31 [1955]: 324).

The part of the book most frequently criticized at length was Schumpeter's evaluation downward of the role of members of the British School, especially Adam Smith's role. Knight remarked on Schumpeter's "predilection," in the treatment of Smith, that "there are scores of generally negative characterizations, especially, emphatic denials of the least originality; and perhaps a dozen disparaging comparisons with other named luminaries, earlier and later" (*Southern Economic Journal* 21 [1955]: 265). Viner summarized by saying that "Schumpeter does not like Smith . . . as theorist, as man, or with respect to his social views. . . . Most references to Adam Smith are hostile" (*American Economic Review* 44 [1954]: 904). Stigler spoke of Schumpeter's "underestimate of the

English tradition of substantive generalization, and especially of its greatest exponent, Adam Smith" (*Journal of Political Economy* 62 [1954]: 345). Taylor disapproved at length of Schumpeter's "deflation of the usual estimate of Adam Smith's work and position in his epoch" (*Review of Economics and Statistics* 37 [1955]: 17). "As for the treatment of Adam Smith," Robbins commented, "I am inclined to regard it as one of the few real lapses in the book. There can be little doubt that Adam Smith was one of Schumpeter's blind spots" (*Quarterly Journal of Economics* 69 [1955]: 71). Little wrote of Schumpeter's "grudging assessments of Smith, Ricardo, Marshall, and Keynes" (*Economic History Review* 7 [1955]: 92), of his "failure to do justice to the whole English classical tradition" (ibid., p. 93), of the "debunking which Smith suffers" (ibid., p. 96), and that "the scattered remarks on Smith add up to something close to malice" (ibid.). Singer pointed out that Schumpeter committed "the unpardonable sin of not devoting to the founder of our science a separate chapter" (*Economic Record* 31 [1955]: 327).

Three reviews noted Schumpeter's treatment of Adam Smith but did not take extensive exception to it. Coats, after finding "the passages most likely to provoke controversy in this country are those dealing with British economic thought since 1776," added that "the overall picture which emerges will, however, be no surprise to readers familiar with Schumpeter's earlier writings" (*Economica,* new ser. 32 [1955]: 172). Richardson judged that "Schumpeter's attitude to Smith is fair if unsympathetic" (*Oxford Economic Papers,* new ser. 7 [1955]: 149). Kuznets pointed out the "partially defensible and partially biased judgment of Adam Smith" (*Journal of Economic History* 15 [1955]: 325).

575   [Spiegel, Henry William (b. 1911), ed.]
      Keizai shiso hatten shi. [Translation by] Shinzaburo Koshimura. Tokyo:
          Toyo Shimpo-sha, 1954–55. 5 v.
      Listed in *Index translationum.*
      American edition: 1952.
      Other histories by Spiegel: 1964, 1971.

576* Villey, Daniel (1911–68)
      Petite histoire des grandes doctrines économiques. Nouvelle [troisième]
          édition, revue et précédée d'úne préface. Paris: Éditions M.-Th. Génin,
          1954. 302 p. 20 cm.
      See entry for first (1944) edition.

577* Zimmerman, Louis Jacques (b. 1913)
      Geschichte der theoretischen Volkswirtschaftslehre. Ins deutsche über-
          tragen nach der dritten holländischen Auflage 1953 von Dr. Wilhelm
          Hankel. Köln: Bund-Verlag GMBH, 1954. 287 p. 23.5 cm.
      Dutch editions: 1947, 1950, 1953, 1955.

578   Zweig, Ferdynand (b. 1896)
      El pensamiento económico y su perspectiva histórica. Traducción de

Martha Chávez. México: Fondo de Cultura Económica, 1954. 216 p. 17 cm.
In U.S.C. Library.
American edition: 1950.

579* Amato, Luigi d'
Da Cantillon a Pareto. Roma: Angelo Belardetti, 1955. 83 p. 22 cm.

580 Bhatnagar, Kalka Prasad (b. 1896), and Bahadur, Satish
A History of Economic Thought. Thoroughly revised and enlarged edition. Kanpur: Kishore Publishing House, 1955. ix, 423, iii p. 23 cm.
In U.S.C. Library.
Other editions: 1954, 1957, 1963, 1965, 1969, 1974.

581* Fanfani, Amintore (b. 1908)
Storia delle dottrine economiche dall'antichità al XIX secolo. Quarta edizione. Milano-Messina: Casa Editrice Giuseppe Principato, 1955. xvi, 527 p. 21.5 cm.
See entry for first (1938) edition.

582 Heilbroner, Robert Louis (b. 1919)
De filosofen van het dagelijks brood: de levens, tijden en ideeën van de grote economische denkers. Vertaling van J. E. Kuiper. Amsterdam: H. J. Paris, 1955. 383 p. 21.5 cm.
Listed in Brinkman's Catalogus van boeken.
See entry for first (1953) American edition.

583 ———
The Great Economists: Their Lives and Their Conceptions of the World. Revised for publication in England with two supplementary chapters by Paul Streeten. London: Eyre & Spottiswoode, 1955 (also dated 1969). 320 p. 23 cm.
In University of Chicago Library.
See entry for first (1953) American edition.

584* Hugon, Paul (b. 1902)
Economistas célebres. Textos selecionados e apresentados pelo autor. São Paulo: Editôra Atlas, 1955. 454 p. 24 cm.
Second edition: 1967.
Another history by Hugon: 1942.
Began with Aristotle and ended with Keynes. Gave an introduction to the economic thought of selected authors and excerpts from their writings.

585 Iz istorije gradjanske ekonomske misli (Smit, Rikardo, Maltus, Bem-Baverk, Kejnz, Šumpeter). Ciklus predavanja održanih na Kolarčevom Narodnom Univerzitetu. Beograd: Kolarčev Narodni Univerzitet,

"Naučna Knjiga," 1955. 171 p. 20 cm.
Listed in *Jugoslovenska retrospektivna bibliografska grada.*

586*   James, Émile (b. 1899)
Cours d'histoire des doctrines économiques, rédigé d'après les notes et avec l'autorisation de M. James. Diplômes d'études supérieures, économie politique—sciences économiques, 1954–55. [Photographically reproduced typescript]. Paris: Les Cours de Droit, 1955. 415 p. 26 cm.
Other editions: 1944, 1959.
Other histories by James: 1950, 1955 (next below).

587*   ———
Histoire sommaire de la pensée économique. Paris: Éditions Montchrestien, 1955. 331 p. 25 cm.
Later editions: 1957, 1965, 1969. Translations: Italian, 1963; Spanish, 1963, 1974; Japanese, 1965; Portuguese, 1970.
Other histories by James: 1944, 1950.
Designed particularly for French students who, "aspirant au doctorat en droit, doivent étudier le 'programme général' d'histoire des doctrines economiques." Though it resembled James's 1950 history, the author said that it was "cependant un tout autre livre" (p. 7).

588   Lajugie, Joseph (b. 1914)
As doutrinas econômicas. [Translation by] J. Guinsburg. São Paulo: Difusão Européia do Livro, 1955. 173 p.
Listed in *Index translationum.*
See entry for first (1949) French edition.

589   Muhs, Karl (b. 1891; professor at Jena)
Kurzgefasste Geschichte der Volkswirtschaftslehre: Hauptströmungen der Nationalökonomie. Wiesbaden: Th. Gabler, 1955. 137 p. 21 cm.
Listed in *Deutsches Bücherverzeichnis.*
Later edition: 1963.

590*   Narasaki, Toshio (b. 1891)
Keizai shiso shi. Tokyo: Gengen-sha, 1955. 357 p. 18 cm.

591   Newman, Philip Charles (b. 1914)
Economie: de ontwikkeling van het economisch denken. s'Gravenhage: Succes, 1955. 494 p. 21 cm.
Listed in *Brinkman's Catalogus van boeken.*
See entry for American (1952) edition.

592*   Piettre, André (b. 1906)
Les Trois âges de l'économie: essai sur les relations de l'économie et de la civilisation de l'antiquité classique à nos jours; économie subordonnée,

économie indépendante, économie dirigée. Paris: Éditions Ouvrières, 1955. 430 p. 23 cm.
Later edition: 1964. Translation: Spanish, 1962.
Other histories by Piettre: 1956, 1959, 1969.

593 Roll, Erich (b. 1907)
Historia de las doctrinas económicas. [Translation by] Florentino Martínez Torner. México: Fondo de Cultura Económica, 1955. 549 p.
Listed in *Index translationum.*
See entry for first (1938) British edition.

594 Rozenberg, David Iokhelevich (1879–1950)
Historia ekonomii politycznej. Warszawa: Państwowe Wydawnictwo Naukowe, 1955. 511 p.
Listed in *Index translationum.*
See entry for first (1934–36) edition.

595* Schumpeter, Joseph Alois (1883–1950)
Diez grandes economistas de Marx a Keynes. Traducción española y advertencia por Fabián Estapé. Barcelona: Libreria Bosch, 1955. xx, 382 p. 21 cm.
See entry for first (1951) American edition.

596 ———
Keizai bunseki no rekishi. [Translation by] Seiichi Tohata. Tokyo: Iwanami Shoten, 1955–62. 7 v.
Listed in *Index translationum.*
See entry for American (1954) edition.

597 Soule, George Henry (1887–1970)
A'qayed-e bozorgtarin olamaye eqtesad. [Translation into Iranian by] Hossein Pirniya. Tehrān: Ebn-e Sina, 1955 (also dated 1961). 224 p.
Listed in *Index translationum.*
See entry for first (1952) American edition.

598* ———
Ideas of the Great Economists. New York: New American Library, 1955. 160 p. 18 cm.
See entry for first (1952) edition.

599* ———
Die Ideen der grossen Nationalökonomen. [Translation by] Erwin Schuhmacher. Frankfurt am Main: Nest, 1955. 290 p. 8°.
See entry for first (1952) American edition.

600* Zimmerman, Louis Jacques (b. 1913)

Geschiedenis van het ekonomisch denken. Vierde, herziene druk. Den Haag: Uitgeverij Albani, 1955. 310 p. 25 cm. Earlier editions: 1947, 1950, 1953. Translation: German, 1954.

601 Żurawicki, Seweryn, ed.
Historia myśli ekonomicznej. Warszawa: Państwowe Wydawnictwo, 1955–57. 2 v. (109, 240 p.).
Listed in Šoškić, "Bibliografija," *Razvoj ekonomske misli.*
Another history by Żurawicki: 1973.

602 Behrens, Fritz (b. 1909; professor at Leipzig)
Grundriss einer Geschichte der politischen Ökonomie. Berlin (East): Akademie-Verlag, 1956. (Als Ms. gedr.) xii, 586 p. 8°.
Listed in *Deutsches Bücherverzeichnis.*
Later edition: 1962–76.

603* Desai, S. S. M.
Economic Doctrines: Being an Account of the Development of Western Economic Thought from Ancient Times to the Present Day. Bombay: C. Jamnadas and Co., 1956. xvi, 523 p. 22 cm.
Later editions: 1963 (Malayalam), 1967.

604 Gide, Paul Henri Charles (1847–1932), and Rist, Charles (1874–1955)
Ching chi ssü hsiang shih. [Translation by] T'ung-sun Lou. Taipei: China Culture Publishing Foundation, 1956–58. 5 v. (1378 p.) 19 cm.
In Indiana University Library.
See entry for first (1909) French edition.

605* Gonnard, Charles René (1874–1966)
Historia de las doctrinas económicas. Traducción de J. Campo Moreno. Revisada y ampliada con arreglo a la última edición francesa, de 1947, por Inocencia Rodríquez-Mellado. [5ª ed.] Madrid: Aguilar, 1956 (also dated 1959, 1967, 1969). 664 p. 22 cm.
Identical with 4ª ed. (1952).
See entry for first (1921–22) French edition.

606 Hugon, Paul (b. 1902)
História das doutrinas econômicas. 5ª edição. São Paulo: Editôra Atlas, 1956. 452 p. 24 cm.
Listed in *Boletim bibliográfico brasileiro.*
See entry for first (1942) edition.

607* Lajugie, Joseph (b. 1914)
Les Doctrines économiques. 4ᵉ édition. Paris: Presses Universitaires de France, 1956. 134 p. 18 cm.
See entry for first (1949) edition.

608   Lipiński, Edward (b. 1888)
      Rozwój myśli ekonomicznej: od merkantylizmu do socjalizmu utopijnego.
      Wyd. 3. Warszawa, 1956. 382 p. 24 cm.
      In Stanford University Library.
      Other editions: 1950, 1953.
      Other histories by Lipiński: 1950, 1968.

609* Marx, Karl (1818–83)
      Theorien über den Mehrwert (vierter Band des "Kapitals"). Berlin
      (East): Dietz, 1956, 1959, 1962. 3 v. (XXXI, 495; 723; 674 p.). 22 cm.
      See entry for first (1905–10) edition.

610   Piettre, André (b. 1906)
      *Cours d'histoire des doctrines économiques, rédigé d'après la sténotypie
      du cours et avec l'autorisation de M. Piettre.* Diplômes d'études
      supérieures, économie politique, histoire du droit, et droit romain, 1955–
      1956. Paris: Les Cours de Droit, 1956. 552 p. 25 cm.
      In Library of Congress.
      Other histories by Piettre: 1955, 1959, 1969.

611* Rogin, Leo (1893–1947)
      The Meaning and Validity of Economic Theory: Historical Approach.
      New York: Harper & Brothers, 1956 (reprinted, 1971). 697 p. 22 cm.

612   Roll, Erich (b. 1907)
      Povijest ekonomske misli. [Translation by] Slobodan Štampar. Zagreb:
      "Kultura," 1956. lxvii, 442 p.
      Listed in *Jugoslovenska retrospektivna bibliografska grada.*
      See entry for first (1938) British edition.

613   Shirasugi, Shoichiro (1909–61)
      Keizaigaku shi. Kyoto: Mineruva Shobo, 1956. 8, 276 p.
      Listed in Svendsen.
      Another history by Shirasugi: 1960.

614   Šoškić, Branislav; Pjanić, Z.; Samardžija, M.; Stamenković, R.;
      Stojanović, R.
      *Iz istorije gradanske ekonomske misli (Smit, Rikardo, Maltus, Bem-Baverk,
      Kejnz, Sumpeter).* Beograd: Naučna Knjiga, 1956. 170 p.
      In University of California Library.
      Another history by Šoškić: 1965.

615* Vecchio, Gustavo del (1883–1972)
      Vecchie e nuove teorie economiche. Seconda edizione. Torino: Unione
      Tipografico-Editrice, 1956. viii, 417 p. 24.5 cm.
The first edition was not a *general* history.

616   Barrère, Alain (b. 1910; professor at Paris)
       Histoire de la pensée économique et analyse des théories contemporaines.
       [Multigraphed]. Paris: Les Cours de Droit, 1957–58. xxxvi, 880 p. 8°.
       Listed in *La Librairie française.*
       Later edition: 1974.

617   Bhatnagar, Kalka Prasad (b. 1896), and Bahadur, Satish
       A History of Economic Thought. 3d, revised edition. Kanpur: Kishore
       Publishing House, 1957 (also dated 1958). 421 p.
       Listed in fourth edition.
       Other editions: 1954, 1955, 1963, 1965, 1969, 1974.

618*   Cole, Arthur Harrison (b. 1889)
       The Historical Development of Economic and Business Literature. Boston:
       Harvard Graduate School of Business Administration, 1957. 56 p. 25 cm.
       Publication Number 12 of The Kress Library of Business and Economics.

619   Heilbroner, Robert Louis (b. 1919)
       Les Grands penseurs de la révolution économique. Paris: Colombe, 1957.
       296 p. 23 cm.
       In Northwestern University Library.
       See entry for first (1953) American edition.

620*   James, Émile (b. 1899)
       Histoire sommaire de la pensée économique. 2ᵉ édition, revue et aug-
       mentée. Paris: Éditions Montchrestien, 1957 (also dated 1959). 421 p.
       26 cm.
       See entry for first (1955) edition.

621   Kim, Il-lo
       Kyŏngjehak sa. [Seoul?], 1957. 2, 8, 489 p. 21 cm.
       In Library of Congress.

622   Marx, Karl (1818–83)
       Joyo kachi gakusetsu shi. [Translation by] Fumio Hasebe. Tokyo: Aoki
       Shoten, 1957–58. 3 v.
       Listed in *Index translationum.*
       See entry for first (1905–10) German edition.

623   Roll, Erich (b. 1907)
       Ching chi ssü hsiang ti fa chan. [Translation by] Hsi-liu Hsu. Taipei:
       Hwa Kuo Pub. Service, [published not later than 1957].
       Listed in *Index translationum.*
       See entry for first (1938) British edition.

624   Schumpeter, Joseph Alois (1883–1950)

De ekonomiska doktrinernas historia till sekelskiftet. Till svenska av Anders Byttner. Stockholm: Natur och Kultur, 1957. 240 p.
Listed in *Svensk bok-katalog.*
See entry for first (1914) German edition.

625* ——

Keizaigaku shi. [Translation by] Ichiro Nagayama. Tokyo: Iwanami, 1957. 6, 3, 355, 9 p. 22 cm.
See entry for first (1914) German edition.

626 Soule, George Henry (1887–1970)
Jaleel-ul-qadar mahereen-i-muashiyat ke afkar. [Translation into Urdu by] Sardar Mohammad Akhtar. Lahore: Franklin Publications, 1957.
Listed in *Index translationum.*
See entry for first (1952) American edition.

627 ——

Al mathahib al iktesadiah al kobra. [Translation in Arabic by] Rashed al Barrarvi. Al Kahira (Cairo): Maktabat al Nahdat al Misriah, 1957 (also dated 1962, 1965). 228 p.
Listed in *Index translationum.*
See entry for first (1952) American edition.

628 Stamenković, Radoš
Istorija ekonomskih doktrina. Beograd: Odbor Udruženja Studenta Ekonomskog Fakulteta, 1957. 2 v. (78, 123 p.) 29 cm. Vol. 1: *Razvoj gradjanske ekonomske misli od Merkantilista do Rikarda;* vol. 2: *Razvoj grandjanske misli ad Rikarda do Kejnza.*
Listed in *Jugoslovenska retrospektivna bibliografska grada.*

629 Stavenhagen, Gerhard
Geschichte der Wirtschaftstheorie. 2., völlig neubearb. Auflage. Göttingen: Vandenhoeck & Ruprecht, 1957. 536 p. 24 cm.
In Columbia University Library.
See entry for first (1951) edition.

630* Taylor, Edward (b. 1884)
Historia rozwoju ekonomiki. Poznań: Państwowe Wydawnictwo Naukowe, 1957–58. 2 v. (xii, 258, 385 p.) 26 cm.
Prybla called it "a clear, incisive, well-balanced and comprehensive manual worthy of the attention of students of the subject" (*American Economic Review* 49 [1959]: 422). A third volume on the development of socialism had been promised.
Taylor was a professor at Poznan from 1919 to 1949, when he was purged. He prepared a script of his lectures on the history of economic thought prior to 1949. He put the script into book form during the period from 1950 to 1956 (when he was reinstated).

631 Wu, Chên-hsiung
Chin tai hsi yang ching chi shih. Kaolan, 1957. 424 p. 21 cm.
In Library of Congress.

632 Yamada, Yuzo (b. 1902)
Kindai keizaigaku shi yo. Tokyo: Shunja, 1957. vi, iv, 181, 4 p. 22 cm.
In Library of Congress.
Other histories by Yamada: 1947, 1951.

633 Abe, Gen'ichi (b. 1904)
Keizai gakuhattatsu shi. Tokyo: Hakutou Shobo, 1958. 375 p. 19 cm.
In Library of Congress.
Other editions: 1950, 1962.

634* Aguirre, Manuel Agustín (b. 1904; "profesor del Colegio Meijía de la Universidad Central")
Apuntes para el estudio de la historia del pensamiento económico. Quito: Editorial Universitaria, 1958–62. 2 v. 22 cm.
Volume 1 covered the period from antiquity to the Physiocrats. Volume 2 covered the Classics and Marx.

635* Capodaglio, Giulio (b. 1910)
Sommario di storia delle dottrine economiche. Quarta edizione, riveduta ed accresciuta. In Appendice: *La storiografia italiana delle dottrine economiche nella prima metà del secolo XX.* Milano: Dott. A. Giuffrè, 1958. 262 p. 24 cm.
Other editions: 1934, 1937, 1941, 1945, 1968.

636 Deguchi, Yuzo (b. 1909), ed.
Keizaigaku shi. [3d edition, revised and enlarged]. Kyoto: Mineruva Shobo, 1958. 58, 508 p.
Listed in *International Bibliography of Economics.*
First edition: 1953.
Another history by Deguchi: 1969.

637 Ferguson, John Maxwell (b. 1890)
Historia de la economía. Traducción de Vicente Polo. Segunda edición en espanõl. México (also Buenos Aires): Fondo de Cultura Económica, 1958. 286 p. 21 cm.
Listed in third Mexican edition.
See entry for first (1938) American edition.

638* Friederichsen, Vittorio Cristiano (b. 1881)
Epoche svolgimenti tendenze nella storia delle dottrine economiche: compendio esegètico. Udine: Del Bianco, 1958. 277 p. 24 cm.
Attempted a different presentation.

639   Gray, Alexander (1882-1968)
       Arthashastra siddhanta ka vikas. [Translation into Hindi by] Viraj.
       Delhi: S. Chand and Co., 1958, vii, 422 p. 18.5 cm.
       Listed in *Index translationum.*
       British edition: 1931.

640   Heilbroner, Robert Louis (b. 1919)
       Los filósofos de la vida material. Madrid: Editorial Aguilar, 1958 (also
       dated 1963).
       Listed in Gómez Granillo.
       See entry for first (1953) American edition.

641*   Horie, Yasuzo (b. 1904)
       Keizaishi. Tokyo: Kobun Sha, 1958 (also dated 1961). 2, 149 p. 21 cm.
       Another history by Horie: 1949.

642   Lakshmi, Narain
       Guide to History of Economic Thought. Meerut: Sri Prakashan, 1958.
       80 p.
       Listed in *Indian Books in Print.*

643   Schumpeter, Joseph Alois (1883-1950)
       Dez grandes economistas. Tradução de Japy Freire. Rio de Janeiro:
       Editôra Civilização Brasileira, 1958. 296 p.
       In Columbia University Library.
       See entry for first (1951) American edition.

644   Soule, George Henry (1887-1970)
       Pikiran sardjana besar ahli ekonomi. [Translation by] L. M. Sitorus.
       Djakarta: Pustaka Rakjat, 1958 (also dated 1967). 305 p.
       Listed in *Index translationum.*
       See entry for first (1952) American edition.

645   Villey, Daniel (1911-68)
       Petite histoire des grandes doctrines économiques. 4. éd. Paris: Éditions
       M.-Th. Génin, 1958. 302 p. 20 cm.
       In University of Texas Library.
       See entry for first (1944) edition.
       Another history by Villey: 1967.

646*   Weiller, Jean (b. 1905; professor at Paris)
       *Cours d'histoire des doctrines économiques, rédigé d'après les notes et
       avec l'autorisation de Jean Weiller.* Droit romain et histoire du droit,
       économie politique, sciences économiques, 1957-1958. Paris: Les Cours
       de Droit, 1958. 253 p. 25 cm.
Ended with Mill.

647   Abraham, V. M.
        History of Economic Thought. Delhi: Jiwan Prakashan, 1959. viii, 344 p.
        21.5 cm.
        Listed in *Indian National Bibliography.*

648   Gide, Paul Henri Charles (1847–1932), and Rist, Charles (1874–1955)
        Istoria tōn oikonomikōn theōriōn apo tōn phusiokratōn mehri sēmeron.
        [Translation by] N. B. Patselēs. Athēnai: Gkonēs, 1959 (also dated
        1961). 448 p. 8°.
        Listed in *Index translationum.*
        See entry for first (1909) French edition.

649   Goetz, Robert (b. 1910; professor at Paris)
        *Cours d'histoire des doctrines économiques, rédigé d'après la sténotypie
        du cours et avec l'autorisation de Robert Goetz.* Droit romain et histoire
        du droit, économie politique. D.E.S., 1958–1959. Paris: Les Cours de
        Droit, 1959. 382 p. 25 cm.
        In Library of Congress.

650*   Hamelin, André (b. 1925)
        Les Doctrines économiques. Paris: Éditions Ouvrières, 1959. 188 p. 19 cm.
Proceeded through Bastiat and then switched to a discussion of the socialists.

651   Heilbroner, Robert Louis (b. 1919)
        Gyeong'je'sa'sang'sa. [Translation by] Yeong-rog Gim. Seoul: Su'do'-
        mun'hwa'sa, 1959. 356 p.
        Listed in *Index translationum.*
        See entry for first (1953) American edition.

652   ———
        Utopister och samhällsomdanare. Till svenska av Anders Byttner. Stock-
        holm: Natur och Kultur, 1959 (also dated 1967). 303 p.
        Listed in *Svensk Bok-katalog.*
        See entry for first (1953) American edition.

653   Hugon, Paul (b. 1902)
        História das doutrinas econômicas. 6ª edição. São Paulo, 1959.
        Listed in seventh edition.
        See entry for first (1942) edition.

654   James, Émile (b. 1899)
        *Cours d'histoire de la pensée économique, rédigé d'après les notes et avec
        l'autorisation de Émile James.* Licence 3ᵉ année, 1958–1959. Paris: Les
        Cours de Droit, 1959. 496 p. 25 cm.
        In Northwestern University Library.
        Earlier editions: 1944, 1955.
        Other histories by James: 1950, 1955.

655   Kruse, Alfred (b. 1912)
       Geschichte der volkswirtschaftlichen Theorien. 4., verb. und erweiterte
       Auflage. Berlin: Duncker & Humblot, 1959. 366 p. 24 cm.
       In University of Chicago Library.
       Earlier editions: 1948, 1953 (3. erweiterte Auflage).
       Another history by Kruse: 1960.

656*   Lekachman, Robert (b. 1920)
       A History of Economic Ideas. New York: Harper, 1959; Delhi: Uni-
       versal Book Stall, 1959. 427 p. 22 cm.
       Translations: French, 1960; Argentine, 1962; Italian, 1971; Brazilian, 1973.
Reviewed by Henderson, who said that "in large part this volume reflects the
dilemma of a shrinking, but courageous, corps of economists who cling to the
idea that it is desirable to offer an undergraduate course in the history of economic thought" (*American Economic Review* 50 [1960]: 199).

657*   Maide, Chogoro (b. 1891), and Yokohama, Masahiko (b. 1917)
       Keizaigaku shi. Tokyo: Kobundo, 1959. 272 p. 21 cm.
       Earlier history by Maide: 1937.

658   Marx, Karl (1818–83)
       Teorie wartości dodatkowej. Tom czwarty "Kapitału." [Translation into
       Polish by] Czeslaw Grabowski, Felicja Romaniukowa, and Władyslaw
       Sadowski (vol. 1); Julian Maliniak (vols. 2 and 3). Warszawa: Ksiażka
       i Wiedza, 1959–66. 3 v. (544, 811, 740 p.)
       Listed in *Index translationum.*
       See entry for first (1905–10) German edition.

659*   Piettre, André (b. 1906; professor at Strasbourg)
       Histoire de la pensée économique et analyse des théories contemporaines.
       Paris: Dalloz, 1959. 520 p. 19 cm.
       Later editions: 1961, 1965, 1966, 1970, 1973.
       Other histories by Piettre: 1955, 1956, 1969.
Contained chronological charts relating the history of economics to other matters.
    In his review, Grayson described it as "an undergraduate textbook in which
the history of economic thought and an analysis of modern theory are combined"
(*American Economic Review* 49 [1959]: 1060).

660   Rozenberg, David Iokhelevich (1879–1950)
       Chêng chih ching chi hsüeh shih. Peking, 1959. 575 p. 21 cm.
       In Library of Congress.
       See entry for first (1934–36) Russian edition.

661   Schumpeter, Joseph Alois (1883–1950)
       'asharah Min A'immat al-Iqtisād 'min Mārkis Ilā Kīnz. [Translation into

Arabic]. al'Qāhirah (Cairo): Maktabit al'Sharq bel-Fajjālah, 1959. 273 p.
Listed in *Index translationum*.
See entry for first (1951) American edition.

662 ———

Storia dell'analisi economica. Traduzione italiana di Paolo Sylos-Labini e Luigi Occhionero. Vol. 1: *Dai primordi fino al 1790;* vol. 2: *Dal 1790 al 1870;* vol. 3: *Dal 1870 ai giorni nostri*. Torino: Edizione Scientifiche Einaudi, 1959–60. 3 v. (1526 p.) 23.5 cm.
Listed in *Bibliografia nazionale italiana*.
Reviewed in *Giornale degli economisti* (1960).
See entry for American (1954) edition.

663 Bartoli, Henri (b. 1918; professor at Paris)
Cours d'histoire de la pensée économique, rédigé d'après la sténotypie du cours et avec l'autorisation de Henri Bartoli. Licence 3ᵉ année, 1959–1960. Paris: Les Cours de Droit, 1960. 988 p. 25 cm.
In Library of Congress.

664 Ch'oe, Mun-hwan (b. 1916; dean at Seoul)
Kyŏngjesa. Seoul, 1960. 515 p. 22 cm.
In Library of Congress.

665 Gide, Paul Henri Charles (1847–1932), and Rist, Charles (1874–1955)
Clásicos de la ciencia económica: Adam Smith, David Ricardo, Saint-Simon, Stuart Mill. Habana: Editorial Lex, 1960. 267 p. 17 cm.
In University of Florida Library.
See entry for first (1909) French edition.

666 Heilbroner, Robert Louis (b. 1919)
Vishva ke mahan arthashastri. [Translation into Hindi by] R. K. Joshi. Bombay: Allied Publishers, 1960. vi, 297 p. 22 cm.
Listed in *Index translationum*.
See entry for first (1953) American edition.

667 ———

Wirtschaft und Wissen: zwei Jahrhunderte Nationalökonomie. [Translation by] Julius Wünsche. Köln: Bund-Vere, 1960. 423, 23 p.
Listed in *Index translationum*.
See entry for first (1953) American edition.

668* Kruse, Alfred (b. 1912)
Nationalökonomie: Ausgewählte Texte zur Geschichte einer Wissenschaft. Stuttgart: K. F. Koehler, 1960. 306 p. 20.5 cm.
Another history by Kruse: 1948.

Arranged, not chronologically, but under eleven subjects. It contains short excerpts from leading writers on each subject, along with some introductory material.

669* Lekachman, Robert (b. 1920)
    Histoire des doctrines économiques de l'antiquité à nos jours. Traduit de
    l'anglais par Bernard de Zélicourt. Paris: Payot, 1960. 437 p. 23 cm.
    See entry for first (1959) American edition.

670 Napolitano, Gaetano (b. 1892; professor at Sassari)
    Gli sviluppi storici dell'economia politica. Milano: A. Giuffrè, 1960. vii,
    194 p. 22 cm.
    In New York Public Library.
Proceeded to Malthus, added a chapter on the liberals and socialists, and finished
with one on the economics of the state and private economics.

671 Sachdeva, T. N.
    History of Economic Thought: Full View at a Glance. New Delhi:
    Sudha Publications, 1960. xii, 198 p. 21.5 cm.
    Listed in *Indian National Bibliography.*
    Later editions: 1962, 1965, 1969, 1973.

672 Scott, William Amasa (1862–1944)
    Ching chi ssü hsiang shih. Taipei: San Ming Bk. Co., 1960. xviii, 592,
    xxiii p.
    Listed in *Index translationum.*
    American edition: 1933.

673 Shirasugi, Shoichiro (1909–61)
    Keizaigaku shi gaisetsu. Kyoto: Mineruva Shobo, 1960. 480 p.
    Listed in *International Bibliography of Economics.*
    Another history by Shirasugi: 1956.

674 Sobajima, Shozo (b. 1903)
    Keizaigaku shi shinko. Kyoto: Seki Shoin, 1960. 401 p.
    Listed in *International Bibliography of Economics.*

675 Soule, George Henry (1887–1970)
    Ozama ke siyas nazriat. [Translation into Urdu by] S. M. Akhtar &
    Gulam Rsul Mehr. Lahore: Board for Advancement of Literature,
    1960. 356 p.
    Listed in *Index translationum.*
    See entry for first (1952) American edition.

676* ———
    Storia del pensiero economico. Traduzione di Gualtiero Da Vià. Intro-

duzione e appendice di Elio Caranti. Bologna: L. Capelli, 1960. 228 p. 19 cm.
See entry for first (1952) American edition.

677*   Spengler, Joseph John (1902; professor at Duke), and Allen, William R. (b. 1924; professor at U.C.L.A.), eds.
Essays in Economic Thought: Aristotle to Marshall. Chicago: Rand McNally & Company, 1960. 800 p. 26 cm.
Translation: Spanish, 1971.
Assembled, in chronological arrangement, 31 articles written by eminent economists on important parts of the history of economics.

678*   Stark, Werner (b. 1909)
Die Geschichte der Volkswirtschaftslehre in ihrer Beziehung zur sozialen Entwicklung. Übertragen von Erich Abt. Dordrecht-Holland: D. Reidel, 1960. viii, 86 p.
See entry for British (1944) edition.

679   Stavenhagen, Gerhard
Historia de las teorías económicas. [Translation by] Adolfo von Ritter-Zahony. Buenos Aires: El Ateneo, 1960. xx, 519 p.
Listed in *Index translationum.*
German editions: 1951, 1957, 1964, 1969.

680*   Stollberg, Rudhard (b. 1931)
Geschichte der bürgerlichen politischen Ökonomie: eine allgemeinverständliche Einführung. Berlin (East): Die Wirtschaft, 1960. 242 p. 22 cm.
Presented the history of economics to Marxians in East Germany. Supporting authorities included many references to Marx's *Theorien über den Mehrwert.*

681*   Taylor, Overton Hume (b. 1897; professor at Harvard University)
A History of Economic Thought: Social Ideals and Economic Theories from Quesnay to Keynes. New York: McGraw-Hill Book Co., 1960. xix, 524 p. 24 cm.
Translations: Argentine, 1965; Portuguese, 1965.
The preface says that the book "is not a complete or comprehensive history of economic thought . . . about one half . . . is devoted to . . . [the] history of philosophical and overall social, ethical, and political thought" (p. ix).

Stigler characterized the book as "a traditional liberal's running commentary, of all degrees of perspicacity, on the philosophical, political, and economic problems of modern times, hung on the framework of a chronological conspectus of economic theory" (*American Economic Review* 51 [1961]: 426–27). Stigler noted the slight attention given to technical economics after 1850 and added that anyone who could read it in its entirety was in a select group.

682   Totomiants, Vakhan Fomich (b. 1875)
Historia de las doctrinas económicas. Habana: Editorial Lex, 1960.
2 v. 17 cm.
In University of Florida Library.
See entry for Russian (1921) edition.

683   Villey, Daniel (1911–68)
Historia de las grandes doctrinas económicas. Traducción de la *Petite histoire des grandes doctrines économiques* por Teresa Vidal. Buenos Aires: Editorial Nova, 1960. 306 p.
Listed in *Index translationum.*
French editions: 1944, 1946, 1954, 1958, 1973.
Another history by Villey: 1967.

684*   Whittaker, Edmund (1897–1956)
Schools and Streams of Economic Thought. Chicago: Rand McNally & Company, 1960; London: John Murray, 1960. 416 p. 24 cm.
Another history by Whittaker: 1940.
The preface said that this volume went farther than the author's *History of Economic Ideas* (1940) "in studying economic writings by author, school, and period; therefore, it does more than the earlier book to show the contemporary integration of ideas" (p. vii).
Reviewed by Spiegel (*American Economic Review* 50 [1960]: 744).

685   Yi, Yŏng-hyŏp
Ilban kyŏngjesa yoron. [Seoul?], 1960. 305 p. 22 cm.
In Library of Congress.

686   Bell, John Fred (b. 1898)
História do pensamento econômico. Tradução de Giasone Rebuá. Revisão de Cassio Fonseca. Rio de Janeiro: Zahar Editôres, 1961. 581 p.
In Library of Congress.
American editions: 1953, 1967.

687*   Beltrán Flórez, Lucas (b. 1911)
Historia de las doctrinas económicas. Barcelona: Editorial Teide, 1961.
376 p. 22 cm.

688   Bhatta, Srikrsnadatta
Arthik vicardhara: udaya se sarvodaya tak [in Hindi]. Varanasi: Akhil Bharat Sarva Seva Sangh, 1961. ix, 483 p. 22 cm.
Listed in *Indian National Bibliography.*

689   Cho, Ki-jun (b. 1917; professor at University of Korea)
Sin Kyŏngjesa. Seoul, 1961. 346, 10 p. 21 cm.
In Library of Congress.

690 Heilbroner, Robert Louis (b. 1919)
The Worldly Philosophers: The Lives, Times, and Ideas of the Great Economic Thinkers. Revised edition. New York: Simon and Schuster, 1961. 309 p. 23 cm.
In Rutgers University Library.
See entry for first (1953) edition.

691 Herz, Ulrich (b. 1913)
Välfärdsideologins förhistoria: från Aristoteles till Marx. Malmö: Rabén & Sjögren, 1961. 243 p. 21 cm.
In New York Public Library.
One of many short histories that ended with Marx.

692 Hong, U. (b. 1913; dean at Tongguk University)
Kyŏngjehak sa. [Seoul?], 1961. 394 p. 21 cm.
In Library of Congress.

693 McConnell, John Wilkinson (b. 1907)
Enseñanzas de los grandes economistas. Buenos Aires: Tipográfica Editora Argentina, 1961. 426 p.
Listed in *Libros en venta.*
American edition: 1943.

694* Piettre, André (b. 1906)
Histoire de la pensée économique et analyse des théories contemporaines. Deuxième édition. Paris: Dalloz, 1961. 517 p. 19 cm.
See entry for first (1959) edition.

695* Schmölders, Günter (b. 1903; professor at Cologne)
Geschichte der Volkswirtschaftslehre. Wiesbaden: Th. Gabler, 1961. 148 p. 24 cm.
Another history by Schmölders: 1962.
Made up of short discussions (with long bibliographies) on Justi, Quesnay, Smith, Thünen, List, Marx, Wagner, Schmoller, Menger, Pareto, Marshall, Wicksell, Veblen, Keynes, and Schumpeter.

696 Soule, George Henry (1887–1970)
Ideas de los grandes economistas. Traducción de Aníbal Leal. Buenos Aires: General Fabril Editora, 1961. 252 p. 19 cm.
In Yale University Library.
See entry for first (1952) American edition.

697 Srivastava, Shri Krishna
History of Economic Thought. Delhi: Atma Ram, 1961 (also dated 1963). xii, 423 p. 22 cm.
Listed in *Impex.*

Other editions: 1963 (in Hindi), 1965, 1969.

698   Stark, Werner (b. 1909)
      Historia de la economía en su relación con el desarrollo social. Traducción
      de Rubén Pimentel y José Manuel Sobrino. México: Fondo de Cultura
      Económica, 1961. 112 p. 22 cm.
      In University of Georgia Library.
      See entry for British (1944) edition.

699* Udal'tsov, Ivan Dmitrievich (1885–1958), ed.
      Istoriia ekonomicheskoĭ mysli: kurs lektsiĭ. Moskva, 1961–64. 2 v. 27 cm.

700   Wendt, Siegfried (b. 1901; professor at Göttingen, Giessen, and Wil-
      helmshaven)
      Geschichte der Volkswirtschaftslehre. Berlin: Walter de Gruyter, 1961.
      182 p.
      In Columbia University Library.
      Second edition: 1968.
Contained a long bibliography.

701   Abe, Gen'ichi (b. 1904)
      Keizai gakuhattatsu shi. Tokyo: Hakutou Shobo, 1962. 401 p. 19 cm.
      In Library of Congress.
      Earlier editions: 1950, 1958.

702* Behrens, Fritz (b. 1909)
      Grundriss der Geschichte der politischen Ökonomie. Band 1: *Die poli-
      tische Ökonomie bis zur bürgerlichen Klassik.* Band 2: *Die Marxsche
      politische Ökonomie.* Berlin (East): Akademie-Verlag, 1962–76. 2 v.
      (231, 368 p.) 24 cm.
      Earlier edition: 1956.
Marxist orientation.

703* Blaug, Mark (b. 1927; professor at London)
      Economic Theory in Retrospect. Homewood, Ill.: Irwin, 1962. 633 p.
      24 cm.
      Revised edition: 1968. Translations: Japanese, 1966–71; Spanish, 1968;
      Italian, 1970; German, 1971–75.
Allen said that "it will serve the splendid purpose of making the specialist in
dead men less disreputable in the eyes of his theory-teaching colleagues" and
that since it was "unencumbered (or unadorned) by biography, sociology of
knowledge, economic history, or noneconomic intellectual history," the book
was delimited in scope and gave "the hard substance of historically developing
theory rather than the usual poetry" (*American Economic Review* 53 [1963]:
173–74).

704* Catlin, Warren Benjamin (1881–1968; professor at Bowdoin College)
      The Progress of Economics: A History of Economic Thought. New
      York: Bookman Associates, 1962. 788 p. 24 cm.
Had a topical approach. In his review Powers said, "The author displays much
more than just a passing acquaintance with the literature of the field, and the
patient research is obvious" (*American Economic Review* 53 [1963]: 466).

705   Cho, Tong-p'il (b. 1919; professor at University of Korea)
      Sin kyŏngjehak sa. [Seoul?], 1962. 452 p. 21 cm.
      In Library of Congress.

706   Chodkiewicz, Zygmunt
      Historia myśli ekonomicznej: zagadnienia wybrane. Warszawa: Pań-
      stwowe Wydawnictwo Naukowe, 1962. 208 p. 24 cm.
      In Library of Congress.

707   Heilbroner, Robert Louis (b. 1919)
      Widaehan gyeongjehagjadeul. [Translation by] Yeong-log Kim. Seoul:
      Sasanggyesa, 1962. 415 p.
      Listed in *Index Translationum.*
      See entry for first (1953) American edition.

708* Hugon, Paul (b. 1902)
      História das doutrinas econômicas. Sétima edição, revista e ampliada.
      São Paulo: Editôra Atlas, 1962. 507 p. 23 cm.
      See entry for first (1942) edition.

709* Kapp, Karl William (b. 1910), and Kapp, Lore L.
      History of Economic Thought: A Book of Readings. New York: Barnes
      and Noble, 1962. viii, 444 p. 21 cm.
First issued as *Readings in Economics* (1949).

710   Koshimura, Shinzaburo (b. 1907)
      Keizaigaku shi. Tokyo: Shunju-sha, 1962. 300 p.
      Listed in *International Bibliography of Economics.*
      Earlier edition: 1953.

711   Lekachman, Robert (b. 1920)
      Historia de las doctrinas económicas. Traducido del inglés por Edgardo
      Guimerans. Buenos Aires: Editorial Victor Lerú, 1962. 424 p. 20 cm.
      In University of Texas Library.
      See entry for first (1959) American edition.

712   Mittala, S. C.
      Arthika vicarom ka itihasa [in Hindi]. 1962. 608 p. 23 cm.

In Library of Congress.
Textbook for postgraduate students.

713   Piettre, André (b. 1906)
       Las tres edades de la economía. [Translation by] Fernando Aguirre de
       Cárcer. Madrid: Rialp, 1962. 515 p.
       Listed in *Index translationum.*
       See entry for first (1955) French edition.

714   Roll, Erich (b. 1907)
       História das doutrinas econômicas. Tradução de Cid Silveira. 2ª ed.,
       rev. e aumentada. São Paulo: Companhia Editôra Nacional, 1962.
       539 p.
       In University of Pittsburgh Library.
       See entry for first (1938) British edition.

715   _____
       Historia de las doctrinas económicas. [Translation by] Florentino
       Martínez Torner. México: Fondo de Cultura Económica, 1962 (also
       dated 1964, 1967, 1969, 1971). 492 p.
       Listed in *Index translationum.*
       See entry for first (1938) British edition.

716   Sachdeva, T. N.
       History of Economic Thought: Full View at a Glance. Second edition,
       radically revised and elaborately enlarged. New Delhi: Sudha Publica-
       tions, 1962. 280 p. 23 cm.
       In Columbia University Library.
       Other editions: 1960, 1965, 1969, 1973.

717   Schmölders, Günter (b. 1903)
       Geschichte der Volkswirtschaftslehre: Überblick und Leseproben. Reinbek
       bei Hamburg: Rowohlt, 1962 (also dated 1967). 360 p. 19 cm.
       In University of Michigan Library.
       Another history by Schmölders: 1961.

718   Schneider, Erich (1891–1971; professor at the University of Kiel)
       Ausgewählte Kapitel der Geschichte der Wirtschaftstheorie [vol. 4 in his]
       Einführung in die Wirtschaftstheorie. Tübingen: J. C. B. Mohr, 1962.
       423 p. 24 cm.
       Listed in *Deutsches Bücherverzeichnis.*
       Second edition: 1965.
Concentrated on theory, especially price theory.

719*   Schumpeter, Joseph Alois (1883–1950)
       Esquisse d'une histoire de la science économique, des origines jusqu'au

début de XXe siècle. Traduit par G. H. Bousquet. Paris: Dalloz, 1962. 222 p. 20 cm.
See entry for first (1914) German edition.

720 Sonachalam, K. S.
Porulatarac cintanai varalaru [in Tamil]. 1962. 223 p. 23 cm.
In Library of Congress.

721 Soule, George Henry (1887–1970)
Idai naru keizaigakusha no shiso. [Translation by] Kiyoshi Kono. Tokyo: Hosei Daigaku Shuppan-kyoku, 1962. 114 p.
Listed in *Index translationum.*
See entry for first (1952) American edition.

722 Tokinaga, Fukashi (b. 1922)
Keizaigaku shi. Tokyo: Gakubun-sha, 1962–68. 2 v. (243, 526 p.) 21.5 cm.
Listed by Mizuta.
Later editions: 1970, 1971.

723* Akademiia nauk SSSR. Institut ekonomiki
Istoriia ekonomicheskikh uchenii. Nikolaĭ Konstantinovich Karataev [ed.] Moskva: Izd-vo Sotsial'no-ekon. Lit-ry, 1963. 549 p. 23 cm.
Translations: Mexican, 1964; German, 1965; Brazilian, 1967.

724* Baldwin, Armand Jean (b. 1917)
A History of Economic Thought. Latrobe, Pa.: Archabbey Press, 1963. 210 l. 28 cm.

725* Bhatnagar, Kalka Prasad (b. 1896), and Bahadur, Satish
A History of Economic Thought. 4th edition. Kanpur: Kishore Publishing House, 1963. xvi, 555 p. 22.5 cm.
Other editions: 1954, 1955, 1957, 1965, 1969, 1974.

726 Cho, Moriyoshi (b. 1900)
Keizaigaku shi. Tokyo: Toyo Keizai Shinbun, 1963. xi, 369, 4 p. 22 cm.
In Library of Congress.

727 Davar, B. C.
History of Economic Thought. Poona: City Book Stall, 1963. ii, 198 p. 21 cm.
Listed in *Indian National Bibliography.*

728 Denis, Henri
Cours d'histoire de la pensée économique, rédigé d'après les notes et avec l'autorisation de M. Henri Denis, professeur agrégé, chargé de cours à

la faculté de droit et des sciences économiques de Paris. Licence 3e année, 1962–1963. Paris: Les Cours de Droit, 1963. 423 p. 25 cm.
In Library of Congress.
Another edition: 1972.
Other histories by Denis: 1966, 1967.
"Ce cours n'est pas une sténographie des leçon prononcées par le Professeur. Il est destiné à compléter ces leçons et à faciliter l'assimilation. Il contient en particulier des analyses assez détaillées d'un certain nombre des textes fondamentaux étudies au cours" (p. 3).

729   Desai, S. S. M., and Yevlekar, C. T.
       Arthasastra vicar vikas [in Malayalam, with English subtitle *History of Economic Thought*]. Poona: Swadhyay Mahavidyalay Prakashan, 1963. xii, 352 p. 21.5 cm.
       Listed in *Indian National Bibliography*.
       English language editions: 1956, 1967.

730*   Ferguson, John Maxwell (b. 1890)
       Historia de la economía. Traducción de Vicente Polo. México (also Buenos Aires): Fondo de Cultura Económica, 1963. 286 p. 22 cm.
       See entry for first (1938) American edition.

731   Gokhle, Ramcandra Mahadev
       Arthasastriya vicaraca itihas [in Malayalam]. Poona: Continental Prakashan, 1963. viii, 368 p. 22 cm.
       Listed in *Indian National Bibliography*.

732*   Guaresti, Juan José (b. 1907; professor at University of Buenos Aires)
       Las doctrinas económicas [vol. 5 in his] *Economía política.* Prólogo del Dr. Ricardo Zorraquin Becú. Buenos Aires: Guillermo Kraft, 1963. 476 p. 24 cm.

733   Heilbroner, Robert Louis (b. 1919)
       Qādat al-fikr al-iqtisadī. [Translation into Arabic by] Rashīd al-Barāwī. Al-Qāhirah (Cairo): Maktabat al-Nahdah al Misrīyah, 1963. 387 p.
       Listed in *Index translationum*.
       See entry for first (1953) American edition.

734   James, Émile (b. 1899)
       Historia del pensamiento económico. Traducción del francés por Ricardo Defarges Ibáñez. Madrid: Aguilar, 1963 (also dated 1967, 1969). xxxv, 414 p.
       Listed in *Libros en venta*.
       See entry for first (1955) French edition.

735   ———
       Storia del pensiero economico. Trad. Umberto del Canuto. Milano:

A. Garzanti, 1963 (also dated 1968, 1970). 502 p. 17.5 cm.
Listed in *Index translationum*.
See entry for first (1955) French edition.

736*   Kuhn, William Ernest (b. 1922; professor at University of Nebraska)
The Evolution of Economic Thought. Cincinnati: Southwestern Publishing Company, 1963. 451 p. 24 cm.
Second edition: 1970.
Reviewed by Lekachman (*American Economic Review* 54 [1964]: 149–51).

737   Legradić, Rudolf
Historija ekonomske teorije. Osijek: Zajednica Studenata Ekonomskog Fakulteta, 1963. 274 p. 29 cm.
Listed in *Jugoslovenska retrospektivna bibliografska grada*.

738*   Madan, Gurmuk Ram (professor at Lucknow University), and Dhooria, H. S.
The History and Development of Economic Thought (an Introductory Analysis). With a foreword by Radhakamal Mukerjee. Delhi: S. Chand, 1963. iii, ii, 311 p. 23 cm.

739   Marx, Karl (1818–83)
Joyo kachi gakusetsu shi. [Translation by] Oshima Kiyoshi, Tokinaga Fakashi, [and] Okazaki Jiro. Tokyo: Otsuki Shoten, 1963–70. 6 v.
Listed in *Index translationum*.
See entry for first (1905–10) German edition.

740*   ———
Theories of Surplus Value (vol. 4 of *Capital*). Translated by Emile Burns from the 1956 German edition. Edited by S. Ryazanskaya. Part 1. Moscow: Foreign Languages Publishing House, 1963. 491 p. 22 cm.
See entry for first (1905–10) German edition.

741   Muhs, Karl (b. 1891)
Kurzgefasste Geschichte der Volkswirtschaftslehre: Hauptströmungen der Nationalökonomie. Wiesbaden: Gabler, 1963. 161 p. 21 cm.
In Library of Congress.
Earlier edition: 1955.

742*   Myrdal, Gunnar (b. 1898)
Das politische Element in der nationalökonomischen Doktrinbildung. Mit einem Nachwort von Paul Streeten. Hannover: Verlag für Literatur und Zeitgeschehen, 1963. 210 p. 24 cm.
See entry for first (1930) Swedish edition.

743* Newman, Philip Charles (b. 1914)
Historia de las doctrinas económicas. Traducción de José Rico Godoy y Joaquín Muns. Barcelona: Editorial Juventad, 1963. 558 p. 22 cm.
See entry for American (1952) edition.
Another history by Newman: 1954.

744* Oser, Jacob (b. 1915)
The Evolution of Economic Thought. New York: Harcourt, Brace & World, 1963. xiii, 399 p. 24 cm.
Later editions: 1970, 1975.

745 Schumpeter, Joseph Alois (1883–1950)
Sepuluh sardjana ekonomi terkemuka. [Translation by] Oh Bian Hong. Djakarta: Bhratara, 1963. 334 p.
Listed in *Index translationum.*
See entry for first (1951) American edition.

746* Silva Herzog, Jesús (b. 1893)
Antologia del pensamiento económico-social. Vol. 1: *De Bodino a Proudhon* [no more published]. México (also Buenos Aires): Fondo de Cultura Económica, 1963. 606 p. 24.5 cm.
A general discussion, "El panorama económico," followed by a consideration of the work of fifty-four political economists, which appraised the work of each and gave excerpts from his writings translated into Spanish.

747 Soule, George Henry (1887–1970)
Qu'est-ce que l'économie politique? [Translation by] Claude Lafarge. Strasbourg: Istra, 1963. 208 p.
Listed in *Index translationum.*
See entry for first (1952) American edition.

748 Srivastava, Shri Krishna
Arthik vicar-dharaem [in Hindi]. Delhi: Atma Ram, 1963. xiii, 415 p. 22 cm.
Listed in *Indian National Bibliography.*
English language editions: 1961, 1965, 1969.

749 Akademiia nauk SSSR. Institut ekonomiki
Historia de las doctrinas económicas. Karataev y otros. México: Grijalbo, 1964. 2 v. (1223 p.).
Listed in *Libros en venta.*
See entry for Russian (1963) edition.

750 Budénová, Rita; Müller, Václav; and Kýn, Oldřich
Kapitoly ke studiu dějin ekonomických teorií. II díl. [Part 1 published later (1966) covering from Mercantilism to Imperfect Competition].

Praha: Státní Pedagogické Nakladatelství, 1964. 87 p. 29 cm.
In Harvard University Library.
From Keynes to present.

751* Cannan, Edwin (1861–1935)
A Review of Economic Theory. 2d edition, with a new introduction by
B. A. Corry. London: Cass, 1964. xx, 448 p. 22 cm.
See entry for first (1929) edition.

752 Gide, Paul Henri Charles (1847–1932), and Rist, Charles (1874–1955)
Historia de las doctrinas económicas. Buenos Aires: Ediciones Arayú,
[1964?]. 2 v.
Listed in Libros en venta.
See entry for first (1909) French edition.

753 Heilbroner, Robert Louis (b. 1919)
100 mannin no keizaigaku. [Translation by] Hamada Kiyofu. Tokyo:
Hara Shobo, 1964. 423 p.
Listed in Index translationum.
See entry for first (1953) American edition.

754 ———
Økonomiens taenkere. [Translation by] Niels Gabe. København: Hassel-
balch, 1964. 355 p.
Listed in Index translationum.
See entry for first (1953) American edition.

755 ———
Vida y doctrina de los grandes economistas. [Translation by] Armando
Lázaro Ros. Madrid: Aguilar, 1964 (also dated 1970). 362 p.
Listed in Libros en venta.
See entry for first (1953) American edition.

756 el-Kaissi, Fawzi, and Kassira, Anwar, eds.
Writings of Great Economists. Bagdad: Matba'at al-Zahrā, 1964. 277,
3 p. 21 cm.
In Stanford University Library.

757 Lajugie, Joseph (b. 1914)
As doutrinas econômicas. Trad. de J. Guinsburg. 3ª ed. São Paulo:
Difusão Européia do Livro, 1964. 146 p. 19 cm.
Listed in Bibliografia brasileira.
See entry for first (1949) French edition.

758 ———
Ē ekonomike theōrie. [Translation by] Sabbas Bassiliou. Athēnai:

Zaharopoulos, 1964. 130 p.
Listed in *Index translationum*.
See entry for first (1949) French edition.

759   Piettre, André (b. 1906)
Les Trois âges de l'économie: essai sur les relations de l'économie et de la civilisation de l'antiquité classique à nos jours. 2e éd. Paris: Fayard, 1964. 458 p. 22 cm.
In Library of Congress.
See entry for first (1955) edition.

760   Scheifler Amézaga, Xavier (professor at Universidad Iberoamericana [Mexico])
Historia del pensamiento económico: apuntes de la cátedra del . . . Scheifler Amézaga. Vol. 1: *La economía subordinada, desde los orígenes hasta el liberalismo.* México, 1964. 23 cm.
In Library of Congress.
Later editions: 1967, 1968.

761   Schumpeter, Joseph Alois (1883–1950)
Síntesis de la evolución de la ciencia económica y sus métodos. Versión, Jorge Petit Fontseré. Madrid: Garcia, 1964; Barcelona: Ediciones de Occidente, 1964. 212 p. 21.5 cm.
Listed in *Index translationum*.
See entry for first (1914) German edition.

762   Spiegel, Henry William (b. 1911), ed.
The Development of Economic Thought: Great Economists in Perspective. Abridged edition. New York: Wiley, 1964. xii., 486 p.
In Columbia University Library.
First edition: 1952.
Another history by Spiegel: 1971.

763*   Stavenhagen, Gerhard
Geschichte der Wirtschaftstheorie. Dritte, neubearbeitete und erweiterte Auflage. Göttingen: Vandenhoeck & Ruprecht, 1964. 649 p. 24 cm.
See entry for first (1951) edition.

764   Uchida, Yoshihiko (b. 1913); Kobayashi, Noboru; Miyazaki, Yoshikazu; and Miyazaki, Saiichi, eds.
Keizaigaku shi koza. Tokyo: Yuhikaku, 1964. 3 v. (2, 5, 306; 2, 5, 280; 2, 5, 502 p.)
Listed by Mizuta.
Another history by Uchida: 1970.

765*   Wilson, George Wilton (b. 1929; professor at Indiana University)

Classics of Economic Theory. Bloomington: Indiana University Press, 1964. 637 p. 22 cm.

Contained "An Essay on the History of Economic Thought" as a brief introduction, followed by long excerpts from Smith, Ricardo, Mill, Marx, Jevons, and Marshall.

766   Akademiia nauk SSSR. Institut ekonomiki
       Geschichte der ökonomischen Lehrmeinungen [von einem] Autorenkollektiv. Redaktionskollegium: N. K. Karatajew u.a. Übersetzung aus dem Russischen (von W. Tuchscheerer u.a.). Berlin (East): Verlag Die Wirtschaft, 1965. 540 p. 22 cm.
       In Library of Congress.
       See entry for Russian (1963) edition.

767   Alvim, Décio Ferraz (b. 1897; professor at Universidade Católica de Campinas)
       História das doutrinas econômicas. 2ª edição. [Date of first edition not ascertained]. Petrópolis: Vôzes, 1965. 111 p. 19 cm.
       In Library of Congress.

From Egypt to the *Rerum novarum* of Leo XIII.

768*   Bhatnagar, Kalka Prasad (b. 1896), and Bahadur, Satish
       A History of Economic Thought. Fourth edition [*sic*]. Kanpur: Kishore Publishing House, 1965. 464 p. 22 cm.
       Other editions: 1954, 1955, 1957, 1963, 1969, 1974.

769*   Brizio, Giuseppe
       Il pensiero economico nei secoli. Prefazione di Librero Lenti. Bergamo: Editrice San Marco, 1965. 293 p. 26 cm.

Published during 1963/64 in 43 weekly installments of *24 ore.* It contained 99 illustrations, of which 58 were portraits of economists, ranging from Socrates to Samuelson.

770*   Gherity, James Arthur (b. 1929; professor at Northern Illinois University), ed.
       Economic Thought: A Historical Anthology. New York: Random House, 1965. xv, 554 p. 21 cm.

A collection of readings from books and articles on, or by, outstanding authors of the past.

771   Heilbroner, Robert Louis (b. 1919)
       Arthanitik daršam o daršanik. [Translation into Bengali by] Parikshit (pseud.). Calcutta: Arts and Letters, 1965. iv, 355 p. 21.5 cm.
       Listed in *Index translationum.*
       See entry for first (1953) American edition.

772 ——————
Introdução à história das idéias econômicas. Trad. de Waltensir Dutra.
Rio de Janeiro: Zahar, 1965 (also dated 1969, 1974). viii, 321 p. 21 cm.
Listed in *Bibliografia brasileira*.
See entry for first (1953) American edition.

773 Heimann, Eduard (1889–1967)
Historia das doutrinas econômicas. Trad. de Waltensir Dutra. Rev. por
Cassio Fonseca. Rio de Janeiro: Zahar Ed., 1965. 252 p. 21 cm.
Listed in *Bibliografia brasileira*.
See entry for first (1945) American edition.

774 James, Émile (b. 1899)
Histoire sommaire de la pensée économique. 3e éd., rev. et cor. Paris:
Montchrestien, 1965. 423 p. 25 cm.
In Washington University (Saint Louis) Library.
See entry for first (1955) edition.

775 ——————
Keizai shiso shi. [Translation by] Kubota Akimitsu & Yamahawa Yoshio.
Tokyo: Iwanami Shoten, 1965. 388 p.
Listed in *Index translationum*.
See entry for first (1955) French edition.

776* Lecce, Michele
Sommario storico del pensiero economico. Milano: Giuffrè, 1965. 322 p.
24 cm.

777* Marx, Karl (1818–83)
Theorien über den Mehrwert (vierter Band des "Kapitals") [vol. 26 in]
Karl Marx—Friedrich Engels Werke. Berlin (East): Dietz, 1965–72.
3 v. (xxiv, 497, 705, 663 p.) 22 cm.
See entry for first (1905–10) edition.
The Vorwort, the Anhang, and the Register are different from those in the
1956–62 edition.

778* Moscow. Akademiia obshchestvennykh nauk
Istoriia ekonomicheskikh uchenii. Redaktsionnaia kollegiia: S. L. Vygod-
skiĭ, V. S. Afanas'ev, and V. I. Gromeka. Moskva: Mysl', 1965. 479 p.
21 cm.

779 Peter, Kattadyil Chacko (b. 1922)
Dhanasastra purogati jivacaritrannali-lute [in Malayalam]. Ernakulam:
C.I.C.C. Book House, 1965. viii, 275, ii, iv p. 19 cm.
In Library of Congress.

780   Piettre, André (b. 1906)
Histoire de la pensée économique et analyse des théories contemporaines.
3e éd. Paris: Dalloz, 1965. 549 p. 18 cm.
Listed in *"Biblio."*
See entry for first (1959) edition.

781* Recktenwald, Horst Claus (b. 1920; professor at Erlangen-Nürnberg), ed.
Lebensbilder grosser Nationalökonomen: Einführung in die Geschichte der politischen Ökonomie. Köln: Kiepenheuer & Witsch, 1965. 666 p. 24 cm.
Later edition: 1971. Translation: British, 1973.
A collection of 61 articles on 28 economists, arranged chronologically to serve as a general history. It supplied portraits of all but two (Cantillon and Gossen).

782   Roll, Erich (b. 1907)
Arthik vicarom ka itihas [in Hindi]. Allahabad: Central Book Depot, 1965. x, 482 p.
Listed in *Index translationum.*
See entry for first (1938) British edition.

783   Sachdeva, T. N.
History of Economic Thought: Full View at a Glance. Fourth edition, radically revised and elaborately enlarged. New Delhi: Sudha Publications, 1965. 304 p. 22 cm.
In University of Florida Library.
Other editions: 1960, 1962, 1969, 1973.

784* Schneider, Erich (1891–1971)
Ausgewählte Kapitel der Geschichte der Wirtschaftstheorie [vol. 4 in his] *Einführung in die Wirtschaftstheorie.* Zweite, durchgesehene Auflage. Tübingen: J. C. B. Mohr, 1965 (also dated 1970). viii, 423 p. 24 cm.
First edition: 1962.

785* Schumpeter, Joseph Alois (1883–1950)
Geschichte der ökonomischen Analyse. Mit einem Vorwort von Fritz Karl Mann. Aus dem Amerikanischen übersetzt von Gottfried & Johanna Frenzel. Göttingen: Vandenhoeck & Ruprecht, 1965. 2 v. (1520 p.) 24 cm.
See entry for American (1954) edition.

786   ———
Gyeongjehagsa. [Translation by] Min-Chae Kim. Seoul: Ilsinsa, 1965. 267 p.
Listed in *Index translationum.*
See entry for first (1914) German edition.

787 ——————

História da análise econômica. Trad. de Alfredo Moutinho dos Reis, José Luís Silveira Miranda, Renato Rocha Capa de Raul Pereira. Rio de Janeiro: Ed. Fundo de Cultura, 1965. 3 v. (472, 461, 574 p.) 21 cm.
Listed in *Bibliografia brasileira.*
See entry for first (1954) American edition.

788 Šoškić, Branislav
Razvoj ekonomske misli. Beograd: Rad, 1965. 328 p. 24 cm.
In Library of Congress.
Later editions: 1968, 1970.
Another history by Šoškić: 1956.
Contained a bibliography of modern books on the history of economics.

789 Srivastava, Shri Krishna
History of Economic Thought. 2d edition. Delhi: Atma Ram, 1965. xvi, 684 p. 21 cm.
In Library of Congress.
Other editions: 1961, 1963 (in Hindi), 1969.

790 Taylor, Overton Hume (b. 1897)
Historia del pensamiento económico. Buenos Aires: TEA, 1965. 609 p.
Listed in *Libros en venta.*
American edition: 1960. Other translation: Portuguese, 1965 (next below).

791 ——————

História do pensamento econômico: ideais sociais e teorias econômicas de Quesnay à Keynes. Rio de Janeiro: Editôra Fundo de Cultura, 1965. 639 p. 21 cm.
In Brooklyn Public Library.
American edition: 1960. Other translation: Argentine, 1965 (next above).

792 Toda, Takeo (b. 1905; professor at Shizuoka University)
Keizai gaku shi no hanashi. Tokyo: Sunbun, 1965. 1, 4, 199 p.
In Library of Congress.

793 Blaug, Mark (b. 1927)
Keizai riron no rekishi. [Translation by] Kubo Yoshikazu, Mazane Kazuo, [and] Sugihara Shiro. Tokyo: Tokyo Keizai Shimpo-sha, 1966–71. 3 v.
Listed in *Index translationum.*
See entry for first (1962) American edition.

794* Boardman, Fon Wyman (b. 1911)

Economics: Ideas and Men. New York: Henry Z. Walck, 1966. 133 p. 25 cm.

Translation: French, 1969.

A book for children.

"Explores the ideas and systems from the time of Plato and Aristotle to the modern theories of John Maynard Keynes. Ages 12-up" (*American Book Publishing Record, Annual Cumulative 1966,* p. 259).

795   Budénová, Rita; Kýn, Ordřich; and Müller, Václav
     Kapitoly ke studiu dějin ekonomických teorií. 1 díl. [Second part published previously (1964)]. Praha: Státní Pedagogické Nakladatelství, 1966. 124 p. 29 cm.
     In Harvard University Library.

Began with Mercantilism and ended with Imperfect Competition.

796   Denis, Henri
     Histoire de la pensée économique. Paris: Presses Universitaires de France, 1966. 756 p. 18 cm.
     In New York Public Library.
     Later editions: 1967, 1971, 1974. Translations: Italian, 1968; Spanish, 1970; Turkish, 1973–74; German, 1975.
     Other histories by Denis: 1963, 1967.

797   Ferguson, John Maxwell (b. 1890)
     Historia de la economía. 4ª ed. México: Fondo de Cultura Económica, 1966 (also dated 1970, 1971). 188 p.
     Listed in *Libros en venta.*
     See entry for first (1938) American edition.

798*   Fusfeld, Daniel Roland (b. 1922; professor at the University of Michigan)
     The Age of the Economist. Glenview, Ill.: Scott, Foresman and Company, 1966. 147 p. 23 cm.
     Later editions: 1968, 1972. Translations: Italian, 1970; Mexican, 1970; German, 1975.

799*   Heilbroner, Robert Louis (b. 1919)
     The Worldly Philosophers: The Lives, Times, and Ideas of the Great Economic Thinkers. Large-type edition. New York: Watts, 1966. 368 p. 29 cm.
     See entry for first (1953) edition.

800   Hugon, Paul (b. 1902)
     História das doutrinas econômicas. Pref. de Abelardo Vergueiro César. 8ª ed. São Paulo: Ed. Atlas, 1966. 481 p. 23 cm.
     Listed in *Bibliographia brasileira.*
     See entry for first (1942) edition.

801   Kobayashi, Noboru (b. 1916; professor at Rikkyo University), ed.
       [*A History of Economics* (in Japanese)]. Tokyo, 1966. 10, 288 p.
       Listed by Mizuta.

802*   Mitchell, Broadus (b. 1892)
       Great Economists in Their Times. Totowa, N.J.: Littlefield, Adams,
       1966. xix, 236 p. 21 cm.

803   Piettre, André (b. 1906)
       Histoire de la pensée économique et analyse des théories contemporaines.
       4ᵉ édition. Paris: Dalloz, 1966. 558 p. 18 cm.
       In Library of Congress.
       See entry for first (1959) edition.

804   Roll, Erich (b. 1907)
       Storia del pensiero economico. 3ᵃ ed. Trad. Nanni Negro. Torino:
       Boringhieri, 1966 (also dated 1967, 1970, 1971). xxi, 558 p. 19.5 cm.
       Listed in *Bibliografia nazionale italiana.*
       See entry for first (1938) British edition.

805   ——
       Toledot ha-mahshava ha-kalkalit. [Translation by] Y. Tishler. Tel-Aviv:
       Hakibbutz Hameuchad, 1966. 409 p.
       Listed in *Index translationum.*
       See entry for first (1938) British edition.

806   Akademiia nauk SSSR. Institut ekonomiki
       História das doutrinas econômicas. Trad. de Renato Guimares. Rio de
       Janeiro: Zahar Ed., 1967. 437 p. 21 cm.
       Listed in *Boletim bibliográfico brasileiro.*
       See entry for Russian (1963) edition.

807*   Barber, William Joseph (b. 1925; professor at Wesleyan University,
       Middleton, Conn.)
       A History of Economic Thought. Harmondsworth, England, or Baltimore,
       Md.: Penguin, 1967. 266 p. 18.5 cm.
       Translations: American, 1968; Swedish, 1971; Spanish, 1971; Italian, 1971;
       Brazilian, 1971; Japanese, 1973.

808*   Bell, John Fred (b. 1898)
       A History of Economic Thought. 2d edition. New York: Ronald Press,
       1967. viii, 745 p. 24 cm.
       First edition: 1953.

809   Denis, Henri
       La Formation de la science économique. Paris: Presses Universitaires de

France, 1967. viii, 371 p. 18 cm.
In New York Public Library.
Other histories by Denis: 1963, 1966.

A book of readings, divided by subject, with texts supplemented by a short description of each author.

810* ———

Histoire de la pensée économique. Deuxième édition, revue et augmentée. Paris: Presses Universitaires de France, 1967. 804 p. 18 cm.
See entry for first (1966) edition.

811* Desai, S. S. M.
History of Economic Thought: Being an Account of the Development of Western Economic Thought from Mercantilism to Alfred Marshall. 2d, revised edition. Poona: Continental, 1967. 2, 7, 382 p. 23 cm.
Earlier editions: 1956, 1963 (Malayalam).

812* Gill, Richard T. (b. 1927)
Evolution of Modern Economics. Englewood Cliffs, N.J.: Prentice-Hall, 1967. viii, 119 p. 24 cm.
Translations: Portuguese, 1968; Swedish, 1968; Japanese, 1969; Mexican, 1969; Italian, 1969.

813* Gómez Granillo, Moisés
Breve historia de las doctrinas económicas. México: Editorial Esfinge, 1967 (also dated 1971, 1973). 275 p. 22 cm.
Later edition: 1975.

814 Hajela, T. N. (formerly lecturer in Economics at Bareilly College, Bareilly, India)
History of Economic Thought. Agra, India: Shiva Lal Agarwala, 1967. 698 p.
In Washington University (St. Louis) Library.
Later editions: 1970, 1972, 1973.

815* Heilbroner, Robert Louis (b. 1919)
The Worldly Philosophers: The Lives, Times, and Ideas of the Great Economic Thinkers. 3d edition, newly revised. New York: Simon and Schuster, 1967. 320 p. 22 cm.
See entry for first (1953) edition.

816 Hugon, Paul (b. 1902)
Evolução do pensamento econômico: economistas célebres, textos selecionados e apresentados pelo autor. 2ª ed., rev. e ampl. São Paulo: Ed. Atlas, 1967. 317 p. 21 cm.
Listed in *Bibliografia brasileira mensal.*
First edition: 1955.

817 ——

História das doutrinas econômicas. 9ª ed. S. Paulo: Ed. Atlas, 1967.
479 p. 21 cm.
Listed in *Boletim bibliográfico brasileiro.*
See entry for first (1942) edition.
Another history by Hugon: 1942.

818   Lajugie, Joseph (b. 1914)
Les Doctrines économiques. 9ᵉ édition, remaniée et mise à jour. Paris:
Presses Universitaires de France, 1967. 136 p. 18 cm.
In Library of Congress.
See entry for first (1949) edition.

819*   Marshall, Howard Drake (b. 1924)
The Great Economists: A History of Economic Thought. New York:
Pitman Publishing Corporation, 1967. 397 p. 25 cm.
Another history by Marshall: 1968.
In his review Gruchy said that "this book is much too condensed" (*American
Economic Review* 58 [1968]: 209).

820*   Mitchell, Wesley Clair (1874–1948)
Types of Economic Theory: From Mercantilism to Institutionalism.
Edited with an Introduction by Joseph Dorfman. New York: A. M.
Kelley, 1967–69. 2 v. (xi, 608; xii, 875 p.) 23 cm.
Earlier versions: 1935, 1949. Translation: Japanese, 1971.
Joseph Dorfman prepared these lectures for publication. The 1967–69 edition
was approximately twice as long as the 1949 edition. It incorporated a newly
edited version of the 1949 edition; made additions from a "1918 typescript" of
a part of the course that Mitchell "arranged for, and at least in part supervised,"
and of which the class obtained copies; and made use of a manuscript "The
Classical Economics," which Mitchell had begun to write in 1916, of outlines
and abstracts that Mitchell left, of the notes that a student took of the course in
1923/24, and of other sources.

821*   Montaner, Antonio (b. 1919; professor at Mainz), ed.
Geschichte der Volkswirtschaftslehre. Köln: Kiepenheuer & Witsch, 1967.
476 p. 24 cm.
A collection of previously published articles on the history of economics, mainly
by German authors.

822*   Myrdal, Gunnar (b. 1898)
El elemento político en el desarrollo de la teoría económica. [Translation
by] José Díaz García. Madrid: Editoral Gredos, 1967. 244 p.
See entry for first (1930) Swedish edition.

823   ——
Seiji gakusetsu to seijiteki yoso. [Translation by] Yuzo Yamada & Ryuzo

Sato. Tokyo: Shunju-sha, 1967. 349 p.
Listed in *Index translationum.*
See entry for first (1930) Swedish edition.

824*   Nešić, Dragoljub
Historija ekonomiskih doktrina. Sarajevo: Univerzitet, 1967. Vol. 1.
283 p. 24 cm.

825*   Rima, Ingrid Hahne (b. 1925; professor at Temple University)
Development of Economic Analysis. Homewood, Ill.: Richard D. Irwin,
1967. xvi, 422 p. 24 cm.
Revised edition: 1972.
Another history by Rima: 1970.

Gruchy ended his review with the statement that "instructors who wish to give
their students in intermediate economic theory an historical orientation for the
concepts and tools that they are analyzing, Rima's book will be found very
useful" (*American Economic Review* 58 [1968]: 211).

826*   Salin, Edgar (b. 1892)
*Politische Ökonomie: Geschichte der wirtschaftspolitischen Ideen von
Platon bis zur Gegenwart.* Fünfte, erweiterte Auflage der Geschichte
der Volkswirtschaftslehre. Tübingen: J. C. B. Mohr (Paul Siebeck),
1967. viii, 205 p. 24 cm.
See entry for first (1923) edition.

In his review, Barthel said that the volume "gives testimony of a learned man
who has assimilated much knowledge; however, the value of many of his conclusions cannot be seen by a world he himself does not trust anymore" (*American
Economic Review* 58 [1968]: 572).

827   Scheifler Amézaga, Xavier
Historia del pensamiento económico. Segunda edición (del autor). Mé-
xico, 1967.
Listed in third edition.
Other editions: 1964, 1968.

828   Schumpeter, Joseph Alois (1883–1950)
Diez grandes economistas de Marx a Keynes. [Translation by] Angel de
Lucas. Madrid: Alianza, 1967 (also dated 1969, 1971). 446 p.
Listed in *Index translationum.*
See entry for first (1951) American edition.

829*   Spann, Othmar (1878–1950)
*Die Haupttheorien der Volkswirtschaftslehre auf lehrgeschichtlicher
Grundlage.* 27., durchgesehene Auflage, eingerichtet von Oskar Müllern
und Adam Reining [vol. 2 in his] *Gesamtausgabe.* Graz, Austria:

Akademische Druck und Verlagsanstalt, 1967 (also dated 1969). xvii,
383 p. 25 cm.
See entry for first (1911) edition.

830   Villey, Daniel (1911–68)
      *Notes d'histoire de la pensée économique, rédigées par M. Jacques
      Anthonioz . . . d'après les cours de M. Daniel Villey.* D. E. S., 1966–
      1967. Sciences économiques et histoire du droit. Paris: Les Cours de
      Droit, 1967. 234 p. 25 cm.
      In Library of Congress.
      Another history by Villey: 1944.

831* Barber, William Joseph (b. 1925)
      A History of Economic Thought. New York: Frederick A. Praeger,
      1968. 272 p. 21 cm.
      Identical with the 1967 Penguin edition except for the added "Biblio-
      graphical Notes."
      See entry for first (1967) British edition.

832   Berni, Giorgio (b. 1913; professor at Instituto Tecnológio y de Estudios
      Superiores de Monterrey)
      Evolución del pensamiento económico. México: Herrero Hermanos, 1968.
      258 p. 23 cm.
      In University of Chicago Library.

833* Blaug, Mark (b. 1927)
      Economic Theory in Retrospect. Revised edition. Homewood, Ill.: Irwin,
      1968. xxiv, 710 p. 24 cm.
      See entry for first (1962) edition.

834* ———
      La teoría económica actual [also with title *La teoría económica en retro-
      spección*]. Traducción por Mario Estartús. Revisión por José M.ª Arau.
      Barcelona: Luis Miracle, 1968. 908 p. 22 cm.
      See entry for first (1962) American edition.

835* Capodaglio, Giulio (b. 1910)
      Breve storia dell'economica. Vol. 1: *Lo svolgimento storico.* Vol. 2:
      Le fonti. Con la collaborazione di Mario Del Viscovo. Milano: A.
      Giuffrè, 1968 ("ristampa inalterata," 1973)–1970. 2 v. (287, 362 p.)
      22 cm.
      Other editions: 1934, 1937, 1941, 1945, 1958.

836* Denis, Henri
      Storia del pensiero economico. Traduzione di Franco Rodano. Milano:
      Il Saggiatore, 1968 (also dated 1973). 2 v. (432, 494 p.) 21 cm.
      See entry for first (1966) edition.

837* Fusfeld, Daniel Roland (b. 1922)
The Age of the Economist. New York: Morrow, 1968. xii, 209 p. 22 cm.
See entry for first (1966) edition.

838* Ghosh, Biswanath
Short History of Economic Thought. With a foreword by Alak Ghosh.
Calcutta: N. M. Raychowdhury, 1968 (also dated 1973). [x], 210 p.
22 cm.

839 Gill, Richard T. (b. 1927)
Den moderna nationalekonomin. Övers. av Ulrich Herz. Stockholm:
Aldus-Bonnier, 1968 (also dated 1974). 163 p.
Listed in *Index translationum.*
See entry for American (1967) edition.

840 ———
Evolução do pensamento econômico. [Translation by] António Labisa.
Lisboa: A. M. Teixeira (Filhos), 1968. 247 p.
Listed in *Index translationum.*
See entry for American (1967) edition.

841 *Histoire de la pensée économique: Notes.* 1e éd. Bruxelles: Les Presses
Universitaires de Bruxelles, 1968. 71 p. 27 cm.
In Library of Congress.

842 Lipiński, Edward (b. 1888)
Historia powoszechnej myśli ekonomicznej do roku 1870. Warszawa:
Państwowe Wydawnictwo Naukowe, 1968. 538 p. 22 cm.
In Library of Congress.
Other histories by Lipiński: 1950 (two entries).

843* Marshall, Howard Drake (b. 1924; professor at Vassar College), and
Marshall, Natalie J. (b. 1929; professor at State University College,
New Paltz, N.Y.)
The History of Economic Thought: A Book of Readings. New York:
Pitman Publishing Corporation, 1968. xvii, 408 p. 25 cm.
Another history by H. D. Marshall: 1967.

844 Marx, Karl (1818–83)
Theorien über den Mehrwert (4. Band des Kapitals). Red., Walter
Schulz. Frankfurt am Main: Europäische Verlagsanstalt, 1968. 3 v.
(497, 705, 663 p.) 22 cm.
In South Bend (Ind.) Public Library.
See entry for first (1905–10) edition.

845 Roll, Erich (b. 1907)
Tārīkh al-fikr al-iqtiṣādī. [Translation into Arabic by] Rāshid al-

157

Barrāwī. al-Qāhirah (Cairo): Dār al-Kātib al-'Arabī, 1968. 524 p.
Listed in *Index translationum*.
See entry for first (1938) British edition.

846* Scheifler Amézaga, Xavier
Historia del pensamiento económico. Tomo 1. Tercera edición. (4ª ed.,
1969). México: Editorial F. Trillas, 1968. xxiv, 371 p. 27.5 cm.
Earlier editions: 1964, 1967.

A standard history, influenced by French histories. This volume stopped with
Mill.

847* Schumpeter, Joseph Alois (1883–1950)
Storia dell'analisi economica. Traduzione di Paolo Sylos-Labini, et di
Luigi Occhionero. Edizione ridotta a cura di Claudio Napoleoni.
Torino: Paolo Boringhieri (Toso), 1968 (also dated 1971, 1972).
xv, 684 p. 19.5 cm.
See entry for first (1954) American edition.

This shortened version omitted sections less directly related to economic analysis.

848 Sekiguchi, Kineo (b. 1925)
Keizai gakusetsu no tenkai. 1968. 306 p. 22 cm.
In Library of Congress.
Published 1967 under title *Keizaigakushi kogi*.

849 Šoškić, Branislav
Razvoj ekonomske misli (Zaključno sa Marksom). Beograd: Institut za
Ekonomska Istraživanja, 1968. 308 p. 24 cm.
Other editions: 1965, 1970.
Another history by Šoškić: 1956.

850* Wendt, Siegfried (b. 1901)
Geschichte der Volkswirtschaftslehre. 2., neubearbeitete Auflage. Berlin:
Walter de Gruyter, 1968. 184 p. 15.5 cm.
First edition: 1961.

851* Behrens, H. H. (b. 1896)
De ontwikkeling in het economisch denken. Utrecht: Het Spectrum, 1969.
512 p. 18 cm.

852* Bhatnagar, Kalka Prasad (b. 1896), and Bahadur, Satish
A History of Economic Thought. 6th edition. Kanpur: Kishore Pub-
lishing House, 1969 (also dated 1970). 483 p. 22 cm.
Other editions: 1954, 1955, 1957, 1963, 1965, 1974.

853 Boardman, Fon Wyman (b. 1911)
Initiation aux doctrines économiques. [Translation by] Odile Valensi-

Lederman. Paris: Istra, 1969. 232 p.
Listed in *Index translationum* (1975).
American edition: 1966.

854* Cole, Charles Leland (b. 1927; professor at California State University, Long Beach)
   The Economic Fabric of Society. New York: Harcourt, Brace and World, 1969. x, 246 p. 21 cm.
"A brief history of economic thought covering writers from Aristotle to J. M. Keynes. An admirably readable essay designed for the non-economist" (*Journal of Economic Literature* 7 [1969]: 494).

855 Deguchi, Yuzo (b. 1909)
   Keizaigaku shi nyumon. Tokyo: Yuhikaku, 1969. 275 p. 19 cm.
   In Library of Congress.
   Another history by Deguchi: 1953.

856* Gill, Richard T. (b. 1927)
   Evolución de la economía moderna. Traducción al español por Manuel Ortuño. México: Unión Tipográfica Editorial Hispano Americana, 1969. 220 p. 17 cm.
   See entry for American (1967) edition.

857 ———
   Keizaigaku shi. [Translation by] Kubo Yoshikazu. Tokyo: Toyo Keizai Shimpo-sha, 1969. 167 p.
   Listed in *Index translationum.*
   See entry for American (1967) edition.

858* ———
   Il pensiero economico moderno. [Translation by] Guiliana De Vergottini. Bologna: Il Mulino, 1969 (also dated 1970). 159 p. 21.5 cm.
   See entry for American (1967) edition.

859 Haney, Lewis Henry (1882–1969)
   Ching chi ssü hsing shih. [Translation by] Ch'i-Fang Tsang. Taipei: Cheng-chung Publishing Co., 1969. 2 v. (848 p.) 21 cm.
   Listed in unpublished letter.
   See entry for first (1911) American edition.

860 Heilbroner, Robert Louis (b. 1919)
   Arthashastrace shilpakar. [Translation into Marathi by] P. L. Gadgil. Bombay: Majestic, 1969. 298 p.
   Listed in *Index translationum.*
   See entry for first (1953) American edition.

861* James, Émile (b. 1899)
Histoire sommaire de la pensée économique. 4ᵉ édition, revue et completée. Paris: Montchrestien, 1969. 453 p. 25 cm.
See entry for first (1955) edition.

862 Kazgan, Gülten
Iktisadî düşünce: veya, politik iktisadm evrimi. Istanbul: Istanbul Üniversitesi, Iktisat Fakültesi, 1969. xxiv, 523 p. 24 cm.
In Library of Congress.

863* Mai, Ludwig Hubert (b. 1898; professor at Saint Mary's University, San Antonio, Texas)
On the Formation of Political Economy. San Antonio, Tex.: Astra Center for Social Studies, St. Mary's University, 1969. 100 p. 20 cm.
Other histories by Mai: 1974, 1975.

864* Marx, Karl (1818–83)
Theories of Surplus Value (Volume IV of Capital). Translated from the German by Emile Burns (pt. 1), Renate Simpson (pt. 2), Jack Cohen and S. W. Ryazanskaya (pt. 3). Edited by S. W. Ryazanskaya and Richard Dixon. Printed in the U.S.S.R. Moscow: Progress Publishers, 1963, 1968, 1971. London: Lawrence and Wishart, 1969–72. 3 v. (506, 661, 637 p.) 22 cm.
See entry for first (1905–10) German edition.

865 Muto, Mitsuro (b. 1914)
Keizaigaku shi no tetsugaku. Tokyo: Sobun-sha, 1969. 284 p. 22 cm.
In Library of Congress.

866* Pearce, Alan
Great Ideas in Economics. London: Maxwell, 1969. xiii, 226 p. 23 cm.

867 Piettre, André (b. 1906)
Histoire économique, essai de synthèse, faits et idées. Paris: Éditions Cujas, 1969. 272 p. 18 cm.
In Library of Congress.
Other histories by Piettre: 1955, 1956, 1959.

868* Sachdeva, T. N., and Sachdeva, S. K.
History of Economic Thought: Full View at a Glance. 6th edition, radically revised and elaborately enlarged. New Delhi: Sudha Publications, 1969. 394 p. 22 cm.
Other editions: 1960, 1962, 1965, 1973.

869 Souza, J. C. Martins de
Economia política: históris dos fatos econômicos, conceitos fundamentais.

São Paulo: J. Bushatsky, 1969. 541 p. 21 cm.
In Library of Congress.

870* Srivastava, Shri Krishna
History of Economic Thought. Fully revised and enlarged third edition.
Delhi: S. Chand, 1969 (also dated 1970, 1974). 680 p. 23 cm.
Earlier editions: 1961, 1963 (in Hindi), 1965.

871 Stavenhagen, Gerhard
Geschichte der Wirtschaftstheorie. 4., durchgesehene und erweiterte
Auflage. Göttingen: Vandenhoeck und Ruprecht, 1969. 710 p. 24 cm.
In University of Chicago Library.
See entry for first (1951) edition.

872* Traa, Pieter Cornelis van (professor at Leiden)
Geschiedenis van de economie: evoluties in een gedachtenwereld. Amster-
dam: J. H. de Bussy, 1969. vii, 198 p. 21 cm.
Schematic treatment of history at end of volume.

873* Blaug, Mark (b. 1927)
Storia e critica della teoria economica. Torino: Boringhieri, 1970 (also
dated 1973). 883 p. 24 cm.
See entry for first (1962) American edition.

874 Bourcier de Carbon, Luc (b. 1913; professor at Paris)
Notes sur l'histoire de la pensée et des doctrines économiques. Licence ès
sciences économiques. 4e année, 1969–1970. Paris: Les Cours de Droit,
1970. 581 p. 24 cm.
In Library of Congress.
Another history by Bourcier de Carbon: 1971–72.

875* Claeys, R. H. (professor at Antwerp)
*Overzicht van de evolutie de ekonomische theorieën van der oudheid
tot heden.* Gent-Leuven: E. Story-Scientia, 1970. ix, 417 p. 24 cm.
From the Greeks to post-Keynesian economics.

876 Denis, Henri
Historia del pensamiento económico. [Translation by] Nuria Bozzo &
Antonio Aponte. Barcelona: Ariel, 1970. 615 p.
Listed in *Index translationum.*
See entry for first (1966) French edition.

877* Fusfeld, Daniel Roland (b. 1922)
La época del economista: el desarrollo del pensamiento económico moderno.
Traductor: Eduardo Suárez. México: Fondo de Cultura Económica,
1970. 253 p. 21 cm.

See entry for first (1966) American edition.

878 ———

Storia del pensiero economico moderno. Traduzione di Vittorio Libera. Milano: A. Mondadori, 1970. 243 p. 18.5 cm.
Listed in *Bibliografia nazionale italiana.*
See entry for first (1966) American edition.

879 Grigorov, Kiril Iordanov
Istoriia na ikonomicheskite ucheniia. Sophiia: Nauk i Iskustvo, 1970 (also in 1963?). 676 p. 23 cm.
In Library of Congress.

880* Hajela, T. N.
History of Economic Thought. 2d, revised edition. Agra: Shiva Lal Agarwala, 1970. 563 p. 25 cm.
Other editions: 1967, 1972, 1973.

881 Heilbroner, Robert Louis (b. 1919)
Arthanitika darshanera itibrtta. [Translation into Bengali by] Mumtazuddin Ahmed. Dacca: Chayanika Prokashani, 1970. 448 p. 22 cm.
In Library of Congress.
See entry for first (1953) American edition.

882 ———

Keizai shiso no nagare. [Translation by] Hamada Kiyofu. Tokyo: Hara Shobo, 1970. 319 p.
Listed in *Index translationum.*
See entry for first (1953) American edition.

883 Ivanciu, Nicolae
Istoria doctrinelor economice. Bucureşti: Editura Didactică şi Pedagogică, 1970. 567 p. 24 cm.
In Library of Congress.

884 James, Émile (b. 1899)
História sumaria do pensamento económico. Vol. 1. Coimbra, 1970.
Listed in *Livraria Portugal.*
See entry for first (1955) French edition.

885* Kuhn, William Ernest (b. 1922)
The Evolution of Economic Thought. 2d edition. Cincinnati: Southwestern Publishing Company, 1970. x, 500 p. 24 cm.
First edition: 1963.

886 Kumagai, Hisao (b. 1914)

"Kindai keizaigaku shi" [in vol. 3 of his] *Kindai keizaigaku.* Tokyo: Yuhikaku, 1970. 302 p. 18 cm.
In Library of Congress.
Emphasized the period since 1871.

887 Lajugie, Joseph (b. 1914)
Al-Madhâheb al-iqtisadyiat. [Translation by] Mamdû'h 'Hiqqi. Beyrouth (Lebanon): Dâr 'Ueidât, 1970. 160 p.
Listed in *Index translationum.*
See entry for first (1949) French edition.

888 Okada, Jun'ichi (b. 1921)
Keizai shiso shi. Tokyo: Keizai Shinshi-sha, 1970. 308 p. 19 cm.
In Library of Congress.

889 Okochi, Kazuo (b. 1905)
Keizaigaku shi nyumon. Tokyo: Aomori Shoin Shin-sha, 1970. 301 p. 19 cm.
In Library of Congress.
Another history by Okochi: 1950–58.

890* Oser, Jacob (b. 1915)
The Evolution of Economic Thought. 2d edition. New York: Harcourt, Brace & World, 1970. xiii, 458 p. 24 cm.
Other editions: 1963, 1975.
"Thoroughly revised, expanded, and brought up to date . . . . Greater emphasis on the continuity of economic thought, the interrelationship among the different schools, and on the carryover into current thinking of some older ideas."

891 Piettre, André (b. 1906)
Histoire de la pensée économique et analyse des théories contemporaines. 5e éd., rev. et mise à jour. Paris: Dalloz, 1970. 562 p. 18 cm.
In Harvard University Library.
See entry for first (1959) edition.

892* Rima, Ingrid Hahne (b. 1925), comp.
Readings in the History of Economic Theory. New York: Holt, Rinehart and Winston, 1970. viii, 303 p. 26 cm.
Other histories by Rima: 1967.

893 Roll, Erich (b. 1907)
Keizai gakusetsu shi. [Translation by] Mikio Sumitani. Tokyo: Yuhi-kaku, 1970. 2 v.
Listed in *Index translationum.*
See entry for first (1938) English edition.

894   Schumpeter, Joseph Alois (1883–1950)
Teoria econômica, de Marx a Keynes. Trad. de Ruy Jungman. Rio de
Janeiro: Zahar, 1970. 290 p. 21 cm.
Listed in *Bibliografia brasileira mensal.*
See entry for first (1951) American edition.

895*   Šoškić, Branislav
Razvoj ekonomske misli. 3., revidirano izdanje. Beograd: Institut za
Ekonomska Istraživanja, 1970 (also dated 1974). viii, 302 p. 24 cm.
Earlier editions: 1965, 1968.
Another history by Šoškić: 1956.

896   Tokinaga, Fukashi (b. 1922)
Keizaigaku shi. Tokyo: Hosei Daigaku, 1970. 468 p. 22 cm.
In Library of Congress.
Other editions: 1962–68, 1971.

897   Uchida, Yoshihiko (b. 1913; dean at Senshu University)
Keizaigaku shi. Tokyo: Chikuma Shobo, 1970. 435 p. 23 cm.
In Library of Congress.
Another history by Uchida et al.: 1964.

898*   Afanas'ev, Vladilen Sergeevich
Etapy razvitiia burzhuaznoĭ politicheskoĭ ekonomii. Moskva: Mysl', 1971.
367 p. 21 cm.

899*   Anikin, Andreĭ Vladimirovich (professor at Moscow)
IUnost' nauki: zhizn' i ideĭ myslitelei-ekonomistov do Marksa. Moskva:
Izd-va Politicheskoĭ Literatury, 1971 (also deluxe reprint, 1975). 382 p.
21 cm.
Translation: German, 1974.
From Aristotle to Robert Owen.

900   Barber, William Joseph (b. 1925)
De ekonomiska idéernas historia. Övers. av Ulrich Hertz. Stockholm:
Aldus/Bonnier, 1971. 266 p.
Listed in *Index translationum.*
See entry for first (1967) British edition.

901*   ———
Historia del pensamiento económico. Traducción por Carlos Solchaga y
Gloria Barba Bernabeu. Madrid: Alianza, 1971 (also dated 1974).
290 p. 13 cm.
See entry for first (1967) British edition.

902*   ———
Storia del pensiero economico. Traduzione dall' inglese di Enrico Facchini.

Milano: Feltrinelli, 1971 (also dated 1975). 263 p. 18 cm.
See entry for first (1967) British edition.

903 ——————

Uma história do pensamento econômico. Trad. de Sérgio Goes de Paula.
Rio de Janeiro: Zahar, 1971. 250 p. 22 cm.
Listed in *Bibliografia brasileira mensal.*
See entry for first (1967) British edition.

904* Blagojević, Obren (professor at Niš)
Ekonomske doktrine. Beograd: Savremena Administracija, 1971. xxx,
488 p. 24 cm.

905* Blaug, Mark (b. 1927)
Systematische Theoriegeschichte der Ökonomie. Aus dem Amerikanischen
übersetzt von Johannes Hengstenberg. München: Nymphenburger
Verlagshandlung, 1971–75. 3 v. (268, 268, 358 p.) 21 cm. Vol. 4 not
published?
See entry for first (1962) American edition.

906* Bourcier de Carbon, Luc (b. 1913)
Essai sur l'histoire de la pensée et des doctrines économiques. Vol. 1:
*De Montchrétien à Karl Marx, trois thèmes centraux: l'état, l'individu,
la société.* Vol. 2: *Aux sources du scientisme et de l'humanisme économiques modernes.* Paris: Montchrestien, 1971–72. 2 v. (427, 534 p.)
25 cm.
Another history by Bourcier de Carbon: 1970.

907* Denis, Henri
Histoire de la pensée économique. 3e édition revue. Paris: Presses Uni-
versitaires de France, 1971. 796 p. 18 cm.
See entry for first (1966) edition.

908* Fanfani, Amintore (b. 1908)
Storia delle dottrine economiche. Quinta edizione. Milano: Principato
Editore, 1971. xix, 577 p. 21.5 cm.
See entry for first (1938) edition.

909* Heilbroner, Robert Louis (b. 1919)
Les Grands économistes. [Translation by] Pierre Antonmattei. Paris:
Éditions du Seuil, 1971 (also dated 1974). 335 p. 20.5 cm.
See entry for first (1953) American edition.

910 Heimann, Eduard (1889–1967)
História das doutrinas econômicas. Trad. de Waltensir Dutra. 2ª ed.
Rio de Janeiro: Zahar, 1971. 232 p. 22 cm.

Listed in *Bibliografia brasileira mensal.*
See entry for first (1945) American edition.

911   Lajugie, Joseph (b. 1914)
Las doctrinas económicas. [Translation by] J. García-Bosch. Barcelona: Oikos-tau, 1971. 124 p.
Listed in *Index translationum.*
See entry for first (1949) French edition.

912   ———
Ekonomik doktrinler. [Translation by] Samih Tiryakioğlu. Istanbul: Varlik Yayinevi, 1971. 190 p.
Listed in *Index translationum.*
See entry for first (1949) French edition.

913   Lekachman, Robert (b. 1920)
Storia del pensiero economico. Trad. Luigi Occhionero. Milano: Franco Angeli, 1971. 415 p. 22 cm.
Listed in *Bibliografia nazionale italiana.*
See entry for first (1959) American edition.

914*   Louis, Paul P. (b. 1918; professor at Dayton)
Readings in the History of Economic Thought. Berkeley, Calif.: McCutchan Publishing Corporation, 1971. v, 248 p. 23 cm. Title changed to *Great Economists of the World* and issued in 1973 by Orient House Publications, Centerville, Ohio.

915*   Marx, Karl (1818–83)
Teorie sul plusvalore (Libro quatro del Capitale). Traduzione e prefazione di Giorgio Giorgetti. Roma: Editori Riuniti, 1971–73. 3 v. (629 p., 646 p.; vol. 3 had not been published as of 1976). 22 cm.
See entry for first (1905–10) German edition.

916   Mitchell, Wesley Clair (1874–1948)
Keizai riron no shokeitai. [Translation by] Kasugai Kaoru. Tokyo: Bungado Ginko Kenkyu-sha, 1971. 382 p.
Listed in *Index translationum.*
American editions: 1935, 1949, 1967–69.

917   Miyagawa, Takeo (b. 1909)
Keizaigaku keisei e no sekkin. Kyoto: Keibun-sha, 1971. 363 p. 22 cm.
In Library of Congress.

918   Myrdal, Gunnar (b. 1898)
To politiko stihio stēn ikonomikē theōria. [Translation by] K. M. Sofoulis. Athēnai: Papazēssēs, 1971. 336 p.

Listed in *Index translationum*.
See entry for first (1930) Swedish edition.

919 ———

Vetenskap och politik i nationalekonomin. Ny omarb. uppl. . . . Återövers.
av Kerstin Lundgren . . . av den engelska utgåvan 1953. Stockholm:
Rabén & Sjögren (Tema); Helsingfors: Schild, 1971 (postdated 1972).
334 p.
Listed in *Svensk bokförteckning*.
See entry for first (1930) Swedish edition.

920* Recktenwald, Horst Claus (b. 1920), ed.
Geschichte der politischen Ökonomie: eine Einführung in Lebensbildern.
Mit einer Abhandlung politische Ökonomie in Gegenwart und Zukunft
und 23 Bildtafeln. Stuttgart: Kröner, 1971. 640 p. 18 cm.
Earlier edition: 1965. Translation: British, 1973.

921 Roll, Erich (b. 1907)
História das doutrinas econômicas. Tr. Cid Silveira. 3ª ed. São Paulo:
National, 1971. xxv, 539 p.
Listed in *Libros novos*.
See entry for first (1938) British edition.

922 Roshan, Ali Mangi
History of Economic Thought. Hyderabad (Pakistan): Naseem Book
Depot, 1971. 200 p. 22 cm.
In Library of Congress.

923* Schachtschabel, Hans Georg (b. 1914; professor at Mannheim)
Geschichte der volkswirtschaftlichen Lehrmeinungen. Stuttgart: W. Kohlhammer, 1971; Düsseldorf: L. Schwann, 1971. 271 p. 21 cm.
Personenregister contains just over 800 authors. *Sachregister* lists just under 800
subjects.

924* Schumpeter, Joseph Alois (1883–1950)
*Esquisse d'une histoire de la science économique, des origines jusqu'au
début de XXᵉ siècle.* Traduit par G. H. Bousquet. Deuxième édition.
Paris: Dalloz, 1971 (also dated 1972). 234 p. 21 cm.
See entry for first (1914) German edition.

925* ———

Historia del análisis económico. Traducción castellana de Manuel Sacristán.
Barcelona: Ediciones Ariel, 1971. 1371 p. 23 cm.
See entry for first (1954) American edition.
Professor Jorge Pasqual added a "Bibliographia traducida al castellano" of books
cited by Schumpeter.

926* ———

Historia del análisis económico: editada de la versión manuscrita por Elizabeth Boody Schumpeter. Traducción de Lucas Mantilla. Revisión de Carlos Villegas. México: Fondo de Cultura Económica, 1971. 810 p. 24 cm.

See entry for first (1954) American edition.

927 Spengler, Joseph John (b. 1902), and Allen, William R. (b. 1924), eds.
El pensamiento económico de Aritóteles a Marshall. Madrid: Technos, 1971. 802 p.
Listed in *Libros en venta.*
American edition: 1960.

928* Spiegel, Henry William (b. 1911), ed.
The Growth of Economic Thought. Englewood Cliffs, N.J.: Prentice-Hall, 1971. xiv, 816 p. 25 cm.
Other histories by Spiegel: 1952, 1964.

From Aristotle to Econometrics. In his review, Kennedy thought its approach "cultural rather than technical" and that its strongest appeal as a text lay in its "lucidity of exposition" (*Journal of Economic Literature* 10 [1972]: 70). Blaug called this history "admirably suited to serious undergraduate teaching" (*Economica,* new ser. 39 [1972]: 122).

929 Sugihara, Shiro (b. 1920), ed.
Keizaigaku keisei shi. Kyoto: Mineruva, 1971. 306 p. 22 cm.
In Library of Congress.

930 Tan, Tjin-kie, and Kalish, Richard J. (b. 1932)
From Mercantilists to Marshall: An Introduction to the Development of Economic Thought. Singapore: University Education Press, 1971. 68 p. 22 cm.
In Indiana University Library.

931 Tokinaga, Fukashi (b. 1922)
Keizaigaku shi. Tokyo: Hosei Daigaku, 1971. 475, 30 p. 22 cm.
In Library of Congress.
Earlier editions: 1962–68, 1970.

932 Tsunoyama, Sakae (b. 1921)
Seiyo keizai shi. Tokyo: Gakubun-sha, 1971. 175 p. 22 cm.
In Library of Congress.

933* Burtt, Everett Johnson (b. 1914; professor at Boston University)
Social Perspectives in the History of Economic Theory. New York: St. Martin's Press, 1972. 297 p. 24 cm.

"Designed to introduce the student of economics and economic theory to the leading economists from the late seventeenth century to the 1930s" (Preface).

934* Cristóbal, Ramiro (b. 1942)
Nombres de la historia económica. Madrid: Las Ediciones de el Espejo, 1972. 319 p. 19 cm.
First published under the title "Galería de economistas" in the *Gaceta del europeo,* October 1970 to December 1971.
It contains short sketches of the lives and original works of 47 economists, Bodin to Samuelson. The final chapter added 9 Spanish economists, Jovellanos to Mallada.

935 Denis, Henri
Cours d'histoire de la pensée économique. Licence 3e année, 1971–1972. [Multigraphié]. Paris: Les Cours de Droit, 1972. 220 p. 25 cm.
Listed in "Biblio."
Earlier edition: 1963.
Other histories by Denis: 1966, 1967.

936* Fusfeld, Daniel Roland (b. 1922)
The Age of the Economist. Revised edition. Glenview, Ill.: Scott, Foresman, 1972. 199 p. 23 cm.
See entry for first (1966) edition.

937* Hajela, T. N.
History of Economic Thought. 3d, revised edition. Agra: Shiva Lal Agarwala, 1972. 551 p. 25 cm.
Other editions: 1967, 1970, 1973.

938 Heilbroner, Robert Louis (b. 1919)
Os grandes economistas. Lisboa, 1972.
Listed in *Livraria Portugal.*
See entry for first (1953) American edition.

939 ———
Vida y doctrina de los grandes economistas. [Translation by] Armando Lázaro Ros. 2ª. ed. Madrid: Aguilar, 1972. 472 p.
Listed in *Index translationum.*
See entry for first (1953) American edition.

940* ———
The Worldly Philosophers: The Lives, Times, and Ideas of the Great Economic Thinkers. 4th edition, completely revised for the 1970s. New York: Simon & Schuster, 1972. 347 p. 22 cm.
See entry for first (1953) edition.

941* Herrerías Tellería, Armando (b. 1918; professor at Universidad Nacional Autónoma de México)

Fundamentos para la historia del pensamiento económico. México: Editorial Limusa-Wiley, 1972 (also dated 1975). 418 p. 23 cm.
Contained an unusual chronological chart and perhaps the longest analytical index of any history.

942   Oguro, Sawako (b. 1930)
      Keizaigaku no riron to rekishi. Tokyo: Aoki Shoten, 1972. 221 p. 19 cm.
      In Library of Congress.

943   Ono, Shinzo (b. 1900)
      Keizaigakushi. Vol. 1. Tokyo: Chikura Shobo, 1972. vi, 22, 282, 31 p.
      22 cm.
      In Library of Congress.
      Another history by Ono: 1935.

944* Reuel', Abram Lazarevich
      Istoriia ekonomicheskikh uchenii. Moskva: Vyšoaia Skola, 1972. 422 p.
      22 cm.

945* Rima, Ingrid Hahne (b. 1925)
      Development of Economic Analysis. Revised edition. Homewood, Ill.:
      Richard D. Irwin, 1972. xiv, 488 p. 24 cm.
      First edition: 1967.
      Another history by Rima: 1970.

946   Sabolović, Dušan (professor at Zagreb)
      Historija političke ekonomije. Zagreb: Sveuciliste, "Informator," 1972.
      xi, 142, 2 p. 24 cm.
      In Library of Congress.

947* Vandewalle, Gaston (professor at Ghent)
      Geschiedenis van het ekonomisch denken. Gent: Gents Akademisch
      Kooperatief, 1972. 2 v. (550 p.) 27 cm.
From Aquinas to Keynes, with chapters on the Scandinavian and Dutch wings of the Marginal Utility School.

948   Barber, William Joseph (b. 1925)
      Keizai shisoshi nyumon. [Translation by] Inage Mitsuharu & Onishi
      Takaaki. Tokyo: Shiseido, 1973. 349 p.
      Listed in *Index translationum.*
      See entry for first (1967) British edition.

949* Cedras, Jacques (professor at Rouen)
      Histoire de la pensée économique, des origines à la révolution marginaliste.
      Paris: Dalloz, 1973. 177 p. 24 cm.
A French university manual.

950   Ch'ien, Kung-po
      Ching chi k'o hsüeh fa chan shih. Taipei, 1973. 2, 6, 234 p. 22 cm.
      In Library of Congress.

951   Denis, Henri
      Ekonomik doktrinler. [Translation by] Attila Tokatli. Istanbul: Ercrivan
      Matbaasi, 1973–74. 2 v.
      Listed in *Index translationum.*
      See entry for first (1966) French edition.

952* Finkelstein, Joseph (b. 1926), and Thimm, Alfred L.
      *Economists and Society: The Development of Economic Thought from
      Aquinas to Keynes.* New York: Harper & Row, 1973. xvi, 366 p.
      25 cm.
The authors, in their preface, state that the "attempt to integrate these economic,
social, and intellectual developments in this brief review makes this volume, we
believe, a modest original endeavor."

953* Gide, Paul Henri Charles (1847–1932), and Rist, Charles (1874–1955)
      *Historia de las doctrinas económicas desde los fisiocratas hasta nuestros
      días.* Vertida al español de C. Martinez Peñalver. Cuarta edición.
      Madrid: Instituto Editorial Reus, 1973. xxiv, 760 p.
      See entry for first (1909) French edition.

954   Hajela, T. N.
      History of Economic Thought. Fourth edition. Agra: Shiva Lal Agar-
      wala, 1973.
      Listed in *Indian Books in Print.*
      Earlier editions: 1967, 1970, 1972.

955   Hirao, Satoshi (b. 1926)
      Keizaigaku shi. Tokyo: Sugiyama Shoten, 1973. 271 p. 22 cm.
      In Library of Congress.

956* Knight, Frank Hyneman (1885–1972; professor at Chicago)
      "Economic History" [2:44–61 in] *Dictionary of the History of Ideas:
      Studies of Selected Pivotal Ideas.* Philip P. Wiener, editor in chief.
      New York: Charles Scribner's Sons, 1973. 28.5 cm.
A discerning compact history by a professor who had often taught the subject.

957   Lekachman, Robert (b. 1920)
      História das idéias econômicas. [Translation by] Gabriele Ilse Leib. Rio
      de Janeiro: Bloch, 1973. 417 p.
      Listed in *Index translationum.*
      See entry for first (1959) American edition.

958 Piettre, André (b. 1906)
Histoire de la pensée économique et analyse des théories contemporaines.
6ᵉ éd. Paris: Dalloz, 1973. 561 p. 18 cm.
In Library of Congress.
See entry for first (1959) edition.

959* Recktenwald, Horst Claus (b. 1920), ed.
Political Economy: A Historical Perspective. London: Collier-Macmillan,
1973. xx, 444 p. 23.5 cm.
German editions: 1965, 1971.

960* Roll, Erich (b. 1907)
A History of Economic Thought. 4th edition, revised and enlarged.
London: Faber and Faber, 1973 (also dated 1974). 626 p. 23 cm.
See entry for first (1938) edition.
In the opinion of Deane, the rewritten and updated eleventh chapter and the
substantially new twelfth chapter supply new material that "is as clear, thoughtful
and lively as the rest of the book, but is more a personal and less a scholar's inter-
pretation of the issues" (*Economic Journal* 83 [1973]: 1356).

961* Sachdeva, T. N., and Sachdeva, S. K.
History of Economic Thought: Full View at a Glance. 7th edition,
radically revised and elaborately enlarged. New Delhi: Sudha Publications, 1973. 430 p. 22 cm.
Earlier editions: 1960, 1962, 1965, 1969.

962* Salin, Edgar (b. 1892)
L'economia politica: storia delle idee da Platone ai giorni nostri. A cura
di Francesca Duchini. Traduzione di Herta Ament. Milano: Vita e
Pensiero, 1973. xii, 276 p. 21 cm.
See entry for first (1923) German edition.

963 Tada, Akira (b. 1915; professor at Chiba University)
Keizaigaku shi. 1973. 185 p. 27 cm.
In Library of Congress.

964* Villey, Daniel (1911–68), and Nême, Colette
Petite histoire des grandes doctrines économiques. Nouvelle édition, revue
et augmentée. Paris: Éditions M.-Th. Génin, Librairies Techniques,
1973. 420 p. 18 cm.
See entry for first (1944) edition.
Another history by Villey: 1967.
In his review, Courthéoux called this history "une oeuvre de synthèse dans un
domaine où les tentations de l'érudition pesante et besogneuse paralyseraient
bien des esprits" (*Revue d'histoire économique et sociale* 51 [1973]: 600).

965* Wolff, Jacques (b. 1928; professor at Paris)
Les Grandes oeuvres économiques. Vol. 1: *De Xénophon à Adam Smith.*
Paris: Éditions Cujas, 1973. 22 cm.

966   Żurawicki, Seweryn (professor at Warsaw)
Historia myśli ekonomicznej. Wrocław: Wysza Szkoła Ekonomiczna we
Wrocławiu, 1973. 187 p.
Listed in *International Bibliography of Economics.*
Another history by Żurawicki: 1955–57.

967   Aimi, Shiro (b. 1918)
Keizaigaku shi kogian. Tokyo: Sanwa Shobo, 1974. 285 p. 21 cm.
In Library of Congress.

968* Anikin, Andreĭ Vladimirovich
Ökonomen aus drei Jahrhunderten. Übersetzer: Günter Wermusch.
Frankfurt am Main: Verlag Marxistische Blätter GmbH, 1974. 388 p.
22 cm.
See entry for Russian (1971) edition.

969* Barrère, Alain (b. 1910)
Histoire de la pensée économique et analyse contemporaine. Tome 1: *Les
Grands systèmes d'économie politique.* Tome 2: *L'Analyse économique
contemporaine.* Cinquième édition. [Reproduced from typescript].
Paris: Les Cours de Droit, 1974. 647, xxx; 698, xxxiii p. 24 cm.
First edition: 1957–58.

970* Beauclair, Geraldo (professor at Universidade Federale Fluminense)
Introdução ao estudo do pensamento econômico: uma abordagem histórica.
Rio de Janeiro: Editora Americana, 1974. xii, 98 p. 21 cm.
A university manual.

971* Bhatnagar, Kalka Prasad (b. 1896); Bahadur, Satish; and Mudgal, B. S.
A History of Economic Thought. 8th edition reprint. Kanpur: Kishore
Publishing House, 1974. 651 p. 22 cm.
Earlier editions: 1954, 1955, 1957, 1963, 1965, 1969.

972* Bladen, Vincent Wheeler (b. 1900; professor at Toronto)
*From Adam Smith to Maynard Keynes: The Heritage of Political Econ-
omy.* Toronto: University of Toronto Press, 1974. xiii, 520 p. 23.5 cm.
This book is included even though the Foreword said at its start. "This is not
a history of political economy." In his review, Coats said that it was a "highly
personal" and "mature distillation of forty years teaching" which contained
"many learned, wise, and illuminating remarks" (*Kyklos* 29 [1976]: 551–53).
    It was also reviewed by Bodkin (*Canadian Journal of Economics* 9 [1976]:
192–94), Cramer (*History of Political Economy* 8 [1976]: 435), Deane (*Eco-*

nomic Journal 85 [1975]: 719), Kuhn (*Journal of Economic Literature* 14 [1976]: 893–94), and McIvor (*Canadian Historical Review* 57 [1976]: 176–77).

973*   Bowden, Elbert V. (b. 1924; professor at State University of New York, Fredonia)
    Economics Through the Looking Glass. San Francisco: Canfield Press, 1974. viii, 163, 10 p. 20.5 cm.
A textbook "for everybody . . . not just the scholarly few," it is written to achieve a "frictionless communication of economic ideas" (*Journal of Economic Literature* 12 [1974]: 1385).
Influenced by Heilbroner's *The Worldly Philosophers.*

974*   Denis, Henri
    Histoire de la pensée économique. 4ᵉ édition. Paris: Presses Universitaires de France, 1974. 774 p. 18 cm.
    See entry for first (1966) edition.

975*   García de Quevedo de la Barrera, José
    Introducción a la historia del pensamiento económico. Prólogo de Andrés Fernández Díaz. Jerez de la Frontera (Spain): Gráficas del Exportador, 1974. 200 p. 22 cm.

976*   James, Émile (b. 1899)
    Historia del pensamiento económico. Traducción del francés por Ricardo Defarges Ibañez. Prólogo de José Antonio Piera Labra. Madrid: Aguilar, 1974. xxxv, 462 p. 22 cm.
    See entry for first (1955) French edition.

977*   Lajugie, Joseph (b. 1914)
    Storia delle dottrine economiche. Traduzione di Dionisia Cazzaniga Francesetti. Messina-Firenze: G. d'Anna, 1974. 192 p. 20.5 cm.
    See entry for first (1949) French edition.

978   Mai, Ludwig Hubert (b. 1898)
    A Primer on Development of Economic Thought. San Antonio, Tex.: Institute of International and Public Affairs, St. Mary's University, 1974. ii, 160 p. 23 cm.
    In Library of Congress.
    Other histories by Mai: 1969, 1975.

979*   Marx, Karl (1818–83)
    Storia delle teorie economiche: libro quarto del "Capitale." Introduzione di Lucio Coletti. Traduzione di Lidia Locatelli. 3 v. (366, 572, 478 p.) Roma: Newton Compton Editori, 1974.
    See entry for first (1905–10) German edition.

980* ———

Teorías de la plusvalía. Madrid: Talleres Gráficos Montaña, 1974. 2 v.
(564, 413 p.) 20.5 cm.
See entry for first (1905–10) German edition.

981 ———

Theories sur la plus-value: livre IV du "Capital." [Translation by] Gilbert
Badia et al. Paris: Éditions Sociales, 1974.
Listed in Index translationum.
See entry for first (1905–10) German edition.

982* Muthukrishnan, K.; Raghavan, P. V.; and Ponnappan, C.
History of Economic Thought. Allahabad: Chaitanya Publishing House,
1974. viii, 292 p. 22 cm.
Covers "the B.A. Degree syllabus of the Madras and other Indian Universities.
Written by members of the Department of Economics at the University of
Madras." Final chapter is on "Indian Economic Thought."

983* Astudillo y Ursúa, Pedro (professor at Universidad Autónoma de México)
Lecciones de historia del pensamiento económico. Textos universitarios.
México: U.N.A.M., 1975. 261 p. 23 cm.

984 Denis, Henri
Geschichte der Wirtschaftstheorien. Rheinfelden: Schäuble, 1975. 2 v.
23 cm.
Listed in Index translationum.
See entry for first (1966) French edition.

985* Ekelund, Robert B. (professor at Texas A & M University), and Hebert,
Robert F. (b. 1943; professor at Auburn University)
A History of Economic Theory and Method. New York: McGraw-Hill
Book Company, 1975. xiii, 507 p. 24 cm.
Schwartz, in his review, called it "a useful primer" that engaged in "retrospective
analytics" (History of Economic Thought Newsletter, no. 15 [Autumn 1975],
pp. 25–26). Murdock estimated that "ancient, medieval, mercantilist, Physiocratic, Smithian, Classical, and all nineteenth-century heterodox thought, including Marxist, plus all developments since 1940 receive less than 80 percent of the
space allotted to the 1870–1940 period" (History of Political Economy 9 [1977]:
302). Also reviewed by Coats (Kyklos 29 [1976]: 552–53) and by Eagly (Journal
of Economic History 36 [1976]: 463–64).

986* Fabiunke, Günter
Geschichte der bürgerlichen politischen Ökonomie. Anschauungsmaterial
für Lehre und Studium. Berlin (East): Verlag Die Wirtschaft, 1975.
296 p. 22 cm.
Prepared as an aid in teaching the economics of "Marxismus-Leninismus." It

began with Aristotle and ended with Stackelberg. Part of the explanation was done with 154 red, white, and black diagrams.

987   Fusfeld, Daniel Roland (b. 1922)
      Geschichte und Aktualität ökonomischer Theorien: vom Merkantilismus bis zur Gegenwart. Übers. von Rudolf Wedekind. Frankfurt (Main): Campus Verlag, 1975. 220 p. 21 cm.
      Listed in *Index translationum.*
      See entry for first (1966) American edition.

988*   Ganesan, Arumugam (b. 1923; professor at A.V.V.M. Sri Pushpam College)
      A Concise History of Economic Thought. Thanjavur, India: Gemeni Printing House, 1975. viii, 256 p. 22 cm.

The preface states that the book was designed "mainly to meet the requirements of the undergraduate students of the Madras University." This history ends with a part titled "Indian Economic Thought."

989*   Gómez Granillo, Moisés
      Breve historia de las doctrinas económicas. Quinta edición, corregida y aumentada. México: Editorial Esfinge, 1975. 325 p. 20.5 cm.
      First edition: 1967.

990*   Heilbroner, Robert Louis (b. 1919)
      I grandi economisti (da Smith a Schumpeter). Edizione italiana a cura di Oscar Nuccio. Roma: Edizioni Bizzarri, 1975. 374 p. 23 cm.
      See entry for first (1953) American edition.

991   Kumagai, Jiro
      Keizaigaku hito to gakusetsu. Tokyo: Fujishobo, 1975. 536 p. 21.5 cm.
      In Library of Congress.

Covered 30 writers, arranged by date of birth, from Quesnay (1694) to Solow (1924)—the last 18 born after 1900.

992   Lu, Yu-chang
      Tzu ch'an chieh chi cheng chih ching chi hsüeh shih. Peking: Jen-min Chu Pan She, 1975. 314 p. 20.5 cm.
      In Library of Congress.

993*   Mai, Ludwig Hubert (b. 1898)
      Men and Ideas in Economics: A Dictionary of World Economists Past and Present. Totowa, N.J.: Littlefield, Adams & Co., 1975. xii, 270 p.
      Other histories by Mai: 1969, 1974.

In his review, Gordon said that the author displayed "admirable catholicity" in his selection of the 700 economists "and others" for whom he supplied brief biographies and assessments of their work (*History of Political Economy* 10 [1978]: 686).

994 Marx, Karl (1818–83)
Sheng yü chia chih li lun. Peking: People's Publisher, 1975. 3 v. in 5.
22 cm.
In Library of Congress.
See entry for first (1905–10) German edition.

995 Nakamura, Ken'ichiro
Keizaigakushi. Tokyo: Gakubunsha, 1975. 281 p. 21.5 cm.
In Library of Congress.

996* Oser, Jacob (b. 1915), and Blanchfield, William C.
The Evolution of Economic Thought. 3d edition. New York: Harcourt
Brace, Jovanovich, 1975. xi, 512 p. 24 cm.
Earlier editions: 1963, 1970.

997* Roll, Erich (b. 1907)
Historia de las doctrinas económicas. [Traducción de Florentino M.
Torner]. [Segunda edición en español]. México: Fondo de Cultura
Económica, 1975. 613 p. 21 cm.
See entry for first (1938) British edition.

998* Routh, Gerald Guy Cumming (b. 1916; reader in Economics at the University of Sussex)
The Origin of Economic Ideas. London: Macmillan Press, 1975; also
White Plains, N.Y.: International Arts and Sciences Press, 1975. x,
321 p. 22 cm.
In his review, Tutton wrote, "This book is a polemic against 'orthodox' economic
theory in the form of a history of economic thought," adding that from "Ricardo
onwards the history of orthodox economic thought is seen as one long disaster"
(*Economic Journal* 86 [1976]: 431–32). Collard called it a "neo-institutionalist
attack on formalism" and listed the principal sections; "The Preposterous
Origins" (Scholastics to Smith), "From Propaganda to Dogma" (Classics),
"Tiny Increments of Economic Change" (neo-Classics), and "The Keynesian
Restoration" (Keynes), in order to show that "the book is at bottom a fairly
straight chronological history of economic thought" (*History of Economic
Thought Newsletter,* no. 16 [Spring 1976], p. 13). The reviewer in the *Econo-
mist* said that it was not "a conventional history of economic thought" and
characterized it as a "rather stale radicalism" (vol. 256 [6 September 1975],
pp. 120–21). On the other hand, Capouya called it "a lively history and critique"
(*Nation,* 15 November 1975, p. 505), and Mitchell admired Routh's "light
touch and lively perception" (*Annals of the American Academy of Political and
Social Science* 428 [November 1976]: 181). It was also reviewed by Miller
(*History of Political Economy* 9 [1977]: 595).

Appendix A
Catalog of Short Histories
Found in General Treatises of Economics
from 1840 to 1975

This Catalog resulted from an examination of more than one thousand general treatises on economics in the University of Kansas Library. Consequently, it may be regarded as having been obtained from a large sample taken from a population of general treatises that itself may be not much more than a few times the size of the sample. The examination revealed that about one out of every five general treatises of economics has contained a short history of the subject.

1840 Potter, Alonzo. "History of Political Economy," pp. 31–41 in his *Political Economy*. New York.

1841 List, Friedrich. "Die Systeme," pp. 451–94 in his *Das nationale System der politischen Oekonomie*. Stuttgart und Tübingen.

1842 Riedel, Adolph Friedrich Johann. "Geschichte und Literatur der Volkswirthschaftslehre" and "Bibliothek der Volkswirthschaftslehre," 3:101–252 in his *Nationalöconomie oder Volkswirthschaft dargestellt*. Berlin.

Valle, Eusebio María del. "Teoría de la ciencia, historia de la misma," pp. 17–27 in the 2d ed. (1846) of his *Curso de economía política*. Madrid.

1843 Golovin, Ivan Gavrilovich. "Histoire de l'économie politique," pp. 25–78 in his *Esprit de l'économie politique*. Paris.

Roscher, Wilhelm Georg Friedrich. "Literärgeschichte," pp. 143–50 in his *Grundriss zu Vorlesungen über die Staatswirthschaft*. Göttingen.

1844 Borrego, Andrés. "Resumen histórica de la ciencia," pp. iii–xxxvi in his *Principios de economía política*. Madrid.

Appendix A

1845 Hamal, Ferdinand de. "Histoire de l'économie politique," "De quelques systèmes," "La Science au XVIIIme siècle," "Principes d' Adam Smith," pp. 17–38 in his *Traité élémentaire d'économie politique*. Bruxelles.

Moreno, Vincenzio. "Prolegomeni," pp. 19–81 in his *Lezioni di publica economia*. Napoli.

Pereira Forjaz de Sampaio, Andrião. "Resumo da historia da economia politica," pp. xvii–xix in his *Elementos de economia politica e estadistica*. Nova edição, reformada e augmentada. Coimbra.

Ungewitter, Franz Heinrich. "Die verschiedenen Systeme der Staatswirthschaft," pp. 414–21 in his *Populäre Staatswissenschaft*. Halle.

1846 Garnier, Joseph. "Rapide coup d'oeil historique sur l'origine et les progrès de la science économique, et courtes biographies de ses principaux fondateurs," pp. 619–26 in the 4th ed. (1860) of his *Traité d'économie politique*. Paris.

Kudler, Joseph. "Geschichte der Volkswirtschaftslehre" and "Literatur," 1:6–48 in his *Die Grundlehren der Volkswirtschaft*. Wien.

1851 Ott, Auguste. "Sur l'histoire et la littérature de la science économique," pp. xi–xvi in his *Traité d'économie sociale*. Paris.

1853 Fonteyraud, Paul Henri Alcide. "Esquisse historique," pp. 166–69 in his *Mélanges d'économie politique*. Paris.

1854 [Albertini, Luis Eugenio.] "Autores economistas de diversas naciones," pp. 149–50 in his *Compendio de economía-política analogo a esta America*. Lima.

Royer de Behr, Auguste Nicolas Maximilien. "Aperçu historique," pp. iii–xiv in the 2d ed. (1857) of his *Traité élémentaire d'économie politique*. Bruxelles.

1856 Carballo y Wangüemert, Benigno. "Resumen histórico de la economía política," 2:279–429 in his *Curso de economía política*. Madrid.

Kosegarten, Wilhelm. "Geschichte der Nationaloekonomie," pp. 15–45 in his *Geschichtliche und systematische Uebersicht der National-Oekonomie*. Wien.

Schulze, Friedrich Gottlob. 1:102–4 in his *Nationalökonomie oder Volks-*

wirtschaftslehre, vornehmlich für Land-, Forst- und Staatswirthe. Leipzig.

Wirth, Max. "Geschichte der Volkswirtschaft," 1:71–180 in his *Grundzüge der National-Oekonomie.* Köln.

1857 Villiaumé, [Nicolas]. "Coup d'oeil sur les fondateurs de la science," 1:74–79 in his *Nouveau traité d'économie politique.* Paris.

1858 Courcelle-Seneuil, Jean Gustave. "Note sur l'histoire de l'économie politique," 2:557–76 in his *Traité théorique et pratique d'économie politique.* Paris.

Pereira Forjaz de Sampaio, Andrião. "Resumida noticia historica da economia politica," 1:XL–LXII in his *Novos elementos de economia politica.* Coimbra.

1859 Bascom, John. "Its History," pp. 16–18 in his *Political Economy.* Andover, Massachusetts.

Minghetti, Marco. "Cenno sulla storia delle dottrine economiche," pp. 32–51 in his *Della economia pubblica.* Firenze.

Schober, Hugo Emil. "Entwickelungsgang der Volkswirtschaftslehre," pp. 45–84 in the 4th ed. (1888) of his *Katechismus der Volkswirtschaftslehre.* Leipzig.

1860 Brasseur, Hubert. "Histoire de l'économie politique," 1:18–45 in his *Manuel d'économie politique.* Gand.

Liljenstrand, Axel Wilhelm. "Historisk öfversigt," 1:27–87 in his *System af samfunds ekonomins läror: ett försök.* Helsingfors.

1861 Garbouleau, Paul Jean. "Historique" and "Systèmes économiques," pp. 21–35 in his *Éléments d'économie politique.* Montpellier.

1864 Biundi, Giuseppe. Pp. 14–32 in his *La economia esposta ne' suoi principi razionali e dedotti.* Milano.

Roesler, Hermann. "Geschichte der Wissenschaft," pp. 35–36 in his *Grundsätze der Volkswirthschaftslehre.* Rostock.

1865 Colmeiro, Manuel. "Historia de la economía política," pp. 26–32 in his *Principios de economía política.* Madrid.

Appendix A

1866   Kleinschrod, Carl Theodor von. "Aeltere Literatur," pp. 2–22 in his *Die Grundprinzipien der politischen Oekonomie*. Wien.

Perry, Arthur Latham. "On the History of the Science," pp. 1–35 in his *Elements of Political Economy*. New York.

1867   Baudrillart, Henri Joseph Léon. "Les Principaux fondateurs de la science économique," pp. 7–11 in his *Éléments d'économie rurale, industrielle, commerciale*. Paris.

Komers, Anton Emmanuel. "Entwicklung der Volkswirtschaftslehre," pp. 2–6 in his *Abriss der National-Oekonomie*. Prag.

Schäffle, Albert Eberhard Friedrich. "Zur Geschichte der Nationalökonomie," pp. 16–20 in his *Das gesellschaftliche System der menschlichen Wirtschaft*. 2d ed. Tübingen.

Umpfenbach, Karl. "Literaturnachweis," pp. 222–28 in his *Die Volkswirtschaftslehre oder National-Oekonomik*. Würzburg.

1868   Mangoldt, Hans Karl Emil von. Pp. 20–25 in his *Volkswirthschaftslehre*. Stuttgart.

1871   Richter, Karl Thomas. "Die Wirtschaftslehre und ihre Geschichte," pp. 188–262 in his *Einleitung in das Studium der Volkswirtschaft*. Prag.

Schuler von Libloy, Friedrich. Pp. 4–15 in his *Politische Oeconomie*. Hermannstadt.

1872   Metzger (professor of history). "Histoire des doctrines économiques," pp. 5–21 in his *Cours d'économie politique*. St. Quentin.

1874   Allér, Domingo Enrique. "Resumen razonada de la historia de la economía política," pp. 235–68 in his *Estudios elementales de economía política*. Madrid.

Bischof, Hermann. "Geschichte und Literatur der Volkswirtschaftslehre," pp. 45–82 in his *Grundzüge eines Systemes der Nationalökonomik oder Volkswirtschaftslehre*. Graz.

Lampertico, Fedele. "Scuole economiche," 1:266–337 in his *Economia dei popoli e degli stati*. Milano.

Parth, J. H. "Die Literatur der Nationalökonomik," pp. 18–23 in his *Das A-B-C der National-Oekonomik*. Graz.

Appendix A

Rampal, Benjamin. "Une Rapide excursion à travers l'histoire de l'économie politique," 1:xli–cxlix in Hermann Schulze-Delitzsch, *Cours d'économie politique.* Paris.

1875 Garelli della Morsa, Giusto Emanuele. "Cenni storici," pp. 26–35 in his *Principii di economia politica.* Torino.

Matteuzzi, Alfonso. "Cenni storici sulla politica economia" and "Vicende dell' economia politica nel secolo XIX," pp. 301–46 in his *Lezioni di economia politica per uso delle scuole secondarie e della classe commerciante.* Torino.

Thompson, Robert Ellis. "History," pp. 13–31 in his *Social Science and National Economy.* Philadelphia.

Walcker, Karl. "Oreintirendes über die Geschichte und Literatur der National-Oekonomie," pp. 147–58 in his *Lehrbuch der Nationalökonomie.* Berlin.

1876 Azcárate, Gumersindo de. "Indicaciones históricas acerca del concepto de la economía," pp. 34–40 in his *Estudios económicas y sociales.* Madrid.

1877 Shadwell, John Emelius Lancelot. "History of Political Economy," pp. 9–20 in his *A System of Political Economy.* London.

1878 Bischof, Alois. "Die Geschichte der Nationalökonomik oder Volkswirthschaftslehre im weiteren Sinne," 1:7–13 in his *Lehrbuch der Nationalökonomie und Volkswirtschaftspolitik.* Graz.

Quaritsch, August. "Geschichtliche Uebersicht," pp. 3–28 in his *Geschichtliche Uebersicht und Grundbegriffe der Nationalökonomie.* Berlin.

Roesler, Hermann. "Geschichtliche Skizze der Volkswirtschaft," pp. 23–72 in his *Vorlesungen über Volkswirtschaft.* Erlangen.

1879 Cauwès, Paul. "Revue sommaire des doctrines et des écoles," 2:690–709 in his *Précis du cours d'économie politique.* Paris.

1880 Adler, Abraham. "Geschichtlicher Überblick," pp. 217–54 in the 4th ed. (1901) of his *Leitfaden der Volkswirtschaftslehre.* Leipzig.

Hervé Bazin, Ferdinand Jacques. "Notions historiques," pp. 4–15 in his *Traité élémentaire d'économie politique.* Paris.

Appendix A

Ponsiglioni, Antonio. "Cenni storici sull' ordinamento delle dottrine economiche," pp. 66–103 in his *Della economia pubblica*. 2d ed. Genova.

Worms, Émile. "Introduction historique," pp. 1–63 in his *Exposé élémentaire de l'économie politique*. Paris.

1881 Cognetti de Martiis, Salvatore. "La dottrine economiche in Grecia, etc.," pp. 9–22 in his *Sunti delle lezioni di economia politica*. Torino.

Leo, Ottoman Victor. "Geschichtliches über Wirtschaftssysteme und nationalökonomische Schulen," pp. 7–27 in his *Allgemeine Nationalökonomie*. Jena.

Schmidberger, Heinrich. "Kurzer Abriss der Geschichte und Literatur der Volkswirtschaftslehre," pp. 314–44 in his *Die Volkswirtschaftslehre oder National-Oekonomik*. Innsbruck.

1882 Conrad, Johannes. "Geschichte der politischen Oeconomie," pp. 76–88 in his *Grundriss zu den Vorlesungen über National-Ökonomie*. Halle.

Scheel, Hans von. "Geschichte der politischen Oekonomie," 1:57–88 in *Handbuch der politischen Oekonomie*, Gustav Schoenberg, ed. Tübingen.

Thompson, Robert Ellis. "History of the Science," pp. 14–31 in his *Elements of Political Economy*. Philadelphia.

1883 Brants, Victor Léopold Jacques Louis. "Tableau de la succession et de la filiation des systèmes économiques," pp. 71–92 in his *Loi et méthode de l'économie politique*. Louvain.

Devas, Charles Stanton. "Economic Literature," pp. 58–82 in his *Groundwork of Economics*. London.

Laranjo, José Frederico. "Factos e systemas economicos," pp. 11–38 in his *Principios de economia politica*. Lisboa.

Stern, Robert. "Geschichte der Volkswirtschaftslehre," pp. 116–33 in his *Grundriss für Vorlesungen über Nationalökonomie*. Wien.

1884 Guillemenot, Pierre. "Coup d'oeil historique," pp. 13–29 in his *Essai de science sociale ou Éléments d'économie politique*. Paris.

1885 Olózaga y Bustamante, José María de. "Historia de la economía política," 1:97–169 in his *Tratado de economía política*. Madrid.

Schroeder, Eduard August. "Litteraturgeschichte der politischen Ökonomie," pp. 85–142 in the 3d ed. (1897) of his *Die politische Ökonomie*. Stuttgart.

1886 Bowker, Richard Rogers. "The Modern History and Literature of Economics," pp. 248–57 in his *Economics for the People*. New York.

1887 Neurath, Wilhelm. "Geschichte der Volkswirtschaftslehre," pp. 7–53 in the 2d ed. (1892) of his *Elemente der Volkswirtschaftslehre*. Leipzig.

1889 Andrews, Elisha Benjamin. "Its Origin . . . The Mercantile System . . . Physiocracy . . . Etc.," pp. 8–27 in his *Institutes of Economics*. Boston.

Ely, Richard Theodore. "The Evolution of Economic Science," pp. 309–26 in his *An Introduction to Political Economy*. New York.

Philippovich von Philippsberg, Eugen. "Literatur," 1:42–49 in the 8th ed. (1900) of his *Grundriss der politischen Oekonomie*. Freiburg im Breisgau.

1890 Marshall, Alfred. "The Growth of Economic Science," pp. 50–77 in his *Principles of Economics*. London.

1891 Dullo, Gustav. "Zur Geschichte der Volkswirtschaft," pp. 5–11 in his *Volkswirtschaftslehre in gemeinverständlicher Darstellung*. 2d ed. Berlin.

Lubenow, Hugo. "Die Geschichte der Nationalökonomie," pp. 88–94 in his *Grundriss der allgemeinen Volkswirtschaftslehre*. Berlin.

1892 Devas, Charles Stanton. "History of Economic Science," pp. 549–60 in his *Political Economy*. London.

Lehr, Julius. "Rechts- und Wirtschaftsordnung," pp. 10–17 in his *Politische Oekonomie in gedrängter Fassung*. München.

Marshall, Alfred. "The Growth of Economic Science," pp. 26–32 in his *Elements of Economics of Industry*. London.

1894 Arnault, Louis. "Coup d'oeil historique," pp. 24–28 in his *Résumé d'un cours d'économie politique*. 2d ed. Toulouse.

Oddi, Carlo. "Determinazione storica del concetto d'economia," pp. 26–56 in his *Nuovo trattato elementare di scienza economica*. Verona.

Appendix A

Villey-Desmeserets, Edmond Louis. "Histoire des doctrines économiques," pp. 16–27 in his *Principes d'économie politique.* 2d ed. Paris.

1895 Prothero, Michael Ernlee Du Sautoy. "Sketch of the Succession of the Theoretic Ideas about Economic Facts," pp. 185–246 in his *Political Economy.* London.

Quaritsch, August. "Geschichtlicher Theil," pp. 8–43 in his *Compendium der Nationalökonomie.* 5th ed. Berlin.

1896 Antoine, Charles. "Exposé des doctrines," pp. 174–83 in his *Cours d'économie sociale.* Paris.

Conrad, Johannes. "Die Geschichte der Nationalökonomie," 4th pt. in his *Grundriss zum Studium der politischen Oekonomie.* Jena.

1897 Piernas y Hurtado, José Manuel. "Historia de la ciencia económica," pp. 48–72 in the 2d ed. (1903) of his *Principios elementales de la ciencia económica.* Madrid.

1898 Degraff, Lawrence. "Historical Development," pp. 11–17 in the 1901 ed. of his *Outlines and Questions on the Principles of Economics.* Chicago.

Körner, Alois. "Abriss der Literaturgeschichte der Volkswirtschaft," pp. 121–45 in the 3d ed. (1905) of his *Grundriss der Volkswirtschaftslehre.* Wien.

1899 Zuckerkandl, Robert. "Die Entwicklung der Volkswirtschaftslehre," pp. 37–64 in his *Volkswirtschaftslehre nach den Vorlesungen.* Prag.

1900 Schmoller, Gustav Friedrich von. "Die geschichtliche Entwickelung der Literatur und die Methode der Volkswirtschaftslehre," 1:75–125 in his *Grundriss der allgemeinen Volkswirtschaftslehre.* Leipzig.

1901 Conrad, Johannes. "Die Geschichte der politischen Oekonomie," pp. 89–100 in the 6th ed. (1910) of his *Leitfaden zum Studium der Nationalökonomie.* Jena.

1902 Boggiano, Antonio. "Cenni storici sull'economia politica," pp. 41–64 in his *Istituzioni di economia politica.* Roma.

Kleinwächter, Friedrich Ludwig von. "Die Methoden und Richtungen der Nationalökonomie," pp. 51–67 in his *Lehrbuch der Nationalökonomie.* Leipzig.

Appendix A

1903   Arduino, Ettore. "Cenno storico," pp. 10–16 in his *Elementi di economia politica*. Livorno.

Boitel, Julien. "Histoire de la science économique," pp. 4–9 in the 9th ed. (1920) of his *Notions d'économie politique*. Paris.

Fiedler, Franz. "Die Entwicklung volkswirtschaftlicher Ideen," pp. 287–92 in his *Lehr- und Lesebuch der Nationalökonomie*. Wien.

Ruhland, Gustav. "Entstehungsgeschichte und Kritik der bisherigen national-ökonomischen Schul-Systeme," 1:43–70 in his *System der politischen Oekonomie*. Berlin.

1905   Seligman, Edwin Robert Anderson. "Development of Economic Thought," pp. 109–24 in his *Principles of Economics*. New York.

Vogt, Gustav. "Einleitung," pp. 1–7 in his *Die Grundlagen des modernen Wirtschaftsleben*. Hannover.

1906   Crozier, John Beattie. Pp. 117–82, 343–62, and 385–512 in his *The Wheel of Wealth*. London.

Mills, Herbert Elmer. "Development of Economic Thought," 1:17–19 in his *Outlines of Economics*. Poughkeepsie, N.Y.

Nazzani, Emilio. "Sviluppo storico dell' economia politica," pp. 101–6 in his *Sunto di economia politica*. 10th ed. Forlì.

1907   Schryvers, Joseph. "Les 3 grandes écoles d'économie politique," pp. 19–76 in his *Manuel d'économie politique*. Roulers.

Toniolo, Giuseppe. "La storia dottrinale dell' economia," 1:69–138 in his *Trattato di economia sociale*. Firenze.

Wagner, Adolph Heinrich Gotthilf. "Literatur," 1:1–21 in his *Theoretische Sozialökonomik*. 4th ed. Leipzig.

1908   Ely, Richard Theodore. "History of Economic Thought," pp. 657–76 in his *Outlines of Economics*. New York.

Fischer, August. "Geschichte der Volkswirtschaftslehre," pp. 131–40 in his *Leitfaden der Volkswirtschaftslehre*. Wien.

Landry, Adolphe. "Histoire de l'économique," pp. 27–38 in his *Manuel d'économique*. Paris.

Appendix A

1909 Gruntzel, Josef. "Die Entwicklung der Volkswirtschaftslehre," 1:140–56 in his *Grundriss der Wirtschaftspolitik*. Wien.

Morgenstierne, Bredo Henrik von Munthe af. "Socialøkonomiens Udwikling," pp. 5–19 in his *Forelaesninger over socialøkonomiens grundtraek*. Kristiania.

Pesch, Heinrich. "Merkantilismus, Physiokratie, Industriesystem, Kollektivismus, sociales Arbeitssystem," 2:9–228 in his *Lehrbuch der National-ökonomie*. Freiburg im Breisgau.

1910 Aschehoug, Torkel Halvorsen. "Socialøkonomikens Historie," 1:33–194 in his *Socialøkonomik*. Kristiania.

Loria, Achille. "Sviluppo storico dell' economia politica," pp. 83–116 in his *Corso completo di economia politica*. Torino.

Rambaud, Joseph. "Les Idées économiques avant les physiocrates . . . Les physiocrates . . . Adam Smith et l'apparition de l'économie politique classique," 1:10–12 in his *Cours d'économie politique*. Paris.

Todd, John Aiton. "History," pp. 7–12 in his *Political Economy*. Edinburgh.

1911 Majorana Calatabiano, Giuseppe. "Cenni storici sull' economia politica," 1:29–47 in his *Lezioni di economia politica*. Catania.

Polier, Léon. "Histoire de l'économie politique," 1:21–87 in his *Cours d'économie politique*. Toulouse.

1912 Murray, Roberto A. "Brevi cenni di storia della scienza economica," pp. 50–60 in his *Lezioni di economia politica*. Firenze.

1913 Burke, Edmund J. "Schools of Political Economy," pp. 7–31 in his *Political Economy*. New York.

Nogaro, Pierre Gabriel Bertrand. "Le Développement de la pensée économique," 2:229–78 in his *Élements d'économie politique*. Paris.

Schønheyder, Kristian Gottlieb Fredrik. "Produktionsteoriens utvikling," pp. 40–60 in his *Teoretisk og politisk økonomi*. Kristiania.

1914 Crew, Albert. "History and Development of Economic Theory," pp. 276–98 in his *Economics for Commercial Students*. London.

Appendix A

Lordier, Charles. "Histoire de l'économie politique," pp. 7–15 in his *Économie politique et statistique*. Paris.

Perreau, Camille. "Notions historiques sur les doctrines," 1:34–63 in the 3d ed. (1925) of his *Cours d'économie politique*. Paris.

1916 Diehl, Karl. "Systeme und Methoden der nationalökonomischen Forschung," 1:143–430 in his *Theoretische Nationalökonomie*. Jena.

1919 Carqueja, Bento. "Historia da sciencia economica," pp. 15–37 in his *Lições de economia politica*. Porto.

1920 Espejo de Hinojosa, Ricardo. "Escuelas económicas," pp. 329–44 in the 11th ed. (1947) of his *Tratado de economía moderna*. Barcelona.

Och, Joseph Tarcisius. "Principal Economic Systems, Schools, and Theories," pp. 10–14 in his *A Primer of Political Economy in Catechism Form*. Columbus, Ohio.

1921 Fallon, Valère. "Aperçu de l'histoire des doctrines économiques," pp. 382–96 in the 2d ed. (1923) of his *Principes d'économie sociale*. Bruges.

Paltarokas, K. Pp. 17–21 in his *Socialis klausimas*. Kaunas.

Simpson, Kemper. "The Development of Economics," pp. 3–4 in his *Economics for the Accountant*. New York.

1923 Silverman, Herbert Albert. "The Development of Economic Thought," pp. 321–26 in the 6th ed. (1929) of his *The Substance of Economics*. London.

1925 Cesari, Emidio. "La storia della scienza," pp. 15–23 in his *Elementi di economica*. Ascoli Piceno (Italy).

Martner, Daniel. "Los sistemas económicos," pp. 34–113 in the 2d ed. (1934) of his *Economía política*. Santiago de Chile.

Reboud, Paul. "Le Développement de la pensée économique," 1:45–81 in the 4th ed. (1930) of his *Précis d'économie politique*. Paris.

1926 Amonn, Alfred. "Die Entwicklung der neueren nationalökonomischen Wissenschaft und die Methodenfrage," 1:346–68 in his *Grundzüge der Volkswohlstandslehre*. Jena.

Appendix A

Carqueja, Bento. "Historia da economia politica," 1:531–631 in his *Economia politica*. Porto.

Truchy, Henri. "Vue d'ensemble des doctrines économiques," 1:16–29 in his *Précis élémentaire d'économie politique*. Paris.

1927 Engliš, Karel. "Aus der Geschichte der Wirtschaftswissenschaft," pp. 497–529 in his *Handbuch der Nationalökonomie*. Brünn.

1928 Silió Beleña, César. "Noción histórica de la economía política," pp. 37–94 in the 2d ed. (1930) of his *Nociones de economía*. Madrid.

Weber, Adolf. 1:24–48 in the 4th ed. (1932) of his *Volkswirtschaftslehre*. München.

193–? Rey Alvarez, Raoul. "La Doctrine et son évolution," pp. 9–16 in his *Notions d'économie politique générale*. [Bruxelles?]

1930 Pringle, William Henderson. Pp. 10–11 in his *An Introduction to Economics*. London.

Vecchio, Gustavo del. "I sistemi teorici di economia," pp. 1–116 in his *Lezioni di economia pura*. 2d ed. Padova.

1931 Bülow, Friedrich. "Entwicklung der Volkswirtschaftslehre," pp. 69–166 in the 3d ed. (1934) of his *Volkswirtschaftslehre*. Leipzig.

Carqueja, Bento. "Historia da sciencia economica," pp. 355–93 in his *Principios de economia politica*. Porto.

Mataja, Victor. "Entwicklung der volkswirtschaftspolitischen Lehrmeinungen," pp. 2–6 in his *Lehrbuch der Volkswirtschaftspolitik*. Wien.

1932 Marques, Hernani. "História das doutrinas económicas," pp. 49–169 in his *Economia política*. Coimbra.

1933 Paris. École Universelle par Correspondance de Paris. "Les Diverses doctrines économiques," 1:21–32 in its *Cours d'économie politique*. Paris.

1934 Leite, João Pinto da Costa. "Esbôço da evolução das doutrinas económicas," pp. 177–94 in his *Noções elementares de economia política*. Coimbra.

1936 Ennes Ulrich, Ruy. "História das doutrinas econômicas," pp. 42–86 in his *Economia política*. Lisboa.

Appendix A

Fanno, Marco. "Cenni storici sulle origini della scienza economica" and "Le scuole economiche," pp. 15–32 in his *Lezioni di scienza economica.* Padova.

1937 Arias, Gino. "Gli elementi dell'economia politica corporativa nella storia del pensiero economico," pp. 1–149 in his *Corso di economia politica corporativa.* Roma.

Divisia, François. "L'Historique de la science économique," p. 4 in his *Cours d'économie politique et sociale.* Paris.

Storm, Ernst. "Kurze Darstellung der volkswirtschaftlichen Lehrmeinungen mit wirtschaftsgeschichtlichen Angaben," pp. 1–65 in his *Volkswirtschaftlicher Grundriss.* Berlin.

Tallada, José María. "Historia de las doctrinas económicas," pp. 15–34 in his *Economía política.* Barcelona.

1939 Francisci Gerbino, Giovanni de. "Il pensiero economico," pp. 83–256 in his *Economia politica corporativa.* 3d ed. Palermo.

Pirou, Gaëtan. "L'Histoire de l'économie politique," 1:207–83 in his *Traité d'économie politique.* Paris.

1941 Soignie, Philippe de. "Histoire des doctrines économiques," pp. 315–29 in the 5th ed. (1947) of his *Leçons familières d'économie politique.* Paris.

1942 Arias, Gino. "Noticias históricas," pp. 45–91 in his *Manual de economía política.* Buenos Aires.

Görner, Alexander. "Die Hauptleben der Nationalökonomie," pp. 75–208 in his *Die Hauptlehren der Nationalökonomie, vom Werden der Volkswirtschaft.* Berlin.

Vallarino, Juan Carlos. "Las doctrinas económicas," pp. 131–241 in his *Tratado de economía política.* Montevideo.

1943 Agarwala, Amar Narain. "Evolution of Economic Science," pp. 1–12 in 1957 reprint of his *Reconstruction of Economic Science.* Allahabad.

Fábregas del Pilar, José María. "Doctrinas económicas," pp. 13–25 in his *Economía política.* Madrid.

Appendix A

Marín Marín, Santiago. "Doctrinas económicas," pp. 16–24 in his *Ensayo de economía política y legislación de hacienda*. Valencia del Cid.

Nogaro, Pierre Gabriel Bertrand. "Le Développement de la pensée économique," 1:61–99 in the 3d ed. (1946) of his *Cours d'économie politique*. Paris.

1945 Amonn, Alfred. "Geschichte der Nationalökonomie," pp. 15–49 in his *Leitfaden zum Studium der Nationalökonomie*. Bern.

Antonelli, Étienne. "Histoire de la pensée économique," pp. 54–114 in his *Manuel d'économie politique*. Montpellier.

1946 Guitart, Ernesto. Pp. 47–95 in his *Economía social*. Barcelona.

1947 Ennes Ulrich, Ruy. "História das doutrinas económicas," pp. 73–209 in his *Introduçao ao estudo da economia politica*. Lisboa.

Fanno, Marco. "Brevi cenni sulle origini della scienza economica," pp. 5–11 in the 12th ed. (1959) of his *Elementi di scienza economica*. Torino.

1948 Vito, Francesco. "Lo svolgimento storico dell' economia politica," pp. 49–182 in the 10th ed. (1954) of his *Introduzione alla economia politica*. Milano.

1949 Bresciani-Turroni, Costantino. "L' Evoluzione del pensiero economico," 1:33–41 in his *Corso di economia politica*. Milano.

Marano, Ignazio. "Definizione e svolgimento storico," pp. 41–48 in his *Manuale di economia politica, statistica e finanza*. Catania.

Weinberger, Otto. "Das Schrifttum der Wirtschaftslehre," pp. 23–30 in his *Grundriss der Volkswirtschaftslehre*. Wien.

1950 Santos, Ernesto Schop. "Sintesis histórica de las ideas económicas," 1:7–57 in his *Elementos de economía política*. Barcelona.

Waffenschmidt, Walter Georg. "Dogmen- und Wirtschaftsgeschichte," pp. 7–60 in his *Anschauliche Einführung in die allgemeine und theoretische Nationalökonomie*. Meisenheim am Glan.

1951 James, Émile. "Histoire de la pensée économique," 1:375–99 in Louis Baudin, ed., *Traité d'économie politique*. Paris.

Appendix A

1953   Castelain, L. "L'Evolution de la pensée économique," pp. 5–7 in his *Économie politique et sociale*. Anvers.

Jong, Frits J. de. "De voortijd van de economische wetenschap en de economischwetenschappelijke scholen in de negentiende eeuw," 2:15–35 in the 2d ed. (1957) of his *De werking van een volkshuishouding*. Leiden.

1954   Akademiia Nauk SSSR. Institut Ekonomiki. "Economic Doctrines of the Capitalistic Epoch," pp. 374–411 in the English translation (1957) of *Politicheskaia ekonomiia*. Moscow.

1956   Ballvé, Faustino. Pp. 1–10 in the American translation (1963) of his *Diez lecciones de economía*. México.

Guitton, Henri. "Histoire des faits et de la pensée," 1:17–64 in his *Économie politique*. Paris.

1957   Barrera de Irimo, Antonio. "La historia económica," pp. 18–24 in his *Notas de economía política*. Madrid.

Parrillo, Francesco. "Sintesi dello svolgimento del pensiero economico," pp. 1–38 in his *Contributo alla teoria della politica economica*. Torino.

1958   Dempsey, Bernard William. "Biography of an Unsatisfactory Science," pp. 1–17 in his *The Functional Economy*. Englewood Cliffs, N.J.

Reynaud, Pierre Louis. "Données sommaires sur l'histoire de la science économique," pp. 17–22 in his *Cours d'économie politique destinés au perfectionnement aux affaires*. Paris.

1959   Görner, Alexander. "Vom Werden der Volkswirtschaft," pp. 47–152 in his *Die Volkswirtschaft: die Wandlungen alter Grundsätze und die Lehre von Heute*. Berlin.

1960   Fellner, William John. Pp. 1–159 in his *Emergence and Content of Modern Economic Analysis*. New York.

Zimmerer, Carl. "Dogmengeschichte," pp. 5–41 in his *Kompendium der Volkswirtschaftslehre*. Düsseldorf.

1961   Hamberg, Daniel. "The Development of Modern Economics," pp. 2–3 in his *Principles of a Growing Economy*. New York.

Appendix A

1962 Dehem, Roger. "Historique de la pensée économique," pp. 11–27 in his *Principes d'économie politique*. Paris.

Dowd, Douglas Fitzgerald. "The Background and Aims of Modern Economics," pp. 1–13 in his *Modern Economic Problems in Historical Perspective*. Boston.

1964 Trenton, Rudolf W. "History of Economic Thought," pp. 6–7 in his *Basic Economics*. New York.

1965 Chenault, Lawrence Royce. "Main Streams in the Development of Economic Thought," pp. 246–68 in his *Economics*. Garden City, N.Y.

1966 Frisch, Heinz. "Geschichte der volkswirtschaftlichen Lehrmeinungen," pp. 250–69 in the 3d ed. (1968) of his *Volkswirtschaft in unserer Zeit*. Bad Homburg.

1967 Hansmeyer, K. H. "Lehr- und Methodengeschichte," 1:15–51 in *Kompendium der Volkswirtschaftslehre*, ed. by Werner Ehrlicher. Göttingen.

1968 Lang, Rikard. "Kratki osvrt na povijest ekonomske misli," pp. 58–74 in his *Politička ekonomija*. Zagreb.

Mundell, Robert A. Preface in his *Man and Economics*. New York.

1969 Flouzat, Denise. "Le Grands courants de pensée économique," pp. 14–25 in *Analyse économique*. Paris.

1970 Tichy, Geiserich Eduard. "Zur Geschichte der politischen Ökonomie," pp. 23–87 in his *Theoretische Grundlegung der politischen Ökonomie*. Berlin.

1971 Meerhaeghe, Marcel Alfons Gilbert van. "Economic Doctrines," pp. 465–80 in his *Economics: A Critical Approach*. London.

Sowell, Thomas. "The Evolution of Modern Economics," pp. 323–41 in *Economics: Analysis and Issues*. Glenview, Illinois.

1973 Robinson, Joan, and Eatwell, John. "Economic Doctrines," pp. 1–51 in their *An Introduction to Modern Economics*. Maidenhead.

Wolozin, Harold. "The Development of Economics," p. 8 in his *Introduction to Economics: An Interdisciplinary Approach*. Boston.

Appendix A

1974 Albrecht, William P. "Economic Thought," pp. 79–98 in his *Economics*. Englewood Cliffs, N.J.

1975 Samuelson, Paul Anthony. "Winds of Change: Evolution of Economic Doctrines," pp. 839–966 in his *Economics*. 9th ed. New York.

Alphabetical List of Authors in Appendix A, by Date of Publication

Adler, Abraham, 1880
Agarwala, Amar Narain, 1943
Akademiia Nauk SSSR. Institut Ekonomiki, 1954
Albertini, Luis Eugenio, 1854
Albrecht, William P., 1974
Allér, Domingo Enrique, 1874
Amonn, Alfred, 1926, 1945
Andrews, Elisha Benjamin, 1889
Antoine, Charles, 1896
Antonelli, Étienne, 1945
Arduino, Ettore, 1903
Arias, Gino, 1937, 1942
Arnault, Louis, 1894
Aschehoug, Torkel Halvorsen, 1910
Azcárate, Gumersindo de, 1876

Ballvé, Faustino, 1956
Barrera de Irimo, Antonio, 1957
Bascom, John, 1859
Baudrillart, Henri Joseph Léon, 1867
Bischof, Alois, 1878
Bischof, Hermann, 1874
Biundi, Giuseppe, 1864
Boggiano, Antonio, 1902
Boitel, Julien, 1903
Borrego, Andrés, 1844
Bowker, Richard Rogers, 1886
Brants, Victor Léopold Jacques Louis, 1883
Brasseur, Hubert, 1860
Bresciani-Turroni, Costantino, 1949
Bülow, Friedrich, 1931
Burke, Edmund J., 1913

Carballo y Wangüemert, Benigno, 1856
Carqueja, Bento, 1919, 1926, 1931
Castelain, L., 1953
Cauwès, Paul, 1879
Cesari, Emidio, 1925

Chenault, Lawrence Royce, 1965
Cognetti de Martiis, Salvatore, 1881
Colmeiro, Manuel, 1865
Conrad, Johannes, 1882, 1896, 1901
Courcelle-Seneuil, Jean Gustave, 1858
Crew, Albert, 1914
Crozier, John Beattie, 1906

Degraff, Lawrence, 1898
Dehem, Roger, 1962
Dempsey, Bernard William, 1958
Devas, Charles Stanton, 1883, 1892
Diehl, Karl, 1916
Divisia, François, 1937
Dowd, Douglas Fitzgerald, 1962
Dullo, Gustav, 1891

Ely, Richard Theodore, 1889, 1908
Engliš, Karel, 1927
Ennes Ulrich, Ruy, 1936, 1947
Espejo de Hinojosa, Ricardo, 1920

Fábregas del Pilar, José María, 1943
Fallon, Valère, 1921
Fanno, Marco, 1936, 1947
Fellner, William John, 1960
Fiedler, Franz, 1903
Fischer, August, 1908
Flouzat, Denise, 1969
Fonteyraud, Paul Henri Alcide, 1853
Francisci Gerbino, Giovanni de, 1939
Frisch, Heinz, 1966

Garbouleau, Paul Jean, 1861
Garelli della Morsa, Giusto Emanuele, 1875
Garnier, Joseph, 1846
Görner, Alexander, 1942, 1959
Golovin, Ivan Gavrilovich, 1843
Gruntzel, Josef, 1909

List of Authors in Appendix A

Guillemenot, Pierre, 1884
Guitart, Ernesto, 1946
Guitton, Henri, 1956

Hamal, Ferdinand de, 1845
Hamberg, Daniel, 1961
Hansmeyer, K. H., 1967
Hervé Bazin, Ferdinand Jacques, 1880

James, Émile, 1951
Jong, Frits J. de, 1953

Kleinschrod, Carl Theodor von, 1866
Kleinwächter, Friedrich Ludwig von, 1902
Körner, Alois, 1898
Komers, Anton Emmanuel, 1867
Kosegarten, Wilhelm, 1856
Kudler, Joseph, 1846

Lampertico, Fedele, 1874
Landry, Adolphe, 1908
Lang, Rikard, 1968
Laranjo, José Frederico, 1883
Lehr, Julius, 1892
Leite, João Pinto da Costa, 1934
Leo, Ottomar Victor, 1881
Liljenstrand, Axel Wilhelm, 1860
List, Friedrich, 1841
Lordier, Charles, 1914
Loria, Achille, 1910
Lubenow, Hugo, 1891

Majorana Calatabiano, Giuseppe, 1911
Mangoldt, Hans Karl Emil von, 1868

Marano, Ignazio, 1949
Marín Marín, Santiago, 1943
Marques, Hernani, 1932
Marshall, Alfred, 1890, 1892
Martner, Daniel, 1925
Mataja, Victor, 1931
Matteuzzi, Alfonso, 1875
Meerhaeghe, Marcel Alfons Gilbert van, 1971
Metzger (professor of history), 1872
Mills, Herbert Elmer, 1906
Minghetti, Marco, 1859
Moreno, Vincenzio, 1845
Morgenstierne, Bredo Henrik von Munthe af., 1909
Mundell, Robert A., 1968
Murray, Roberto A., 1912

Nazzani, Emilio, 1906
Neurath, Wilhelm, 1887
Nogaro, Pierre Gabriel Bertrand, 1913, 1943

Och, Joseph Tarcisius, 1920
Oddi, Carlo, 1894
Olózaga y Bustamente, José María de, 1888
Ott, Auguste, 1851

Paltarokas, K., 1921
Paris. École Universelle par Correspondance de Paris, 1933
Parrillo, Francesco, 1957
Parth, J. H., 1874
Pereira Forjaz de Sampaio, Andrião, 1845, 1858
Perreau, Camille, 1914
Perry, Arthur Latham, 1866
Pesch, Heinrich, 1909
Philippovich von Philippsberg, Eugen, 1889
Piernas y Hurtado, José Manuel, 1897
Pirou, Gaëtan, 1939
Polier, Léon, 1911
Ponsiglioni, Antonio, 1880
Potter, Alonzo, 1840
Pringle, William Henderson, 1930
Prothero, Michael Ernlee Du Santoy, 1895

Quaritsch, August, 1878, 1895

Rambaud, Joseph, 1910
Rampal, Benjamin, 1874
Reboud, Paul, 1925
Rey Alvarez, Raoul, 193–?
Reynaud, Pierre Louis, 1958
Richter, Karl Thomas, 1871
Riedel, Adolph Friedrich Johann, 1842
Robinson, Joan, and John Eatwell, 1973
Roesler, Hermann, 1864, 1878
Roscher, Wilhelm Georg Friedrich, 1843
Royer de Behr, Auguste Nicolas Maximilien, 1854
Ruhland, Gustav, 1903

Samuelson, Paul Anthony, 1975
Santos, Ernesto Schop, 1950
Schäffle, Albert Eberhard Friedrich, 1867
Scheel, Hans von, 1882
Schmidberger, Heinrich, 1881
Schmoller, Gustav Friedrich von, 1900
Schober, Hugo Emil, 1859
Schønheyder, Kristian Gottlieb Fredrik, 1913
Schroeder, Eduard August, 1885
Schryvers, Joseph, 1907
Schuler von Libloy, Friedrich, 1871
Schulze, Friedrich Gottlob, 1856
Seligman, Edwin Robert Anderson, 1905
Shadwell, John Emelius Lancelot, 1877

List of Authors in Appendix A

Silió Beleña, César, 1928
Silverman, Herbert Albert, 1923
Simpson, Kemper, 1921
Soignie, Philippe de, 1941
Sowell, Thomas, 1971
Stern, Robert, 1883
Storm, Ernst, 1937

Tallada, José María, 1937
Thompson, Robert Ellis, 1875, 1882
Tichy, Geiserich Eduard, 1970
Todd, John Aiton, 1910
Toniolo, Giuseppe, 1907
Trenton, Rudolf W., 1964
Truchy, Henri, 1926

Umpfenbach, Karl, 1867
Ungewitter, Franz Heinrich, 1845

Vallarino, Juan Carlos, 1942
Valle, Eusebio María del, 1842
Vecchio, Gustavo del, 1930
Villey-Desmeserets, Edmond Louis, 1894
Villiaumé [Nicolas], 1857
Vito, Francesco, 1948
Vogt, Gustav, 1905

Waffenschmidt, Walter Georg, 1950
Wagner, Adolf Heinrich Gotthilf, 1907
Walcker, Karl, 1875
Weber, Adolf, 1928
Weinberger, Otto, 1949
Wirth, Max, 1856
Wolozin, Harold, 1973
Worms, Émile, 1880

Zimmerer, Carl, 1960
Zuckerkandl, Robert, 1899

Appendix B
Courses in the History of Economics in German, American, French, and Italian Universities

This appendix aims to illuminate the development of university courses in the history of economics. It is confined to aspects of their development in Germany, the United States, France, and Italy, four countries in which these courses began, flourished, and still endure. A more complete study should also include sections on Japan, Spain, England, Russia, India, Brazil, and Mexico. There would then still remain unmentioned thirty-five additional countries in which histories had been published and, consequently, in which universities, at some time, may have offered a course of study in the history of economics.[1] Translations of the histories provided a principal avenue by which these courses have moved into new countries.

University courses[2] warrant a place in the historiography of economics not only because the lectures delivered in them stood as effective audible histories but also because they influenced the supply of, and the demand for, book-length histories. Often the professors turned their worked-over lecture notes into manuscripts which increased the supply of published histories. At the same time, the principal demand for published histories centered in these very courses, whose professors and students were nowhere at ease without textbooks.

By a wide margin, Germany led the world in offering university courses on the history of political economy. Professor Johann Friedrich Eiselen gave the earliest German course of this kind during the winter semester of 1820/21 at the progressive eleven-year-old University of Berlin.[3] He named his course "Die Geschichte der National-Oekonomie." A startling forty-odd years intervened before a similar university course appeared in any other nation.

Preparation of the German ground had begun as early as 1727, when Frederick William I added two cameralist professorships to the widely admired system of German universities. In the following years, the courses in Cameralism multiplied and were followed, after 1750, by published studies of its history.[4] The subject of political economy first entered the German universities as part of these general courses in Cameralism. Not until 1809, however, did separate courses in *National-Oekonomie* (the first popular German word to describe what was called "political economy" in English) begin to appear.[5] Eiselen had lectured on the general subject of *National-Oekonomie* in 1819/20. The history of the subject, which he offered the next year, provided a supplement. It was a "public" course, as were most of the later courses on the history of *National-Oekonomie,* and one that he did not repeat.

Some details of the German teaching of the history of political economy in the early years appear in the calendar in table 1. It is incomplete, for I have only been able to examine about half the lecture lists published by the universities.[6] Consequently, the calendar ought to be regarded as a large sample of such courses. It covers a period of 52 years during which 57 courses in the history of political economy are found in this large sample drawn from the 21 operating German universities. It is unlikely that a complete calendar would show more than 100 of these courses during this period. The 1871/72 semester is the last for which such incomplete data need be used. From the summer semester of 1872 to the winter semester of 1941/42, a complete list of the German courses appeared in *Deutscher Universitäts-Kalender* (title varies).

Table 2 offers a compact view of the courses on the history of economics given in German universities between the summer semester of 1873 and the winter semester of 1933/34. It provides a complete list of these courses in each of 11 years chosen at intervals from the 61 that constitute the period, and it identifies the 49 professors in 21 universities who taught 69 courses in the history of economics during these 11 years. If the extent of such courses were similar in the unrecorded years, the total number of courses given in Germany would have been approximately 380. During this period the frequency of courses increased from just over 4 per year from 1873 to 1901 to almost 9 per year from 1902 to 1933/34. In the banner year of 1929, 15 courses were taught. The number dropped to 8 in 1933.

During the war years the German courses in the history of economics disappeared: none were mentioned either by *Minerva* in 1952 or by the *World of Learning* from 1947 to 1960. In the 1960s they began their return to West German universities. An examination of 20 catalogues late in the 1970s showed seven courses then being offered,[7] approximately the same number as in 1933.

In the United States, professors may have put short histories of political economy into their general courses earlier, but the first college-catalogue recognition of such a history did not come until 1870. From 1870 to 1874 the *Catalogue* at the University of Rochester listed President Martin B. Anderson as teaching "Constitutional Law and Political Economy, Lectures and Blanqui." "Blanqui" meant Blanqui's *Histoire,* then a widely known history of political economy, that had not yet been translated into English. This reference to Blanqui could have been expected, since President Anderson had announced that "so profoundly am I impressed with the historical method in study, that I would extend it to every department of instruction, even to grammar and logic."[8] "In this step," his biographer said, "he was in advance of the traditions and customs of the college, and he was thought to be too much out of line with the established order of a correct course of study. He became a little unpopular on account of this innovation."[9]

Appendix B

A CALENDAR OF COURSES IN THE HISTORY OF POLITICAL ECONOMY GIVEN IN GERMAN
UNIVERSITIES, 1820/21 TO 1871/72

SEMESTER	PROFESSOR. TITLE. UNIVERSITY
1820/21	Eiselen, Johan Friedrich. "Die Geschichte der National-Oekonomie." University of Berlin.
1827/28	Weber, Friedrich Benedict. "Über oekonomischen Literatur" (also under the title "Oekonomische Literatur" in 1831). University of Breslau.
1829	Kaufmann, Peter K. "Ueber die drey vorhandenen staatswirtschaftlichen Systeme" (also with the title "Geschichte der staatswirtschaftlichen Systeme" in 1837/38 and 1839/40). University of Bonn.
1831	See Weber, 1827/28.
1834/35	Helwing, Ernst. "Geschichtliche Darstellung der verschieden Systeme der National-Ökonomie." University of Berlin.
1837/38	See Kaufmann, 1829.
1839/40	See Kaufmann, 1829.
1840	Thomas, Karl. "Die Darstellung der Hauptpunkte aus der Litteraturgeschichte der Staatswissenschaften." University of Königsberg.
1840/41	Kosegarten, Wilhelm K. "Historische und systematische Einleitung in die politische Oekonomie." University of Bonn.
1843/44	Dönniges, Wilhelm. "Volkswirtschaftslehre nebst einer historischen Ausführung der nationalökonomischen Systeme" (also in 1846 with the title "Nationalökonomie und Geschichte der nationalökonomischen Systeme"). University of Berlin.
1846	See Dönniges, 1843/44.
1847	Hermann, Benedikt Wilhelm. "Geschichte und Literatur der politischen Oekonomie." University of Muenchen.
1850	Helferich, Johann Alfons Renatus von. "Geschichte der Systeme der politischen Ökonomie." University of Tübingen.
	Weiss. "Geschichte der politischen Oekonomie in Europa, von dem Alterthum an bis auf unsere Tage." University of Freiburg im Breisgau.
1850/51	Friedländer, Karl Jacob. "Geschichte der politischen Ökonomie." University of Berlin. (Repeated with change in title in 1851, 1852/53, 1853/54, 1854, 1854/55.)
	Glaser, Johann Carl. "Die Geschichte der Nationalökonomie." University of Berlin. (Repeated 1853/54.)
	Riedel, Adolph Friedrich Johann. "National-Ökonomie, verbunden mit der Geschichte der nationalökonomischen Systeme und allgemeiner Gewerkskunde." University of Berlin. (Repeated with some change in title in 1852/53, 1853/54, 1859/60, 1862/63, 1863/64.)
1851	See Friedländer, 1850/51.
1851/52	Roscher, Wilhelm Georg Friedrich. "Geschichte der politischen und socialen (national-ökonomischen) Theorien bis auf die neueste Zeit." University of Leipzig. (Repeated with some change in title in 1853/54, 1855/56, 1857/58, 1858/59, 1859/60, 1869, 1871.)
1852/53	Fraas, Karl F. "Geschichte der Nationalökonomie." University of Muenchen. (Repeated with some change in title in 1854/55, 1855/56, 1858/59, 1864/65, 1866/67.)
	See Friedländer, 1850/51.
	Kiesselbach, Wilhelm. "Geschichte der politischen Oekonomie." University of Heidelberg. (Repeated with some change in title in 1853/54.)

Appendix B

TABLE 1 *(concluded)*

SEMESTER	PROFESSOR. TITLE. UNIVERSITY
	See Riedel, 1850/51.
1853	Pickford, E. "Geschichte der Oekonomie und ihrer Wissenschaft, seit Anfang der 18ten Jahrhunderts bis auf die Gegenwart." University of Heidelberg. (Repeated with some change in title in 1859.)
1853/54	See Friedländer, 1850/51.
	See Glaser, 1850/51.
	See Kiesselbach, 1852/53.
	See Riedel, 1850/51.
	See Roscher, 1851/52.
1854	See Friedländer, 1850/51.
1854/55	See Fraas, 1852/53.
	See Friedländer, 1850/51.
1855/56	See Fraas, 1852/53.
	See Roscher, 1851/52.
1857	Dietzel, Karl August. "Geschichte der Volkswirtschaft und der Volkswirtschaftslehre." University of Heidelberg. (Repeated at the University of Bonn in 1859/60.)
1857/58	See Roscher, 1851/52.
1858/59	See Fraas, 1852/53.
	Glaser, Johann Carl. "Geschichte der Staatswissenschaften seit Anfang der 18. Jahrhunderts." University of Königsberg. (Repeated with some change in title in 1860, 1860/61, 1861. Also see Glaser, 1850/51.)
	See Roscher, 1851/52.
1859	See Pickford, 1853.
1859/60	See Dietzel, 1857.
	See Riedel, 1850/51.
	See Roscher, 1851/52.
1860	Gerstner, Ludwig Joseph. "Geschichte und Literatur der staatswirtschaftlichen Systeme." University of Wurzburg.
	See Glaser, 1858/59.
1860/61	See Glaser, 1858/59.
1861	See Glaser, 1858/59.
1862	Helferich, Johann Alfons Renatus von. "Geschichte der Staatswissenschaft." University of Göttingen.
	Hermann, Friedrich Benedikt Wilhelm von. "Geschichte und Literatur der National-Oeconomie und Finanzwissenschaft." University of Muenchen.
1862/63	See Riedel, 1850/51.
1863/64	See Riedel, 1850/51.
1864/65	See Fraas, 1852/53.
1866/67	See Fraas, 1852/53.
1869	See Roscher, 1851/52.
1871	See Roscher, 1851/52.
1871/72	Brentano, Lujo. "Die Geschichte der Volkswirtschaftslehre." University of Berlin.
	Dühring, Eugen Karl. "National-Ökonomie, mit Berucksichtigung ihrer Geschichte." University of Berlin.

TABLE 2

COMPACTED VIEW OF COURSES IN THE HISTORY OF ECONOMICS GIVEN IN GERMAN UNIVERSITIES FOR SELECTED YEARS BETWEEN 1873 AND 1934

UNIVERSITY	PROFESSOR										
	1873/74	1877/78	1882/83	1887/88	1890/91	1897/98	1902/3	1907/8	1913/14	1928/29	1933/34
Berlin	Wagner					Wenckstern	Wenckstern		Oppen-heimer		
Bonn	Held	Held				Gothein				Schumpeter	
Breslau	Brentano	Brentano						Wenckstern			
Frankfurt					Adler					Grünberg	Budge; Biermann
Freiburg							Fuchs	Liefmann	Mombert	Liefmann	Wilken
Giessen							Liefmann			Sommer	
Göttingen			Sartorius von Waltershausen						Oldenberg	Oldenberg	
Greifswald	Baumstark							Oldenberg	Oldenberg	Biermann	
Halle	Eisenhart	Eisenhart	Eisenhart; Conrad			Diehl				Aubin	
Hamburg										Zimmer-mann	Heimann

TABLE 2. (Concluded)

University	Professor										
	1873/74	1877/78	1882/83	1887/88	1890/91	1897/98	1902/3	1907/8	1913/14	1928/29	1933/34
Heidelberg		Knies		Leser			Leser			Berg-strasser	Schuster
Jena							Pierstorff	Pierstorff	Pierstorff	Albrecht; Elster	
Kiel							Adler			Held; Petersen	
Leipzig	Roscher	Roscher		Walcker	Warschauer	Miaskowski					
Marburg			Glaser	Paasche			Oldenberg	Köppe	Biermann		
München								Bonn	Bonn	Halm	Gerhardt; Schmitt
Other Universities			Neumann (Tübingen)				Diehl (Königsberg)		Schmöle (Münster)	Wiese und Kaiserwaldau (Köln)	Meier (Erlangen)

SOURCE: *Deutscher Universitäts Kalender.* Full names of professors: **Georg Adler, Gerhardt Albrecht, Gustav Aubin, Eduard Baumstark, Arnold Bergstrasser, Wilhelm E. Biermann, Moritz J. Bonn, Lujo Brentano, Siegfried Budge, Johannes Conrad, Karl Diehl, Hugo Eisenhart, Ludwig Elster, Karl J. Fuchs, Johanns Gerhardt, Johann K. Glaser, Eberhard Gothein, Carl Grünberg, Georg Halm, Sven Helander, Adolf Held, Eduard Heimann, Karl G. E. Knies, Hans Köppe, Emanuel Leser, Robert Liefmann, Ernst Meier, August von Miaskowski, Paul Mombert, Frederic J. Neumann, Karl Oldenberg, Franz Oppenheimer, Hermann Paasche, Carl Petersen, Julius Pierstorff, Wilhelm G. F. Roscher, August Sartorius von Waltershausen, Alfons Schmitt, Josef Schmöle, Joseph A. Schumpeter, Ernst Schuster, Artur Sommer, Adolf Wagner, Karl Walcker, Otto F. Warschauer, Adolf von Wenckstern, L. M. W. Wiese und Kaiserwaldau, Folkert Wilken, Waldemar F. L. F. Zimmermann.**

Appendix B

Another professor to use Blanqui's name in the title of a first course in political economy was Charles Franklin Dunbar in 1874/75. The course was "Phil. 7. Political Economy—Fawcett's Manual—Blanqui's Histoire—Bagehot's Lombard Street," given to 14 juniors and 19 seniors out of a total Harvard enrollment of 1,196 students. Like Anderson at Rochester, Dunbar had a historical outlook. Frank William Taussig wrote that Dunbar had "not only a strong historical bent, but a streak of antiquarianism."[10]

The number of general courses in which the history of political economy came to play a part increased in the eighteen eighties. One reason for the increase was that textbooks in English became available for the first time. In 1880 both Blanqui's *Histoire* and Cossa's *Guida* were translated into English, and in 1886 Ingram provided a new textbook with the publication of his *History*.[11]

The influence of the translations of 1880 was immediately apparent. At Bucknell in 1880/81 the catalogue showed that Blanqui's *History of Political Economy* was used as one of several books suggested for the political-economy course required of seniors. In the 1881 *Catalogue* of the University of South Carolina the first term of the senior year-long political-economy course was described as "History of Political Economy, its different systems and its fundamental principles . . . Blanqui's History of Political Economy."[12] At Michigan the 1881 *Catalogue* showed that the first section of Henry C. Adam's "Elementary Course" began with Mercantilism and continued through the traditional stages of thought. The *Johns Hopkins University Register* for 1882 specified that "courses in the Elements and History of Political Economy must also be followed." At Princeton in 1884 Alexander Johnston offered "Political Economy, covering the historical development of the science, in all its phases and schools." At the University of Nebraska in 1885/86 the description of a course in "Political Economy" began with a "History of the science." In the same year at Miami (Ohio) the catalogue said that the third term of the senior course in political economy would be given to its history and would use Cossa's *Guide* as a textbook. After 1886 the fresh stimulus of Ingram's newly published *History* increased the rate at which courses in political economy that contained historical sections appeared in college catalogues. Such a course was given by Professor J. J. Wheat at the University of Mississippi (1887), Professor Woodrow Wilson at Bryn Mawr (1887), Simon Nelson Patten at the University of Pennsylvania (1888), Professor E. B. Andrews at Cornell (1888), and Professor Frank W. Blackmar at Kansas (1889). From these instances it is clear that the expanded political-economy course of the eighteen eighties often contained a section on the history of political economy. It was ready to break out and to become a separate course as soon as the course of study grew sufficiently to begin to subdivide.

The first college course in the United States with a title that clearly restricted its contents to the history of economics was described in the Harvard *Catalogue* of 1883. It was Dunbar's "Political Economy 2" with the title "History of Economic Theory and a Critical Examination of Leading Writers."[13]

Two other universities that had a good start in the teaching of the history of economics in the eighteen eighties were Johns Hopkins and Columbia. It was brought to Johns Hopkins by Richard T. Ely and to Columbia by Edwin R. A. Seligman. These two American economists did much to spread the teaching of the history of economics in the United States.[14] Henry Carter Adams, who taught a course in 1887 on the "Development of Economic Thought" at the University of Michigan, and E. J. James, who was at the Wharton School at the University of Pennsylvania, were two other professors who influenced the teaching of the history of economics. At the beginning of the eighteen nineties the University of Chicago opened and began in turn to be an influence.[15]

The further establishment of the history of economics in the colleges and universities of their country was carried on principally by the graduate students from Harvard, Columbia, Johns Hopkins, Wisconsin, Michigan, Chicago, and Pennsylvania as they began to teach the history of economics. These graduate schools furnished both the models to follow and the professors to teach.

Table 3 shows the spread of this subject in the colleges and universities of the United States. It gives the date of the *Catalogue* in which a specialized course in the history of economics was first announced. In case of a date such as 1895/96, the earlier date only is given. Certainly courses were given without having been entered in the catalogue, and likewise, courses were mentioned in catalogues without being given. Only the catalogues of the principal universities and colleges have been examined. A study of the table should give a good view of the general path that the introduction of courses in the history of economics followed. Teaching of these courses was widespread by 1900.

The remaining colleges and universities soon adopted similar courses. Once in the catalogues, there they stayed. All of the American universities listed above still offered courses in the history of economics in their catalogues in 1978/79. Further, all fifty state universities did likewise. As also did, in a north-south-east-west sample of four states, all colleges and universities, provided they had an enrollment of at least one thousand students and offered a degree in economics. In considering these statistics, it must be taken into account that college and university catalogues usually contain some "window dressing," in which case, though the course may be infrequently taught, or not taught at all, it is at least considered to be respectable "window dressing."

In France, the first courses in political economy were given, not in the universities, but in the Athénée, the Conservatoire des arts et métiers, the École speciale du commerce et d'industrie de Paris, and the Collège de France. J. B. Say presented the earliest public lectures on political economy in France at the Athénée in 1815. He began his lectures at the Conservatoire in 1820, and continued them long after his health failed in 1823. In 1832, shortly before he died, he received a professorship at the Collège de France. J. A. Blanqui, Say's protégé, became Professeur d'histoire et d'économie industrielle in 1825 at the École speciale du commerce and, in the same year, a professor at the Athénée. In the

Appendix B

TABLE 3

<small>Date of the Establishment at American Universities of Courses in the History of Economics, 1883–1900</small>

Year	University	Title of Course	Professor
1883	Harvard	History of Economic Theory	Charles F. Dunbar
1884	Johns Hopkins	History of Political Economy	Richard T. Ely
1885	Indiana	History of Economic Theories	Arthur B. Woodward
1886	Columbia	History of Economic Theories	E. R. A. Seligman
1887	Michigan	Development of Economic Thought	Henry Carter Adams
1888	M.I.T.	History of Economic Theory	David Rice Dewey
1890	Rochester	History of Economical Theories	William C. Morey
1891	Haverford	History of Political Economy	Allen Clapp Thomas
	Iowa State	Political Economy . . . the Subject Being Viewed from the Historical Standpoint	Edgar W. Stanton
	Ohio State	History of Economic Thought	George W. Knight
	Princeton	History of Economic Thought	Woodrow Wilson
	Vermont	History of Political Economy	Frederic Eli Dewhurst
	Wesleyan	History of Political Economy	Winthrop More Daniels
	Wisconsin	History of Political Economy	Richard T. Ely
1892	Chicago	History of Political Economy	William Caldwell
	Colorado	History of the Science of Economics	Lindley M. Keasberg
	Columbian	History of Economics	Andrew Fuller Craven
	Oberlin	History of Economic Thought	John William Black
1893	Cornell	Historic Development of Economic Theories	Charles Henry Hull
	Dartmouth	History of Economic Theory and Socialism	David K. Wells
	Minnesota	Economic History, Comprising an Account of Leading Economic Schools and Movements	William W. Folwell
1894	Illinois	Study of Economic Theory beginning with the Physiocrats	David Kinley
	Iowa	History of Political Economy	Isaac Altheus Loos
	Knox	History of Economic Theories	John P. Cushing
	Marietta	History of Economic Thought	John Wilson Simpson
	Syracuse	History of Political Economy	James Henry Hamilton
	Western Reserve	Economic Theory from Adam Smith to the Present Time	Stephen Francis Weston
1895	Boston	Historical Development of Economic Theories	Fay S. Baldwin
	Colgate	History of Political Economy	Charles Worthen Spencer
	Nebraska	History of Economics	W. G. L. Taylor
	New York	History of Political Economy	Frank M. Colby
	Oregon	History of Economic Thought	Frederick G. Young
	Trinity (Conn.)	History of Economic Thought	
1896	Ohio	History of Political Economy	

Appendix B

TABLE 3 *(continued)*

Year	University	Title of Course	Professor
	Pacific	History of Political Economy	Rockwell Dennis Hunt
1897	West Virginia	History of Economics	Jerome Hall Raymond
	Yale	History of Political and Economic Theories	Arthur Twining Hadley
1898	Lehigh	History and Development of Economic Ideas and Systems	
	South	History of Political Economy	
	Stanford	History of the Growth of Economic Thought	Frank A. Fetter
1899	Kansas	Critical History of Economics	Ralph Waldo Cone
	Washington and Lee	History of Economic Thought	Henry Parker Willis
	Tufts	History and Literature of Political Economy	Henry C. Metcalf

year following Say's death, Blanqui added to his duties those of the professorship at the Conservatoire. Blanqui continued to lecture until his own death in 1854. Both Say and Blanqui treated the history of political economy as a small part of their public lectures.[16]

Pelligrino Rossi delivered, from 1838 to 1840 at the Collège de France, the first lectures in France that dealt exclusively with the subject of the history of political economy.[17] Rossi, who had been appointed to the chair in 1833, the year after Say's death, was replaced in 1840 by Michel Chevalier, who himself undertook lectures on an aspect of the general history of political economy, of which some part was published in 1869.[18] A chair "d'histoire des doctrines économiques depuis Adam Smith," promised in the foundation of the École libre des sciences politiques in 1871, did not materialize until 1882.[19]

Courses in the history of political economy did not appear in the French universities until 1895, long after they had been established in Germany. This lag, in part, resulted from the tardy introduction of the subject of political economy into the French universities. Several early attempts had failed. The first success came in 1864 when, partly as a result of a discussion of the question of its introduction in 1863 at the Société d'économie politique,[20] the University of Paris offered such a course. The Universities of Nancy, Toulouse, and Marseilles soon followed the example of Paris. The movement then rested for thirteen years.

It was finally pushed on by the decree of 26 March 1877, the supporters of which sought to temper the judicial content of the law degree. This decree necessitated the immediate introduction of a single course in political economy at each of the French law schools. There followed a twenty-year period with little change: each law school had at least one professor of political economy; only Paris, Aix, Grenoble, and Rennes had as many as two professors.

The change, when it finally came, followed an alteration, in 1889, of the

Appendix B

laws governing military conscription that permitted a reduction in compulsory military service from three years to one for those who could obtain the doctorate in law before the age of twenty-six. This created a burst of candidates for the doctorate in law, which heightened the realization that splitting the doctorate in law would best suit the candidates, many of whom did not aspire to be magistrates.

The split, made by the decree of 30 April 1895, created "le doctorat ès sciences politiques et économiques." It required a course in the history of economic doctrines. Why was history chosen rather than public finance or some other division of political economy as the second course? René Worms, who inaugurated the course in the history of doctrines in 1897 at the University of Caen, attributed it "au grand courant qui a étendu dans nos Universités . . . la place attribuée aux recherches historiques."[21]

By 1900, thirteen French universities offered the "doctorat ès sciences politiques et économiques." Professors who at that time taught the courses in the "Histoire des doctrines économiques" in France are listed in table 4.[22]

Every Faculté de droit in France still offered this same course in 1914.[23] From 1914 to the present, despite widespread changes in university regulations, a course on the history of economics has remained in every French university that granted a degree in economics. As an example, the professors who taught "Histoire" in two pivotal years are listed in table 5.[24]

The course name was altered, during the nineteen sixties, from its original form "Histoire des doctrines économiques" to "Histoire de la pensée économique."[25] The substitution of "pensée" for "doctrines" reflected a modernized content. At present it is required by all Facultés des sciences économiques, often for two semesters, in the third year of study for the Licence ès sciences économiques.

Apparently no Italian university offered a separate course in the history of

TABLE 4

COURSES IN THE HISTOIRE DES DOCTRINES ÉCONOMIQUES AT FRENCH UNIVERSITIES IN 1900

UNIVERSITY	PROFESSOR
Paris	Auguste Deschamps
Aix	Alfred Jourdan
Bordeaux	Charles de Boeck
Caen	René Worms
Dijon	Henri Trucy
Grenoble	Joseph Hitier
Lille	Auguste Dubois
Lyon	Charles Guernier
Montpellier	Charles Gide
Nancy	Jules Joseph Liégeois
Poitiers	J. Gustave Chéneaux
Rennes	Charles Marie Joseph Turgeon
Toulouse	Pierre Maria

Appendix B

TABLE 5

Professors of "Histoire" in French Universities in 1929/30 and 1943/44

University	Professor	
	1929/30	1943/44
Paris	Auguste Deschamps	Gaëtan Pirou
Caen		Joseph Lajugie
Dijon	Louis Baudin	André Marchal
Lille	Georges Lasserre	Georges Lasserre
Nancy	Bernard Lavergne	Robert Goetz
Poitiers	Auguste Dubois	Daniel Villey
Rennes	Pierre Fromont	Henri Denis

economics before 1926. At least *Minerva,* the standard international source, listed none, and those few scattered Italian university catalogues *(annuari)* that are available for inspection contained none. Of course, the histories of political economy had had many earlier connections with Italian universities but, in the sphere of university courses, they appeared mixed into the general courses on political economy, rather than being displayed as distinct courses. In line with his teaching, Luigi Cossa, who was the first Italian to be preponderantly concerned with this subject and who was the author of the Italian histories with the greatest international influence, started his histories with a theoretical (or general) part and did not use the word "history" in their titles.

Reforms in Italian universities during the early nineteen twenties resulted in a decree in 1926 that the course in "Storia delle dottrine economiche" be offered by the Facoltà di giurisprudenza in state universities. In 1938, *Minerva* reported the courses in "Storia delle dottrine economiche" that are listed in table 6.

The state of the history of economics at the Italian universities in 1971/72 is well presented by an article "La storia delle dottrine economiche nelle università italiane," in the first issue of *Storia del pensiero economico: bollettino di informazione* (1973). This is the only article ever written that attempts a full

TABLE 6

Courses in Storia delle dottrine economiche at Italian Universities in 1938

University	Professor
Bari	Giuseppe di Nardi
Cagliari	Spiro Barbieri
Milano (Sacro Cuore)	Amintore Fanfani
Napoli	Mario de Luca
Palermo	Francesco Gallini
Perugia	Aldo Adolfo Crosara
Pisa	Filippo Carli
Roma	Renato Spaventa
Torino	Luigi Einaudi

Appendix B

picture of the courses in the history of economics given in one country in a single year. It lists the courses, names the professors, cites the textbooks, and outlines the materials covered by the courses. It shows, for the year 1971/72, that the history of economics was being presented in sixteen of the twenty-two Italian universities that offered a degree in economics. Possibly some of the remaining six universities were omitted because of the difficulty in assembling information of this kind.

Appendix C
The Geography of Translations

Since translations accounted for more than one-quarter of all the histories of economics that have been published, this subject was marked as an international one. From the start, translations played an important part in the historiography of economics. The first short general history of political economy underwent three translations during the year of its original publication. The year was 1769; the historian, Beccaria; the country of origin, Italy; and the translations of the same year, British, French, and Swiss.

In the succeeding years the growth in numbers of translations at first resulted from the increasing popularity of general treatises of political economy that contained them. The foreign demand for the general treatises, rather than for the histories themselves, precipitated the first translations. Of the 84 often fragmentary histories that were published before 1839, 20 had translations. At least 109 translations of these 20 histories were published before 1839, the year when the first translation of a book-length history appeared. These numerous translations provided avenues through which, by 1839, abbreviated histories had passed from their original center in France, England, Germany, and Italy to 11 additional nations.

This bibliography does not list separately under their dates the translations of these short histories that were incorporated in general treatises. It does, however, mention them, along with their dates, in the entries for the 20 original editions. Table 7 summarizes the translations in the years through 1838.

The first two book-length histories of political economy to be published outside the countries of their origins were those of Villeneuve-Bargemont (1836–38) and of Blanqui (1837–[1838]). In 1839, pirated editions of both appeared in Belgium. These are classed in this bibliography as translations. There was also a Spanish translation in 1839. These three translations were the first of the 278 book-length translations that are separately listed in this bibliography.

However, the years from 1840 to 1877 brought astonishingly few book-length translations. Only two were added after 1839—the German and Dutch translations of Blanqui's history. Only one of the 16 new book-length histories that appeared during this period was ever translated, and it not until after 1877.

TABLE 7

Paths Taken by 109 Translations of General Histories of Political Economy before 1839

Originally	Translations to										
	French	German	American	Spanish	Swiss	Belgian	Italian	Austrian	British	Danish	Other
British 56	21	9	8	3	7		1	1		1	2 Dutch 1 Polish 1 Portuguese 1 Russian
French 44		10	9	9	1	5	4	2	2	1	1 Swedish
Italian 4	2				1				1		
German 3	1							1		1	
Russian 2	1	1									
109	25	20	17	12	9	5	5	4	3	3	6

Note: The following list shows the entry numbers in this Bibliography, the authors' surnames, and the dates of the original works that were translated during this period, each followed, in parentheses, by the number of translations appearing: 4—Dupont, 1768 (2); 6—Beccaria, 1769 (3); 9—Young, 1774 (2); 10—Smith, 1776 (37); 11—Dohm, 1778 (1); 16—Stewart, 1794 (3); 25—Malthus, 1803 (5); 26—Say, 1803 (27); 32—Schmalz, 1808 (1); 33—Ganilh, 1809 (4); 37—Storch, 1815 (2); 41—Schmalz, 1818 (1); 44—Sismondi, 1819 (2); 46—Malthus, 1820 (2); 56—McCulloch, 1824 (2); 60—McCulloch, 1825 (2); 62—Blanqui, 1826 (1); 69—Flórez Estrada, 1828 (3); 71—Pecchio, 1829 (1); 73—Say, 1829 (8).

216

TABLE 8

Paths Taken by 66 Translations of General Histories of Political Economy from 1839 to 1877

Originally	Translated to *						
	French	German	American	Spanish	Belgian	Italian	Other
British 28	8	2	3	7	3	3	1 Russian 1 Venezuelan
French 27 [5]		2 [1]	17	1 [1]	4 [2]	1	1 Danish 1 [1] Dutch
German 4				2	1	1	
Other 2		Italian—1				Russian—1	
61 [5]	8	5 [1]	20	10 [1]	8 [2]	6	4 [1]

*The numbers in brackets represent book-length histories; unbracketed numbers represent essay-length histories.

Note: The following list shows the entry numbers in this Bibliography, the authors' surnames, and the dates of the original works that were translated during this period, each followed, in parentheses, by the number of translations appearing. The translated book-length histories were: 82—Villeneuve-Bargemont, 1836–38 (1); and 83—Blanqui, 1837–[1838] (4). The translated essay-length histories were: 10—Smith, 1776 (11); 25—Malthus, 1803 (6); 26—Say, 1803 (18); 37—Storch, 1815 (1); 44—Sismondi, 1819 (1); 46—Malthus, 1820 (2); 49—Jakob, 1821 (2); 61—McCulloch, 1825 (5); 62—Blanqui, 1826 (3); 65—Rau, 1826 (2); 69—Flórez Estrada, 1828 (4); 71—Pecchio, 1829 (1); and 73—Say, 1829 (5).

TABLE 9

Paths Taken by 46 Translations of Book-length General Histories of Economics from 1878 to 1929

Originally	Translated to								
	German	Russian	French	Spanish	British	Czechoslovak	Italian	Yugoslav	Other
British 13	2	2	2	1		1	1	1	1 Japanese 1 Polish 1 Swedish
French 12	3	2		1	1	1		1	1 American 1 Polish 1 Romanian
German 7		3	1				1		1 American 1 Swedish
Italian 7	1		1	3	2				
Russian 7	2		2			1	1	1	
46	8	7	6	5	3	3	3	3	8

Note: The following list shows the entry numbers in this Bibliography, the authors' surnames, and the dates of the original works that were translated during this period, each followed, in parentheses, by the number of translations appearing: 83—Blanqui, 1837-[1838] (2); 129—Cossa, 1876 (7); 148—Cohn, 1885 (1); 151—Ingram, 1888 (13); 175—Bunge, 1895 (1); 196—Oncken, 1902 (1); 208—Marx, 1905-10 (4); 226—Gide, 1909 (10); 236—Spann, 1911 (1); and 271—Totomiants, 1921 (6).

Appendix C

TABLE 10

Paths Taken by 47 Translations of Book-length General Histories of Economics from 1930 to 1949

Originally	Translated to								
	Mexican	Spanish	Chinese	Italian	Japanese	Argentine	Portuguese	Canadian	Other
French 13	2	4			1	1	2		1 British 1 Bolivian 1 Greek
German 12	1	1	2	2	2	1			1 American 1 Swedish 1 Yugoslav
British 7	3		1	1					1 Brazilian 1 Indian
American 6	2		1						1 German 1 Swedish 1 Turkish
Russian 4		1		1	1				1 Yugoslav
Swedish 3				1	1				1 German
Other 2			1 (Japanese)					1 (Portuguese)	
47	8	6	5	5	5	2	2	1	13

Note: The following list shows the entry numbers in this Bibliography, the authors' surnames, and the dates of the original works that were translated during this period, each followed, in parentheses, by the number of translations appearing: 151—Ingram, 1888 (2); 208—Marx, 1905–10 (3); 226—Gide, 1909 (6); 234—Haney, 1911 (1); 236—Spann, 1911 (7); 270—Gonnard, 1921–22 (5); 271—Totomiants, 1921 (2); 283—Salin, 1923 (2); 299—Bousquet, 1927 (1); 304—Kobayashi, 1927 (1); 311—Cannan, 1929 (3); 323—Myrdal, 1930 (3); 332—Philippe, 1931 (1); 357—Rozenberg, 1934–36 (2); 376—Crobaugh, 1937 (1); 385—Ferguson, 1938 (1); 389—Roll, 1938 (2); 403—Whittaker, 1940 (1); 413—Hugon, 1942 (1); 426—McConnell, 1943 (1); and 442—Heimann, 1945 (1).

219

Appendix C

There were, of course, in addition to the five translations of book-length histories, the translations of the essay-length histories that had appeared as parts of general treatises before 1839. Table 8 presents the details of this lull in translation.

A brisker pace in the publication of translations of histories of economics began with the issue of the Spanish version of Cossa's *Guida* in 1878. Later, the multiple translations of the histories of Ingram, Gide, and Totomiants maintained this increased rate. In all, 46 translations of book-length histories came out between the start of 1878 and the end of 1929. During these 52 years, 13 countries received book-length views of the history of economics through translation. Table 9 displays other features of these translations.

First the Depression and then World War II braked the publication of translations between 1930 and 1949. Nonetheless, these 20 years saw the publication of translations equal in number to that of the preceding 52 years. Ten countries received their first translations, bringing the total of issuing countries to 26. For 6 of the 10, the translations were the first histories of economics published within the countries. As during the earlier periods, France, Germany, and Great Britain together provided the bulk (68 percent) of the translations. Table 10 provides a geography of translations for this period.

The period from 1950 to 1975 surpassed in two ways all that had preceded, as the condensed statement in table 11 shows. Details about the translations during this period are set forth in table 12.

TABLE 11

TRANSLATIONS OF BOOK-LENGTH GENERAL HISTORIES OF ECONOMICS FROM 1839 TO 1975

	1839–1949	1950–75
Total number of separately listed translations	98	180
Translations from American histories	6	87

Appendix C

TABLE 12

Paths Taken by 180 Translations of Book-length General Histories of Economics from 1950 to 1975

Originally	Translated to																Other
	Spanish	Italian	Japanese	Brazilian	Mexican	German	Argentine	French	British	Chinese	Indian	Swedish	Egyptian	Greek	Portuguese	Korean	
American 87	10	11	11	7	7	4	3	5	1	2	4	5	3	1	3	2	1 Danish 2 Dutch 2 Indonesian 1 Iranian 2 Pakistani
French 29	10	3	2	2		1	2			1				2	1		1 Cuban 1 Israeli 1 Lebanese 2 Turkish
German 27	2	5	4				1	3	5	1		1				1	1 American 1 Polish 1 Russian 1 Yugoslav
British 22		3	3	4	4		1			1	2		1	1			1 Dutch 1 Israeli 1 Yugoslav

TABLE 12. (Concluded)

ORIGINALLY	TRANSLATED TO																
	Spanish	Italian	Japanese	Brazilian	Mexican	German	Argentine	French	British	Chinese	Indian	Swedish	Egyptian	Greek	Portuguese	Korean	Other
Russian 8			1	1	1	2				1							1 Cuban 1 Polish
Swedish 5	1		1			1			1					1			
Other 2						1 (Dutch)	1 (Italian)										
180	23	22	22	14	12	9	8	8	7	6	6	6	4	4	4	3	22

NOTE: The following list shows the entry numbers in this Bibliography, the authors' surnames, and the dates of the original works that were translated during this period, each followed, in parentheses, by the number of translations appearing: 83—Blanqui, 1837–[1838] (1); 208—Marx, 1905-10 (16); 226—Gide, 1909 (7); 234—Haney, 1911 (1); 247—Schumpeter, 1914 (8); 270—Gonnard, 1921–22 (2); 271—Totomiants, 1921 (1); 283—Salin, 1923 (1); 323—Myrdal, 1930 (5); 329—Gray, 1931 (1); 348—Scott, 1933 (1); 357—Rozenberg, 1934-36 (3); 363—Mitchell, 1935 (1); 385—Ferguson, 1938 (3); 389—Roll, 1938 (14); 426—McConnell, 1943 (1); 436—Stark, 1944 (3); 437—Villey, 1944 (1); 442—Heimann, 1945 (4); 468—Zimmerman, 1947 (1); 485—Griziotti Kretschmann, 1949 (1); 491—Lajugie, 1949 (8); 517—Zweig, 1950 (1); 525—Schumpeter, 1951 (9); 526—Stavenhagen, 1951 (1); 539—Newman, 1952 (3); 541—Soule, 1952 (10); 542—Spiegel, 1952 (1); 544—Bell, 1953 (1); 548—Heilbroner, 1953 (22); 574—Schumpeter, 1954 (7); 587—James, 1955 (5); 592—Piettre, 1955 (1); 656—Lekachman, 1959 (4); 677—Spengler, 1960 (1); 681—Taylor, 1960 (2); 703—Blaug, 1962 (4); 723—Akademiia nauk SSSR, 1963 (3); 781—Recktenwald, 1965 (1); 794—Boardman, 1966 (1); 796—Denis, 1966 (4); 798—Fusfeld, 1966 (3); 807—Barber, 1967 (6); 812—Gill, 1967 (5); and 899—Anikin, 1971 (1).

Notes

1. James Bonar, ed., *A Catalogue of the Library of Adam Smith* (London: Macmillan and Co., 1932), p. 120.

2. *Die geschichtliche Entwickelung der National-Oekonomik und ihrer Literatur* (no. 115 in this bibliography), 1:36 n.

3. Wilhelm Georg Friedrich Roscher, *Geschichte der National-Oekonomik in Deutschland* (Muenchen: R. Oldenbourg, 1874), pp. 328–29; Edwin Cannan, "Morhof, Daniel Georg," in *Dictionary of Political Economy*, ed. R. H. I. Palgrave (London: Macmillan and Co., 1896), 2:820; Theo Surányi-Unger, *Die Dogmengeschichte der Nationalökonomie als selbständige Wissenschaft* (Budapesth: "Internationaler Donau Lloyd," [1922]), p. 38.

4. *Bibliographie der Kameralwissenschaften* (Köln: Kurt Schroeder, 1937), p. 39.

5. "Ergaenzungen und Anmerkungen zu des Herr Prof. D. Schrebers Geschichte der Cameralwissenschaften," in Daniel Gottfried Schreber, *Neue Cameralschriften,* sechster Teil (Halle: gedrukt und verlegt von Johann Jacob Curt, 1766), pp. 646–56.

6. Dupont blamed this omission on the absence, between countries, of easy communications "qui s'opposent tant au progrès des lumières." In this case, however, the always present lack of communication was probably not crucial. Beccaria, Adam Smith, and David Hume all read French, and each spent some time in Paris during the year 1766, the heyday of Physiocracy. Smith, who had arrived shortly before Hume departed, left on the day Beccaria arrived. These three foreigners, on their visits to the Capitol of the Enlightenment, shared the same friend and counselor, the Abbé Morellet, who knew the Physiocrats and was adept at arranging invitations. What did they learn of Physiocracy during their stay? We can surmise that they learned something, but we have nothing but bare circumstantial evidence that they learned anything. The main reason that they may have learned little or nothing about Physiocracy in their 1766 visits is that before their Paris visits they had developed only minor interests in the subject that was coming to be known as "political economy." Their connections with "political economy" were not prominent and were largely unknown in Paris. While they were in Paris, Beccaria shone as the author of the enormously successful book *Dei delitti e delle pene,* Hume was extravagantly admired as a historian and philosopher, and Smith appeared as Hume's philosopher friend whose *Theory of Moral Sentiments,* two years before, had been translated into French. As others thought of them, so probably did they think of themselves. The only one of the three ever to publish anything concerning the Physiocrats was Smith, and the materials for his publication, which did not appear until ten years after his 1766 visit, may be found in his own library in French books published after he had returned to England. Hume's only remark about them, made in a letter to Morellet some three years after his visit to Paris—that they were "the set of men the most chimerical and most arrogant that now exist"—did not disclose either the extent of his knowledge of Physiocracy or the source of that knowledge. Beccaria never mentioned the Physiocrats at any time in public or known private sources. All notice of them may have escaped him while he was in Paris, not only because he was hailed as a jurist and pursued largely a jurist's interests, but also because personal

difficulties isolated him during much of his sojourn, in what Morellet called "une triste expérience de la faiblesse humaine" (*Mémoires* [1821], 1:161).

7. The term "économie politique" had been used in the same year (1769) by André Morellet, earlier by James Denham Steuart (1767) and Jean Jacques Rousseau (1758), and far back by Antoyne de Montchrétien (1615). Although these four writers infrequently used the term "économie politique" or its English equivalent, they always incorporated it in the titles of their publications, where it would be noticed. None of them used it in quite the sense it later acquired.

8. The subject bibliographers of political economy who preceded Morellet in the eighteenth century were Germans: Julius Bernhard von Rohr (1688–1742), Justus Christoph Dithmar (1677–1737), Georg Heinrich Zincke (1692–1768), and Heinrich Ludwig Bergius (1718–81). Morellet was not acquainted with these bibliographers.

9. Arthur Young had written: "System upon system was framed, and their authors looked upon themselves as the founders of a new science; the *oeconomical Science*" (*Political Arithmetic* [London: W. Nicoll, 1774], p. 209). In Smith's *Wealth of Nations,* "system upon system" was rendered as "systems," which stands out since it it not symmetrical with his expression "commercial system." Smith did not mention Young's *Political Arithmetic* in his *Wealth of Nations,* but there was a copy in Smith's library at the time of his death.

10. There was an earlier history of this subject in August Ludwig von Schlözer, *Theorie der Statistik* (Göttingen: in Vandenhoek und Ruprechtschem Verlag, 1804), pp. 6–8. A later history, by Jacques Peuchet, was "Apperçu historique des écrivains qui ont traité de la statistique française," in his *Statistique élémentaire de la France* (Paris: Chez Gilbert et Compagnie, 1805), pp. 36–52.

11. McCulloch's first book appeared in both a short and an expanded version during the same year. The title of the expanded version was *An Essay on the Question of Reducing the Interest of the National Debt; in which the Justice and Expediency of that Measure are fully Established* (Edinburgh: David Brown, 1816).

12. McCulloch may have seen the *Bibliotheca Britannica* before he published his first history of political economy, since it came out in eleven parts, the first four in Glasgow (1819–20), the others in Edinburgh (1821–24). Later he had a copy in his library and called it a work of "great utility." However, at most he received only help and encouragement, for he did not follow Watt's work in the details, and he included many items in his history that Watt omitted.

13. Born in Modena, Bosellini studied jurisprudence and received a doctor of laws. Study and travel in England and France gave his political economy a Utopian outlook, colored by the French Revolution. Events after 1789 disappointed him and eventually led him to quit public life for private studies. His principal work, *Nuovo esame delle sorgenti della privata e pubblica ricchezza* (1816–17) was withheld for a time from publication for political reasons.

14. In 1821, American colleges had been provided with an introduction to the history of political economy by the publication in Boston of the English translation of Say's *Traité.*

15. The copy in the University of Kansas Library was a presentation to J. C. Herries (1778–1855), a Tory politician.

16. McCulloch divided the *Historical Sketch* into three parts. For the first part, which he called the "Rise and Progress of the Science of Political Economy up to the Publication of the 'Wealth of Nations,' " he used the second edition of the *Discourse,* omitting parts, rewriting sections, and reinserting—in an altered and expanded form—substantial segments on the English mercantilists that he had removed from his *Encyclopaedia Britannica* article when he had adapted it for the *Discourse.* His second part, "Publication of the 'Wealth of Nations'— Principal Merits and Defects of that Work," was four times as long as the comparable section in the *Discourse,* the added matter being critical rather than historical. The third part, "Progress of the Science of Political Economy since the Publication of the 'Wealth of Nations,' " was similar to that in the *Discourse* except for the final pages on Ricardo.

17. "I think I am entitled to say, after a pretty careful investigation, that I have specified most of those [tracts] in which any of the distinguishing and peculiar prejudices of the age

were openly attacked, or in which any of those germinal truths were elicited that have sub-sequently served as the foundation of systems" (p. 50 n).

18. McCulloch sought specifically to "prove the indisputable priority of the English" (p. 51). He dismissed the Italians on the grounds that they had not written on debasement as well, or as early, as Sir Robert Cotton did in his speech before the Privy Council in 1626 and that their strictly commercial works came later than, and were inferior to, those of Child and North (pp. 51–52). He said of Boisguilbert's *Détail de la France* (1695) and Vauban's *Projet d'une dixme royale* (1707) that "economical science" occupied "only a subsidiary and subordinate place in them" (p. 54). He gave de Gournay credit for having the reputation of being an influential thinker but one who never published (p. 56). McCulloch "was disposed to think" Herbert's *Essai sur la police générale des grains* (1753) the best book on the Continent prior to the writings of Quesnay (p. 56).

19. All pre-Smithian arguments "had somewhat of an empirical aspect, and failed of making that impression which is always made by reasonings logically deduced from well-established principles, and shown to be consistent with experience" (p. 57).

20. Especially by *Reasons for a limited Exportation of Wool* (1677) and by John Asgill, *Several Assertions Proved* (1696), p. 62 n.

21. McCulloch announced that Joseph Massie, in *An Essay on the Governing Causes of the Natural Rate of Interest* (1750), had showed, before Hume (who had been supposed to be the first), that the "rate of interest did not depend on the abundance or scarcity of money, but on the abundance or scarcity of disposable capital compared with the demands of the borrowers, and the rate of profit" (p. 27 n). He wrote that William Petty, in his *A Treatise of Taxes and Contributions* (1667), "seems to have been the first person who has distinctly laid down, though only in a cursory and incidental manner, the fundamental doctrine, that the value of commodities is determined by the quantities of labour required for their production" (p. 30). Although earlier (1651) Thomas Hobbes, in the *Leviathan,* was said to be one of the first "who was fully impressed with a conviction of the vast importance of labour in the production of wealth" (p. 35). This discussion marks the introduction into the history of political economy of the subject of value. Later the histories became, to a large degree, histories of value theory, in part because political economy became increasingly concerned with that subject. McCulloch pointed out here (pp. 34–35) that up to the time of Hobbes and Petty "no one had thought of investigating the sources whence they [commodities] derive their value in exchange, or their power or capacity of exchanging for or buying others. This, however, is plainly the most elementary and fundamental inquiry in the whole science; and it was quite impossible that it could ever assume a systematic shape until some considerable progress had been made in its elucidation." He mentioned the "speech of Sir Robert Cotton at the Council table, the 2d September 1626" as the earliest respectable argument against tampering with the currency (p. 51 n). In connection with the development of the theory of rent he wrote that the "rise in the price of raw produce, occasioned by the decreasing fertility of the soils to which every advancing society must resort, was, I believe, first [1766] distinctly shown in a work . . . *Principes de tout Gouvernement*" (p. 94). The author was Claude François Joseph d'Auxrion. McCulloch's article in the *Supplement to the Fourth, Fifth, and Sixth Editions of the Encyclopaedia Britannica* (7:277) mentioned Josiah Tucker as having an early statement of Say's Law in his *Queries on the late Naturalization Bill* (1752). This title is incorrect, perhaps a shelf title. McCulloch evidently referred to "Part II, Containing Important Queries Relating to Commerce, — The Employment of the Poor, — . . ." of *Reflections on the Expediency of a Law for the Naturalization of Foreign Protestants* (London: T. Tyre, 1752).

22. Blanqui announced that he had intended to write a different kind of history of political economy. He knew either that he could follow Say, Sismondi, and McCulloch on the course of political economy after Quesnay, "en y ajoutant quelques mots de politesse pour les siècles qui précèdent," or that he could "lier l'économie politique à l'histoire générale, en signalant leur influence réciproque depuis les anciens jusqu'à nos jours" (*Histoire de l'économie politique* [no. 83 in this bibliography], 1:xxi). He chose, as had Villeneuve-Bargemont, to combine the history of nations with the history of political economy, hoping that one would illuminate the other.

23. The discussion of Saint-Simon, Fourier, and Owen by both Blanqui and Villeneuve-Bargemont was in part the result of the three influential articles by Marie Roch Louis Reybaud that appeared in the *Revue des deux mondes*. These articles, "Les Saint-Simoniens" (1 August 1830), "Charles Fourier" (15 November 1837), and "Robert Owen" (1 April 1838) were published, with some changes, as *Études sur les réformateurs contemporains* (Paris: Guillaumin et Cie., 1840). This is an early example of the influence of a monograph on the content of the general histories.

24. *Karl Marx, Friedrich Engels: Historisch-kritische Gesamtausgabe* (Moscow: Verlagsgenossenchaft ausländischer Arbeiter in der UdSSR), vol. 6 (1933), pp. 602, 613–14.

25. Karl Marx, *Theorien über den Mehrwert*, herausgegeben von Karl Kautsky (Stuttgart: Verlag von J. H. W. Dietz Nachf.), vol. 1 (1905), pp. 47, 281 n. From the Russian edition of 1954, Karl Marx, *Theorien über den Mehrwert (vierter Band des "Kapitals")* (Berlin [East]: Dietz Verlag), vol. 1 (1956), pp. 27, 137.

26. The pamphlet gave the author as "W.S." A later edition (1757) erroneously took "W.S." to stand for William Shakespeare. By the time that Twiss wrote, this attribution had been disproved, and the name of William Stafford offered instead. Since 1891, the accepted author has been John Hales and the date of composition given as 1549. The correct title is *A Compendious or Briefe Examination of Certayne Ordinary Complaints, of Divers of Our Country Men in These Our Dayes: Which Although They Are in Some Part Unjust and Frivolous, Yet Are They All by Way of Dialogues Thoroughly Debated and Discussed.*

27. Twiss was a fellow of University College at Oxford from 1830 to 1863, being active on occasion as bursar, dean, and tutor. He briefly held the Chair of International Law at King's College, London, and later was, for fifteen years, the Regius Professor of Civil Law at Oxford. On the subject of law he wrote many volumes. He also practiced extensively in the ecclesiastical courts. He designed, at the invitation of the King of Belgium, a charter for the Congo Free State. He wrote in other fields as well, editing a four-volume edition of Livy, publishing a two volume *Epitome of Niebuhr's History of Rome,* and contributing two books on the Oregon Question. He was knighted, and his wife was twice presented at court. As the result of the strange turn of events in a spectacular law suit, he chose to spend the last twenty-five years of his life in retirement, working on other things, mainly legal archeology.

28. Grieb compiled a successful two-volume English-German and German-English dictionary (1842, 1847). His last publication was a translation of John Brown's *Slave Life in Georgia* (1855). All his books were published at Stuttgart.

29. Kautz also had mentioned Gossen in *Die National-Oekonomik* the same year, and he repeated the mention in his history in 1860. It was from Kautz that Adamson had learned Gossen's name and then informed Jevons of this predecessor of the Marginal Utility School. Gray (*The Development of Economic Doctrine* [no. 329 in this bibliography], p. 337) said that the life of Gossen's reputation as a predecessor had hung by a footnote in Kautz. Actually this was a second thread.

30. Friedrich Engels, *Herr Eugen Dühring's Revolution in Science* (New York: International Publishers, 1939), p. 254. Engels attributed the part of this book that dealt with Dühring's work on the history of political economy to Karl Marx.

31. Among these were reviews by Oldenberg (*Jahrbuch für Gesetzgebung, Verwaltung und Volkswirtschaft im Deutschen Reich* 17 [1893]: 463–66; 37 [1899]: 461–63); Caldwell (*Journal of Political Economy* 2 [1893/94]: 300–303); and Jenks (*Annals of the American Academy of Political and Social Science* 4 [1894]: 981–83).

32. The law school at Pavia had 185 students in 1879/80 and 212 in 1893/94, all of whom attended the course in political economy during their second year (see Minerva, *Jahrbuch der gelehrten Welt,* 1892/93 to 1896/97).

33. Of the other three, two were primers, one on general economics (1875) and the other on public finance (1876). The third (1878) contained a collection of articles, some on the history of political economy. The popularity of these books led to many editions and translations after 1878.

34. It replaced the article that McCulloch had written for the *Encyclopaedia Britannica* sixty-two years earlier (no. 54 in this bibliography). It remained in the *Encyclopaedia Britannica*

until the eleventh edition (1911), although a nonhistorical article on "Economics" had been included in the ten supplementary volumes, which, when added to the fourth edition (1902), had constituted the tenth edition.

35. Up to 1878, Ingram's only obvious connection with political economy was his regular attendance at the meetings of the Statistical and Social Inquiry Society of Ireland, which he had helped to found. In its journal he published four speeches made at its meetings. They were on the subjects of Irish emigration, Irish poor laws, and the boarding out of pauper children. They contained no sign of an interest in either the generalities or the history of political economy.

36. Later, Ingram held the presidencies of the Statistical and Social Inquiry Society of Ireland, the Royal Irish Academy, the Library Association of the United Kingdom, the Board of Visitors of the Science and Art Museum (Dublin), and the Dublin University Shakespeare Society. He also held several vice-presidencies.

37. For the previous twenty-five years, Ingram had been a professor at Dublin University, first of oratory and English literature, and then, for the last twelve years, of Greek. In his youth he had had a local reputation both as a mathematician and as a poet.

38. After the Belfast meeting in 1852, where Ingram served as one of the secretaries, there is no record that he attended any other meetings of the British Association until 1878. He was not a life member or a subscriber to the British Association at the time of the 1857 Dublin meeting. It is certain that, before 1878, he had never been an officer of the British Association or read a paper at any of its meetings.

39. Cliffe Leslie's "On the Philosophical Method of Political Economy" had appeared in 1876 in *Hermathena*, a journal that Ingram helped to edit. Ingram mentioned this article in the biography of Leslie that he wrote for Palgrave's *Dictionary* and also in the biography that he prepared for the *Britannica*, where he called the article "a memorable one" (9th ed. [1882], 14:477).

40. Ingram's first acquaintance with Comte, according to his own account, came from reading John Stuart Mill's *A System of Logic* (1843). This early influence did not show anywhere in his writings prior to 1878. From that time on, however, Comte's influence over Ingram grew to the extent that Ingram's last books dealt exclusively with Comte. As Edgeworth said, "We may well describe the relation of Comte to his follower by the term 'master,' for Ingram himself repeatedly employs the word" (Francis Ysidro Edgeworth, "Obituary, John Kells Ingram," *Economic Journal* 7 [1907]: 299–301).

41. Ingram urged political economists to make fuller use of other social sciences, avoid abstract reasoning and unreal simplifications, substitute the historical for the deductive method, and express their findings in a less absolute form. In Comte's language, he suggested that political economy move from the metaphysical stage to become a positive science.

42. Shaw-Lefevre, president of the London Statistical Society, spoke of Ingram's "most able address" (*Journal of the Statistical Society* 41 [1878]: 573). Bonamy Price, a president of the National Association for the Promotion of Social Science, also called it an "able address" (ibid., 642). It made a lasting unfavorable impression on Lord Bramwell, who, in his presidential address to Section F in 1888, said that Ingram's argument "attracted a good deal of notice, but for my part I confess I never understood it" (*Report of the Fifty-eighth meeting of the British Association for the Advancement of Science* [London: John Murray, 1887], p. 749). Ely, a student in Germany in 1878, recalled the impression that the address had made in Germany (Ingram, *A History of Political Economy*, 1915 [no. 249 in this bibliography], p. x).

43. Printed in the *Report of the Forty-eighth Meeting of the British Association for the Advancement of Science* (London: John Murray, 1879), pp. 641–58. Before the *Report* appeared, the address came out "Revised, with Notes and Additions" as an appendix, with separate subtitle and pagination, to the *Journal of the Statistical and Social Inquiry Society of Ireland*, pt. 54 (extra). This revised address was published (1878) in Dublin by Ponsonby and in London by Longmans & Co. It also appeared in the *Journal of the Statistical Society* 41 (1878): 602–29.

44. Scheel, the translator, dated his preface January, 1879.

45. Bryce said that Smith "took infinite pains to find the most competent writers" (*Studies in Contemporary Biography* [New York: Macmillan Co., 1903], p. 312). It was something more than competence that led Smith to choose Ingram. The special quality that won him attention was his somewhat heretical outlook—he thought he had broken with the past. Ingram's attitude was shared by Smith, who had been tried for heresy as a result of a number of his publications, beginning with his article in 1875 on "Angel" for the *Encyclopaedia Britannica.*

46. *Dictionary of National Biography, Second Supplement* (London: Smith, Elder & Co., 1912), 2:339. This kind of statement had appeared earlier in the *Times* obituary, which said that "those who had worked with Dr. Ingram in Trinity College were persuaded that he was the best educated man in Europe" (2 May 1907, pp. 9–10).

47. Charles Scribner's Sons, the American publishers of the *Encyclopaedia Britannica,* often reprinted the encyclopaedia articles as textbooks. In 1879 they reported the separate publication of no less than 32 *Britannica* articles for use as textbooks at Yale (*Adam & Charles Black, 1807–1957: Some Chapters in the History of a Publishing House* [London: Adam & Charles Black, 1957], p. 43).

48. In the Seligman correspondence at Columbia University Library. Early in September, Taussig sent Seligman a reminder: "Messrs. Scribner inform me that the reprinted copies of Ingram's 'Political Economy' article in the *Britannica* have been shipped from Edinburgh. Will you kindly let me know how the matter stands? Whether you want any, and if so, how many, and to whom they are to be addressed and charged?" A favorable response must have come soon thereafter, for Taussig wrote in November: "I have an unexpectedly large number of men in my Course 2, and if you want to get rid of some copies of Ingram's article I shall possibly be able to dispose of them." Seligman's own copy of the reprint is in Butler Library at Columbia.

49. Ely wrote that the encyclopaedia article was "printed separately in America for the use of economic students . . . at the suggestion of Professor F. W. Taussig" (Ingram, *A History of Political Economy,* 1915 [no. 249 in this bibliography], p. xi). Its use in Ely's class at Johns Hopkins is suggested by a copy of the reprint in the University of Kansas Library, which contains a bookplate of Frank W. Blackmar, who had studied at Johns Hopkins from 1886 to 1889.

50. Ashley, who felt a kinship with Ingram, later tried to alter Seligman's opinion by writing: "I know you *Political Science Quarterly* people rather sniff at Ingram and I have been saddened to see how much he used other people, e.g. Kautz—but . . . the appearance of his book in England was 'epoch making' " (letter to Seligman of 11 March 1890 in Seligman correspondence at Columbia University).

51. After early scholarly successes, Espinas went to the École normale in 1864. After graduating, he entered the French school system, concentrating on natural history. The War of 1871 and its aftermath turned his attention to social questions and to the study of Comte and Spencer. He came to believe that a scientific study of society would profit from the study of animal societies. The result was his *Des sociétés animales, études de psychologie comparée* (1877), which made his reputation and led him to the universities, first to Bordeaux and then to the Sorbonne, where his interests continued in psychology, philosophy, and pedagogy. See André Lalande, "La Vie et l'oeuvre d'Alfred Espinas," *Revue internationale de sociologie* 33 (1925): 113–44.

52. The *Quarterly Journal of Economics* noticed a publication announcement and commented that it was "apparently" a "posthumous work."

53. Gide published his *Principes d'économie politique* (1884), made his early connection with the cooperative movement by helping to found *L'Émancipation* (1886), was a cofounder of the *Revue d'économie politique* (1887), and published *La Coopération* (1904).

54. The comparison of a sample of Ely's half-sheets that were used by Haney showed that almost none of Haney's book came directly from these notes, which were, in fact, "rough" notes.

55. A short French review by Pierre Moride also missed the special flavor in Spann's *Haupttheorien* (*Revue d'économie politique* 26 [1912]: 257). It was also missed by Emanuel

H. Vogel in his review of the second edition (*Archiv für die Geschichte des Sozialismus und der Arbeiterbewegung* 8 [1919]: 158–59).

56. The more substantial reviews were: Theo Surányi-Unger, *Jahrbuch für Gesetzgebung, Verwaltung und Volkswirtschaft im Deutschen Reiche,* vol. 51 (1927), pt. 2, pp. 151–54; Herbert Schack, *Jahrbücher für Nationalökonomie und Statistik,* 3d ser. 72 (1927): 1017–20; W. Sulzbach, *Zeitschrift für die gesamte Staatswissenschaft* 84 (1928): 174–78; Leo Rogin, *American Economic Review* 21 (1931): 291–93; Frank H. Knight, *Journal of Political Economy* 39 (1931): 258–60; M. T. Rankin, *Economic Journal* 41 (1931): 469–73; Manuel Garcia Pazos, *Revista de ciencias económicas,* 1935, pp. 398–400; Luigi Einaudi, *Rivista di storia economica* 1 (1936): 258–63; and Otto Weinberger, *Zeitschrift für die gesamte Staatswissenschaft* 107 (1951): 482–87.

Appendix B

1. Histories of economics also have been published in Switzerland, Hungary, Sweden, Belgium, Austria, Holland, Czechoslovakia, Poland, Portugal, Yugoslavia, Romania, Greece, China, Norway, Argentina, Bolivia, Peru, Canada, Australia, Turkey, Bulgaria, Israel, Korea, Iran, Pakistan, Egypt, Ecuador, Indonesia, Cuba, Denmark, Iraq, Bangladesh, Lebanon, Singapore, and East Germany.

2. The word "course" is used here in the sense of "a unit of instruction consisting of recitations, lectures, or the like, in a particular subject."

3. Eiselen had lectured for five years before 1820, and he continued to lecture, first at Breslau and then at Halle, for almost forty-five years afterward; but he never lectured on the history of political economy, either earlier or later. It also seems strange that Eiselen's three books that deal with political economy show no trace of the subject's history. Perhaps the explanation lies in the fact that Eiselen started his university lectures at Berlin as a historian but soon changed completely to political economy. Between 1815 and 1817 he had taught Greek History, the History of Migration, German History, the History of the Development of Human Customs, Ancient History, English History, and European History. After 1817 he began to turn to the different subjects then offered as political economy, for a while teaching almost all the courses offered under the heading of *Kameralwissenschaften.* After he had taught other courses in political economy for three years, he gave a public course on its history.

4. See entry no. 3 (Schreber) supra.

5. Separate courses in *National-Oekonomie* had been offered in 1809 by Professor Karl Christian Gottlieb at the University of Jena and by Professor Heinrich Wilhelm Crome at the University of Giessen (see *Jenaische allgemeine Literatur-Zeitung, Intelligenzblatt,* vol. 1 [1809], p. 202, and vol. 2 [1809], p. 620). The first use of the word *National-Oekonomie* in book titles had been in 1805 by Professor Ludwig Heinrich von Jacob (see entry no. 30 supra) and by Friedrich Julius Heinrich Soden (in his *Die Nazional-Oekonomie*). A similar Italian expression, "economia nazionale," had been used by Giammaria Ortes in titles in 1771, 1774, and 1790. In 1804 the publications by Ortes had been reprinted in Custodi's *Scrittori classici italiani di economia politica.*

6. During the first half of the nineteenth century the *Intelligenzblatt* of the *Allgemeine Literatur Zeitung* published regularly the *Verzeichnis des Vorlesungen* of many of the German Universities, although those of a few (Heidelberg and Muenchen particularly) never were included. During the years 1850 to 1872 no single publication covered any group of German universities regularly. Information for the period 1850 to 1872 can be found only in the separate *Index Lectionum, Index Scholarum,* and *Verzeichnis der Vorlesungen,* published each semester for the students at the twenty-one German universities. Only a part of these publications are in the libraries of the United States. Two other publications, the *Jahrbuch der deutschen Universitäten von Heinrich Wuttke* (which is available at the New York Public Library), 1842, and the *Deutscher Universitäts-Almanach für 1859,* cover all German universities for these two years.

7. The following seven German universities offered courses in the history of economics in 1975/76: Frankfurt am Main (Jan Jacob van Klaveyn), Heidelberg (Eckhart Schremmer),

Köln (Rolf Nettig), Mainz (Antonio Montaner), Marburg (Walter Braeuer), München (Knut Borchardt), and Regensberg (Fritz Blaich).

8. Part of an address "The University of the 19th Century," read before the National Baptist Educational Convention, Brooklyn, 19 April 1870. *Papers and Addresses of Martin B. Anderson* (Philadelphia, 1895), 1:80.

9. Asahel C. Kendrich, *Martin B. Anderson, LL.D.: A Biography* (Philadelphia: American Baptist Publication Society, 1895), pp. 70, 167–68.

10. Frank William Taussig, "Introduction," in Charles Franklin Dunbar, *Economic Essays* (New York: Macmillan Company, 1904), p. xxi.

11. It would be enlightening to know how the translations of 1880, Blanqui's in the United States and Cossa's in England, came to be made. Both had prefaces by political economists of the time who shared an interest in the history of the subject: William Stanley Jevons for Cossa's work and David Ames Wells for Blanqui's. Whoever influenced publishers influenced the development of courses in the history of economics. Perhaps Jevons influenced Macmillan to publish the translation of Cossa's *Guida* and Wells brought Blanqui's *Histoire* to the attention of Putnam and Sons. Wells, who once had been a special partner in G. P. Putnam's Sons, was a long-time friend of George Haven Putnam. Wells also had an interest in the history of political economy. G. H. Putnam wrote about Wells's "studies in the history of economic science" and about the library in Wells's Norwich, Connecticut, home which had "one of the most complete collections of economics books and pamphlets that had been brought together in this country" (George Haven Putnam, *Memories of a Publisher, 1865–1915* [New York: G. P. Putnam's Sons, 1915], pp. 35, 39), Jevons was a book collector and a historian of political economy who had had previous books published by Macmillan.

12. We would know more about the rate at which the introduction of the history of economics into American universities progressed during the 1880s if we could examine the sales records of G. P. Putnam's Sons and Macmillan.

13. Since 1883 there has always been a course in the history of economics in the Harvard catalogue. This is not an exceptional occurrence; most American universities likewise have kept the course in the universities' catalogues from the dates of their first appearance to the present. At Harvard, the description of "Political Economy 2" (from 1892 on "Economics 2") changed slightly and was taught by several other people after Dunbar gave it up in 1886. Frank William Taussig, in his first year (1886) as an assistant professor, took over Economics 2 from Dunbar and still offered it in 1893/94 and 1897/98. The biographies of Taussig never mention him as a teacher of the history of economics, since the biographers are his students of a later period when his historical course had been forgotten. As an undergraduate at Harvard, Taussig took honors in history in 1879. He also spent the winter semester of 1879/80 at the University of Berlin studying Roman history and political economy, a semester in which Adolf Wagner had lectured on "Nationalökon. m.d. Literargesch. dies. Wissenschaft." In 1901/2, Thomas Nixon Carver changed Economics 2 from a course in history to a course in theory.

Meanwhile, the arrival at Harvard in 1892 of William S. Ashley led to the creation of other historical courses. The first of these was Economics 11, "History of Economic Theory, down to Adam Smith," which was given in 1892 by Ashley as a half-course. Its successor, Economics 15, lasted longer. Ashley taught it most of the time from 1896 to 1900 under such titles as "The History and Literature of Economics to the Middle of the Nineteenth Century." In 1899 it first was marked as "primarily for graduates." In 1903, a few years after Ashley left, Charles Jesse Bullock began to teach it and continued (the number being changed to 14 in 1912/13) until he retired in 1935. It was then taken over by A. E. Monroe and J. A. Schumpeter. Bullock's thirty-one years constituted a long, stable period in the teaching of the history of economics at Harvard.

There had been supplements to Bullock's course. One was Edwin F. Gay's "Outlines of the Development of Economic Thought in Germany in the Nineteenth Century," started in 1902. It went through many changes of numbers, name, and subject and was last taught by Gay in 1914. In 1920, Allen Young revived it under the title "Modern Schools of Economic Thought" and kept it until he left for the London School of Economics in 1927. These economic-history courses at Harvard had remained "primarily for graduates" from 1899 to 1920. In 1920 A. E. Monroe began to teach a course for undergraduates which, with a change of title in 1932, continued to the Second World War. At the beginning of the nineteen thirties, O. H. Taylor commenced to offer a series of courses that bore on the history of economics.

14. Their early academic careers were similar, and hence they brought the same influences to the subject. Both had graduated from Columbia College (Ely two years ahead), and both went to Germany to study. In Germany they encountered in some degree the German courses in the history of political economy, Ely more than Seligman, for he was at Halle for a year where the subject was lectured on regularly. Both became book collectors, Seligman being the more enterprising. Both joined growing graduate schools and quickly gained reputations, thus influencing graduate students and helping to supply the Ph.D.'s to open the new economics departments in the expanding universities of the United States. These new Ph.D.'s taught what they had been recently taught, which almost always included a course in the history of political economy. Harvard also supplied Ph.D.'s who had studied the history of political economy.

Ely was at Johns Hopkins from 1882 to 1892. He taught a course in the "History of Political Economy" in each of those ten years. After he went to Wisconsin, his students—first Sidney Sherwood and then Jacob Hollander—continued his emphasis at Johns Hopkins on the history of economics. At Wisconsin, Ely again taught a course in the history of economics for twenty years and brought in, as an assistant in this subject, one of his students at Johns Hopkins, William Amasa Scott.

Seligman began to teach his course in the "History of Economic Theories" at Columbia in 1886/87, which he continued to offer down to his retirement in 1931. In 1886 Taussig offered Seligman, for his use in class, bound copies of Ingram's historical article on "Political Economy" from the *Encyclopaedia Britannica* (see entry no. 150 supra). Seligman, who accepted the offer, used Ingram's book at first, but never liked it. Later, Seligman prepared readings in which the recommended textbook was Cossa's. Once he distributed a printed eight-page outline, divided into 60 sections, each of which covered roughly the topic for a day's class. It outlined a book that Seligman never found time to write.

15. The first catalogue of the University of Chicago listed the "History of Political Economy," taught by William Caldwell, who had been a student at Jena, Paris, Cambridge, Berlin, Freiburg, and Edinburgh, and who had taught at Cornell. At the same time, Thorstein Veblen gave the "History of Socialist Theories." When Caldwell left after a short time, Veblen taught both courses. Robert Franklin Hoxie took Veblen's place in 1907/8, when Veblen departed. Hoxie in turn was succeeded in 1916/17 by John Maurice Clark. By the middle of the nineteen twenties, Jacob Viner and Frank Knight had begun to teach the history of economics after Clark had left for Columbia.

16. A version of the part of Say's lectures at the Conservatoire that covered the history is found in volume 6 of his *Cours complet* (1829). In the introduction to his *Histoire de l'économie politique*, Blanqui acknowledged that this book had resulted from the attempt to be simultaneously a professor of history and a professor of political economy at the École spéciale du commerce.

17. The first *leçon* was published in 1842: see entry no. 95 supra.

18. "Histoire de l'économie politique par l'histoire de la liberté du travail," *Journal des économistes,* 3d ser. 13: 185–224 (Paris, 1869).

19. Émile Levasseur, *Résumé historique de l'enseignement de l'économie politique et de la statistique en France de 1882 à 1892* (Paris: Librairie Guillaumin, 1893).

20. Société d'économie politique, Paris, *Annales de la société d'économie politique* 5 (1862–64): 298–318.

21. René Worms, "Leçon d'ouverture d'un cours d'histoire des doctrines," *Revue international de l'enseignement* 36 (1898): 499.

22. *The Universities of France: A Guide for American Students.* Published by the Franco-American Committee (Paris, 1900).

23. *Les Universités et les écoles française* (Paris: Larousse, 1914).

24. Presumably, the universities of Aix, Bordeaux, Caen (in 1929/30), Grenoble, and Toulouse offered the same courses but did not designate them as such in the *Annuaire général de l'université et de l'enseignement français* (Paris: L'Information Universitaire), from which the information for these two years was obtained.

25. See entry no. 95 supra for the origin of the expression "Histoire des doctrines économiques." Due to French influence, it became the world's most widespread title for a history of economics. The title *History of Economic Thought* was first used as a title for a general history by Lewis Henry Haney in 1911 (see entry no. 234 supra). The translation of it, although it had been used earlier, did not become popular in France until the 1960s. It had been used as a title for a university course in 1891 by George W. Knight of Ohio State and by Woodrow Wilson at Princeton. H. C. Adams had used the related title "Development of Economic Thought" at Michigan in 1887.

Index of General Histories,
by "Nationality" and Entry Number

Index of General Histories

234

Index of Authors of General Histories, by Entry Number

Index of Authors of General Histories

Chang, Yü-shan, 395
Chao, Nai-po, 470
Chevalier, Jean, 439, 447, 460
Ch'ien, Kung-po, 950
Chin, T'ien-hsi, 375
Cho, Ki-jun, 689
Cho, Moriyoshi, 726
Cho, Tong-p'il, 705
Chodkiewicz, Zygmunt, 706
Ch'oe, Ho-jin, 545
Ch'oe, Mun-hwan, 664
Choumanidēs, Lazaros Th., 532
Chuprov, Aleksandr Ivanovich, 162, 191, 202, 203, 209, 210, 215, 220, 221, 232, 240
Claeys, R. H., 875
Cohn, Gustav, 148, 172
Cole, Arthur Harrison, 618
Cole, Charles Leland, 854
Condorcet, Marie Jean Antoine Caritat, Marquis de, 15
Contzen, Karl Wilhelm Heinrich, 128, 139
Cooper, Thomas, 63
Coquelin, Charles (with Urbain Gilbert Guillaumin), 107
Cossa, Luigi, 129, 131, 132, 135, 136, 145, 163, 164, 169, 188
Costa, Affonso Augusto da, 192
Coux, Charles de, 75
Cracco, W., 390, 421
Cristóbal, Ramiro, 934
Crobaugh, Mervyn, 376, 383, 410
Custodi, Pietro, 24

Daire, Eugène, 90
Damaschke, Adolf Wilhelm Ferdinand, 205, 206, 225, 229, 233, 237, 241, 250, 253, 254, 257, 273, 313
Davar, B. C., 727
Deguchi, Yuzo, 546, 636, 855
Denis, Hector, 183, 204
Denis, Henri, 728, 796, 809, 810, 836, 876, 907, 935, 951, 974, 984
Desai, S. S. M., 603, 729 (with C. T. Yevlekar), 811
Deschamps, Auguste, 343, 344
Dhooria, H. S. (with Gurmukh Ram Madan), 738
Diepenhorst, Pieter Arie, 230, 238, 258, 354, 448
Dohm, Christian Conrad Wilhelm von, 11
Dubois, Auguste, 199
Dühring, Eugen Karl, 122, 126, 133, 193
Dupont de Nemours, Pierre Samuel, 4, 5, 7
Du Puynode, Michel Gustave Partounau, 116, 118

Eisenhart, Hugo, 140, 157
Ekelund, Robert B. (with Robert F. Hebert), 985
Espinas, Alfred Victor, 158

Fabiunke, Günter, 986
Fanfani, Amintore, 384, 391, 411, 440, 581, 908
Farini, Luigi, 176
Fenoglio, Giulio, 319, 327
Ferguson, John Maxwell, 385, 471, 500, 637, 730, 797
Ferrara, Francesco, 103, 154
Finkelstein, Joseph (with Alfred L. Thimm), 952
Fiore-Goria, Ferdinando Maria, 121
Fiorese, Sabino, 137
Fix, Théodore, 78
Flórez Estrada, Alvaro, 69
Fridrichovičz, Eugen, 239
Friederichsen, Vittorio Cristiano, 638
Fusfeld, Daniel Roland, 798, 837, 877, 878, 936, 987

Ganesan, Arumugam, 988
Gangemi, Lello, 337
Ganilh, Charles, 33, 36
García de Quevedo de la Barrera, José, 975
Garnier, Germain, Comte, 22
Gayer, Arthur D. (with Philip Charles Newman and Milton H. Spencer), 570
Gay y Forner, Vicente, 422
Geigel, Martin, 141
Gemähling, Paul, 294, 345
Gherity, James Arthur, 770
Ghio, Paolo Arnaldo (later Paul), 184, 222, 279, 296
Ghosh, Biswanath, 838
Gide, Paul Henri Charles (with Charles Rist), 226, 242, 243, 244, 248, 259, 260, 261, 268, 269, 274, 280, 297, 298, 301, 320, 386, 423, 429, 461, 462, 472, 483, 519, 547, 604, 648, 665, 752, 953
Gill, Richard T., 812, 839, 840, 856, 857, 858
Głabinski, Stanisław, 392
Godinho, António Maria, 441
Goetz, Robert, 649
Gokhle, Ramcandra Mahadev, 731
Gómez Granillo, Moisés, 813, 989
Gonnard, Charles René, 270, 287, 321, 328, 387, 406, 412, 430, 473, 533, 605
Gray, Alexander, 329, 639
Graziani, Augusto, 484
Grieb, Christoph Friedrich, 101
Grigorov, Kiril Iordanov, 879

236

Index of Authors of General Histories

Index of Authors of General Histories

Louis, Paul P., 914
Lu, Yu-chang, 992
Lueder, August Ferdinand, 40

McConnell, John Wilkinson, 426, 492, 693
McCulloch, John Ramsay, 51, 54, 56, 60, 61, 64, 70, 98
Macleod, Henry Dunning, 181
Madan, Gurmukh Ram (with H. S. Dhooria), 738
Mai, Ludwig Hubert, 863, 978, 993
Maide, Chogoro, 377, 657 (with Masahiko Yokohama)
Malon, Benoit, 130, 144
Malthus, Thomas Robert, 25, 46
Mantilla Pérez de Ayala, José María, 408
Mariotti, Francesco, 127
Marshall, Howard Drake, 819, 843 (with Natalie J. Marshall)
Marshall, Natalie J. (with Howard Drake Marshall), 843
Martello, Tullio, 125
Marx, Heinrich Karl, 208, 211, 212, 282, 289, 369, 432, 493, 521, 538, 552, 553, 568, 569, 609, 622, 658, 739, 740, 777, 844, 864, 915, 979, 980, 981, 994
Maslov, Stepan Alekseevich, 47
Miklashevskiĭ, Aleksandr Nikolaevich, 227
Mill, James, 42
Miller, Adolph Caspar, 213
Mitchell, Broadus, 802
Mitchell, Wesley Clair, 363, 494, 820, 916
Mittala, S. C., 712
Miyagawa, Takeo, 917
Miyazaki, Saiichi (with Noboru Kobayashi, Yoshikazu Miyazaki, and Yoshihiko Uchida), 764
Miyazaki, Yoshikazu (with Nobaru Kobayashi, Saiichi Miyazaki, and Yoshihiko Uchida), 764
Mohl, Robert von, 112
Molster, Johannes Adriaan, 105
Mombert, Paul, 305
Montaner, Antonio, 821
Morellet, André, 8
Morhof, Daniel Georg, 1
Moscow. Akademiia obshchestvennykh nauk, 778
Mudgal, B. S. (with Kalka Prasad Bhatnagar and Satish Bahadur), 971
Müller, Johann Anton, 48
Müller, Václav (with Rita Budénová and Oldrich Kýn), 750, 795
Muhs, Karl, 589, 741
Muthukrishnan, K. (with C. Ponnappan and

P. V. Raghavan), 982
Muto, Mitsuro, 865
Myrdal, Gunnar, 323, 340, 415, 427, 554, 742, 822, 823, 918, 919

Nakamura, Ken'ichiro, 995
Napolitano, Gaetano, 670
Narasaki, Toshio, 590
Natan, Zhak, 495
Nathusius, Martin von, 171
Neff, Frank Amandus, 454, 510
Nême, Colette (with Daniel Villey), 964
Nešić, Dragoljub, 824
Newman, Philip Charles, 539, 555, 570 (with Arthur D. Gayer and Milton H. Spencer), 591, 743
Nogaro, Pierre Gabriel Bertrand, 433

Oberndorfer, Johann Adam, 52
Oguro, Sawako, 942
Okada, Jun'ichi, 888
Okinaka, Tsuneyuki, 346, 455
Okochi, Kazuo, 511, 889
Oncken, August, 196, 223, 276
Ono, Shinzo, 364, 398, 943
Oser, Jacob, 744, 890, 996 (with William C. Blanchfield)
Otsuka, Kinnosuke, 347

Patterson, Samuel Howard, 341
Paulet, Pedro E., 399
Pearce, Alan, 866
Pecchio, Giuseppe, 71
Peck, Harvey Whitefield, 365
Périn, Charles, 138, 143
Peter, Kattadyil Chacko, 779
Peuchet, Jacques, 20
Pfeiffer, Johann Friedrich von, 13
Philippe, Charles Émile, 332, 393
Piettre, André, 592, 610, 659, 694, 713, 759, 780, 803, 867, 891, 958
Pino-Branca, Alfredo, 333
Pjanić, Z. (with M. Samardžija, B. Šoškić, R. Stamenković, and R. Stojanović), 614
Polak, Siegfried, 255, 308
"Political Economy—History of the Science," in *The Penny Cyclopaedia of the Society for the Diffusion of Useful Knowledge,* 92
Ponnappan, C. (with K. Muthukrishnan and P. V. Raghavan), 982
Prato, Giuseppe, 443
Price, Langford Lovell Frederick Rice, 161, 334, 378
Pryme, George, 38

Index of Authors of General Histories

Index of Authors of General Histories